# BEYOND 401(k)S

## FOR

# SMALL BUSINESS OWNERS

*A Practical Guide to Incentive, Deferred Compensation, and Retirement Plans*

**JEAN D. SIFLEET**

WILEY

John Wiley & Sons, Inc.

Published by John Wiley & Sons, Inc., Hoboken, New Jersey.
Published simultaneously in Canada.

For general information on our other products and services please contact our Customer Care Department within the United States at (800) 762-2974, outside the United States at (317) 572-3993 or fax (317) 572-4002.

Wiley also publishes its books in a variety of electronic formats. Some content that appears in print may not be available in electronic books. For more information about Wiley products, visit our web site at www.wiley.com.

*Library of Congress Cataloging-in-Publication Data:*

Sifleet, Jean D., 1948–
    Beyond 401(k)s for small business owners : a practical guide to incentive, deferred compensation, and retirement plans / Jean D. Sifleet.
        p. cm.
    Includes index.
    ISBN 0-471-27268-X (pbk.)
    1. Employee fringe benefits.   2. Small business—Management.   3. Pensions.
    4. Incentive awards.   I. Title.
    HD4928.N6S57      2003
    658.3'22—dc21

                                                          2003041101

Printed in the United States of America.

10   9   8   7   6   5   4   3   2   1

This book is dedicated with great respect to small business owners who overcome incredible obstacles and create prosperity for themselves, their families, and employees.

# PREFACE

The goal of this book is to provide information, in clear ordinary language, that enables small business owners to move ahead with confidence and take advantage of many tools to enhance compensation and retirement benefits.

In preparing this book, I owe thanks to many people. My family and friends endured many months of my questions and requests for feedback. Special thanks are owed to my contributing experts who generously shared their knowledge and experience so that this book would tell you candidly how to avoid pitfalls.

Extra special thanks go to Michael Hamilton and the full extended team from John Wiley & Sons, without whose commitment this book would not have happened.

# CONTENTS

# BEYOND 401(k)S

## FOR

# SMALL BUSINESS OWNERS

# 1

# WHAT ARE
# YOU TRYING
# TO ACCOMPLISH?

Running a business can be so all-consuming that it is easy to lose sight of long-term goals. It is important to take time out to regain perspective on what you are trying to accomplish:

- Attract and retain key employees?
- Reduce taxes?
- Plan for retirement income?

*Employees* are a key challenge for small business owners. The success of the business depends on attracting and retaining high-performing employees. Top performers want more than basic salary, benefits, and vacation days. Motivating key employees requires recognition and rewards. If used effectively, incentive compensation can be a powerful tool to reward excellent performance.

*Reducing taxes* is always attractive to business owners, as is *planning for retirement*. After achieving profitability, smart business owners start to think about deferring current income and putting money into retirement plans. The tax advantages are clear: You can reduce current tax liability, both personally and for the business, while allowing invested assets to grow tax-deferred. Although many business owners and their employees are concerned about deferring current income and planning for their retirement, the reality is that a plan is seldom in place. Many of the 26 million small businesses in the United States, which employ 51 percent of this nation's workers, have a compelling need for retirement planning.

## DIFFERENT GOALS NEED DIFFERENT PLANS

Since personal and business goals should drive the planning process, this chapter includes checklists and forms to assist you in prioritizing goals. As you read, ask yourself, "What is really important to me down the road?"

1. Comfortable retirement?
2. Do not want to pay for employees' retirement (maximize owner compensation)?
3. Reduce taxes?
4. Share profits with employees without sharing ownership?
5. Encourage employee ownership?
6. Personal goals _____ (insert your personal goals)?

## COMPENSATION AND BENEFITS EVOLVE
## AS THE BUSINESS GROWS

Compensation and benefits often develop on an *as needed* basis to fill specific requirements during the development of a business. Many companies start with basic pay and benefits,

Table 1.1    Examples of Benefits

Basic Benefits

    Medical and dental insurance

    Vacation and holidays

    Sick leave and unpaid personal leave

    Business expense reimbursement (car, travel)

Additional Benefits

    Life and disability insurance

    Dependent care and health care reimbursement accounts (also called Section 125 plans)

and then add other benefits as the business becomes able to afford the expense (see Table 1.1).

Small businesses have to be creative with compensation since few of them can match the pay and benefits offered by larger companies (see Table 1.2).

Flexibility and the opportunity to share in future growth are major attractions for employees of small businesses. Providing employees with incentive compensation that matches the goals of the business (and business owner) is critical.

Table 1.2    Creative Compensation Incentives

| | |
|---|---|
| On-site gym/fitness center, basketball | Day care |
| Ice cream/pizza days | Bringing child to work |
| Coffee | Bringing dog to work |
| Car, travel | Company outings |
| Flexible hours, work from home | Free turkey at Thanksgiving |

## "BE CAREFUL WHAT YOU ASK FOR"

There is an old saying: "Be careful what you ask for—because you may get it." Employees respond to incentives, so it is important to align your incentives with the company goals. If the two do not match, you will not get the desired results. Poorly designed incentive compensation can backfire and be counterproductive, whereas rewarding excellent performance with well-designed incentive compensation can create a prosperous business environment (see Table 1.3).

## FOR A CURRENT TAX DEDUCTION, YOU NEED A "QUALIFIED PLAN"

To get a tax deduction for contributing funds to a "qualified plan," you must comply with strict rules for including employees and limiting contributions. Examples of qualified plans include 401(k), SEP (Simplified Employee Pensions), SIMPLE (Savings Incentive Match Plans for Employees), and ESOP (Employee Stock Ownership Plans). In addition, there are investment options and differences between defined-benefit (DB) and defined-contribution (DC) plans (see Table 1.4).

Table 1.3   Incentive and
Deferred Compensation Plans

---

Commission and bonus plans

Profit sharing

Stock options (qualified and nonqualified)

---

Table 1.4    Qualified Plans (Current Tax Deduction)

401(k) program

Simplified Employee Pension (SEP)

Savings Incentive Match Programs for Employees (SIMPLE)

Defined benefit (DB)

Defined contribution (DC)

Employee Stock Ownership Plan (ESOP)

## TO LIMIT PARTICIPATION IN THE PLAN, YOU NEED A "NONQUALIFIED PLAN"

Nonqualified plans allow you to limit the participants in the plan. This means that you can exclude some employees and only include the principals or selected members of your team. Although you will not get a current tax deduction for your contributions, you can achieve aggressive financial benefits with nonqualified plans.

With these plans, there is no tax deduction until the employee begins receiving benefits (usually at retirement). When the employee begins reporting income, the employer can deduct the payment. Examples of nonqualified plans include Supplemental Executive Retirement Plans (SERP), excess benefit plans, and split dollar plans (see Table 1.5).

Nonqualified plans that enhance retirement benefits can be powerful tools to attract and retain key employees. "Forfeiture" provisions (also called "golden handcuffs") encourage employees to stay with their present employer instead of leaving to work for a competitor.

Table 1.5   Nonqualified Plans
(No Current Tax Deduction)

| |
| --- |
| Supplemental Executive Retirement Plans (SERP) |
| Excess benefit plans |
| Split dollar plans |

## LOOK AT THE BIG PICTURE BEFORE
## DIVING INTO THE SPECIFICS

It is important to step back and reassess what you are trying to
accomplish before focusing on specifics. Incentives, deferred
compensation, and retirement planning are components of the
overall compensation plan for the company. Since compensation drives business performance, you need to align your compensation strategies with your business goals.

## THE BEWILDERING ARRAY OF ALTERNATIVES

Evaluating the alternatives can be overwhelming for small
business owners who focus primarily on running the business.
Examining the options can be like getting lost in the "trees"
(details and issues) and losing sight of the "forest" (the business goals). Large corporations hire compensation experts to
perform analyses, design models, and create complex, multi-
faceted compensation programs. Most small business owners,
however, have neither the time nor personnel for such elabo-
rate processes.

    In choosing a plan for your business, cost and complexity of
administration are major factors. So it makes sense to focus on
that perspective when looking at your options. As we discuss

Table 1.6   Options Framework by Complexity and
Cost of Administration

| Easy/Inexpensive | More Complicated/Costly | Complex/Expensive |
| --- | --- | --- |
| Bonus | Defined contribution | Stock options |
| SEP | 401(k) | Nonqualified plans |
| SIMPLE | Defined benefit | ESOP |

the alternatives, we will view them from the perspective of easy and inexpensive to administer, to more complicated and costly, to complex and expensive. This framework will help you evaluate the pros and cons and make a choice that is a good fit for your business (see Table 1.6).

If you already have a plan in place, changing is tricky. You must carefully plan any changes and clearly communicate them to motivate employee performance and achieve business results. Changes are disruptive and raise concerns with employees. To ensure a positive outcome, think about compensation in a comprehensive manner. Do not just add a 401(k) plan without looking at the overall picture.

So, step back and reassess what you are trying to accomplish before tackling the specifics of the options. Filling out Worksheet 1.1 will pinpoint your long-term objectives and enable you to make informed choices about the options available.

Different situations require different plans. Writing down this information will make it easier to pull together a request for proposals later. It will also help you avoid the following common mistakes.

WORKSHEET 1.1
**Company Background Information Worksheet**

Name of Company _____

Address of Company _____

Employer Identification Number (EIN) _____

Organization Form

____ S-Corp     ____ C-Corp     ____ LLC     ____ Unincorporated

Year Founded _____

Type of Product or Service _____

| Names of Owners | Percentage of Ownership | Age |
|---|---|---|
| _____ | _____ | _____ |
| _____ | _____ | _____ |

Number of Employees _____     Family Members Work
in the Business _____

Employee Ages _____     Employee
Salary Range _____

   (See also the Employee Data Table Worksheet 4.1 on p. 36.)

Affiliated Companies
(Is there common ownership of any other companies?)

_____

How is the business doing?

Stable or increasing revenues?

Can you make a fixed annual commitment to fund a plan?

Do you need to determine plan contribution annually?

How much employee turnover do you experience?

What is the competition doing?

How strong are your administrative systems?

Do you outsource payroll and benefits administration?

Do you want to minimize administrative requirements?

What are your business problems?

_____

_____

_____

_____

What are your goals?

How many years until you retire?

Do you plan to sell the business?

Do you want to maximize owner compensation?

Do you want to share rewards with employees without sharing ownership?

Do you want to encourage employee ownership?

What do you want to avoid?

What is your worst fear for your business?

What is most important to you?

## COMMON MISTAKES IN RETIREMENT PLANS

Cynthia Sechrest, CPA, co-owner of Sechrest Financial Services, LLC, a fee-only financial planning firm located in Acton, Massachusetts, and on the Internet at www .sechrestfinancialservices.com, shares her insights and experience.

In her tax practice, Cindy met many small business owners with successful businesses but a short-term financial perspective. Cindy saw a need to help her clients with long-range financial planning for small business owners and individuals.

In working with her clients, Cindy sees some recurring patterns:

**1.** Not taking the time to think about retirement planning

Business owners just do not take the time to think about retirement planning. "Turning 50" is a triggering event for many people to get serious about retirement planning.

**2.** Picking a plan that is too complicated for their business

It is quite common for a business owner to implement a 401(k) plan that sounds great. In reality, for a business with 10 or fewer employees, the cost can be prohibitive and the complexity overwhelming.

**3.** Underestimating the amount of time needed to educate employees about the plan

Communicating with employees about the plan takes a lot of time. It is not uncommon for an employer to put a plan in place that achieves only low employee participation. This causes the plan to fail the "nondiscrimination" tests and triggers a big administrative hassle. If employees are not English-speaking, the complexity of communication is significantly greater.

**4.** Not understanding how the plan is funded

In looking closely into some plans, Cindy found that they were funded with life insurance or variable annuity contracts. These business owners thought they were dealing with a "pension consultant," but in reality they were dealing with a life insurance salesperson. If the person's business card says "securities offers through . . ." or "registered with . . ." you are talking with someone who is selling products, not just offering advice about retirement plans.

### Life Insurance Is Not Appropriate for Funding Retirement Plans

Cindy feels strongly that although life insurance is an important part of personal financial plans, it may not be appropriate for retirement plans.

A business owner should ask these key questions:

- "Am I locked in?"
- "Are there surrender charges?"
- "Can I change my investments?"

In conclusion, Cindy encourages business owners to carefully assess what is necessary to successfully implement the retirement plan before jumping in.

# 2

# WHY HAVE A COMPENSATION PLAN?

Compensation is critical to hiring and retaining key employees. Like your key customers, loyal employees are critical to your company's success. Hence, your compensation plan is as important as your marketing plan, operations plan, and financial plan. Compensation is a critical element of your overall business plan.

Having a written compensation plan actually simplifies life. Without a plan, compensation decisions are made on an ad hoc basis and can easily become fragmented and disconnected from the company's goals. Creating a written plan for all employees forces you to look at compensation in an integrated way. An employee handbook is a useful way to provide this information for employees.

## COMPENSATION REFLECTS YOUR COMPANY'S VALUES

If you have a consistent and well-thought-out compensation plan, your company's values and rewards will be clear to the employees. If you do not develop such a plan, politics will prevail and employees will make their own inferences about company values. Worse, if you allow ad hoc compensation decisions, you may find yourself with new hires who are being paid more than long-term, highly skilled employees. This can have disastrous results, and you may find yourself defending an age-discrimination lawsuit.

I have heard many an outraged business owner complain about employees who leave to start competing firms. It is a fact of life—high-performing employees (who are poorly compensated) will leave. They will go where they will be rewarded. They will work for competitors or start competing firms unless you make staying with your company a more attractive choice. Noncompete agreements are far less effective in retaining key employees than a well-constructed compensation plan.

## BASE PAY AND BENEFITS

Compensation should be designed to reward the behaviors that make the business successful. Base pay is a stated pay rate—the employee receives the same salary or the same amount per hour of work every payday. Benefits are also part of the employee's regular compensation.

It is preferable to keep base pay to a modest level. This approach has several advantages. A lower base payroll can help you weather a slow period in business without layoffs. A lower base payroll also leaves room to reward specific employee accomplishments with a bonus or profit-sharing plan. Employees share in the upside of good times, and you reduce the downside risk of high payroll through lean times. It is much easier to cut bonuses than it is to cut base pay or lay off employees.

## WHAT DO YOU CURRENTLY OFFER?

Worksheet 2.1 provides a framework for assembling information about benefits offered, compensation paid, and results achieved. It is a framework for integrating the components of the compensation plan and making informed business decisions.

---

### WORKSHEET 2.1
### Current Compensation and Benefits Summary

| Benefits Summary | Employer Cost | Employee Cost/ Participation % |
| --- | --- | --- |
| Insurance | | |
|   Medical | _____ | _____ | _____ |
|   Dental | _____ | _____ | _____ |
|   Life | _____ | _____ | _____ |
|   Disability | _____ | _____ | _____ |
| Paid time off | | |
|   Vacation | _____ | _____ | _____ |
|   Sick leave | _____ | _____ | _____ |
|   Personal leave | _____ | _____ | _____ |
|   Holidays | _____ | _____ | _____ |
|   Bonus program | _____ | _____ | _____ |
| Retirement program | | |
|   401(k) | _____ | _____ | _____ |
|   Other | _____ | _____ | _____ |

## HOW DOES YOUR PAY COMPARE?

You need to compare your compensation and benefits with that of other employers and industry standards in your area. You can obtain this information from sources such as the chamber of commerce, recruiting firms, industry associations, and studies conducted by firms and government agencies. Online sources include www.salaries.com and www.salaryticker.com. With this information, you will have a baseline for evaluating your compensation plan.

## USE COMPENSATION TO MOTIVATE EMPLOYEES

Most employees respond positively to incentives. Incentive compensation is additional money for achieving specific pre-established objectives or milestones. In most businesses, paying salespeople a commission for sales made is standard practice. Commissions are usually highly effective in motivating salespeople. One approach is to extend the sales commission model of rewarding specific accomplishments to other positions in your company. For example, employees might receive a commission or bonus for achieving specific milestones such as completing a project on time, meeting budget objectives, or attaining a quality level.

## WHAT BEHAVIORS DO YOU WANT TO ENCOURAGE? DISCOURAGE?

Workplace incentives should be designed to produce behavior that will make the business successful. All too often, the wrong people receive rewards. If you want fantastic front-line customer service, you need to recognize and reward the people delivering the service, not just the group manager.

---

**WORKSHEET 2.2**
**Behaviors and Outcomes**

1. List employee behaviors that are desired.

2. List employee behaviors that you want to discourage in the workplace.

3. List outcomes that you want to reward.

—how do you fund?

---

In our family, we rewarded our kids for doing their homework. It took us a while to figure out that if they did the homework every day, desirable grades would follow. So, think about whether you are asking for an outcome without rewarding the behavior that will produce that outcome.

The next step in designing your incentive compensation plan is to list the behaviors that you want to encourage. Then ✓ list the behaviors that you want to discourage. Finally, list the outcomes that you want to reward. Worksheet 2.2 can help you complete this task.

## WRITING YOUR COMPENSATION PLAN

The real benefit of writing your plan is getting the information out of your head and onto paper. This process helps you to be objective and to identify what is going on in your company.

Table 2.1   Benefits of Writing a Plan

It is inexpensive.

It gets your information on paper.

It provides an objective look at the data.

It allows you to examine alternatives.

It surfaces your assumptions.

It enables you to get feedback from others.

Writing a plan is easy to put off, but putting your plan on paper is *critical*. Planning is an inexpensive way to look at and test out alternatives before you spend any money. You may find it helpful to think of writing your plan as being sort of like following an exercise regimen. Although it is easy to put off the effort because the results are not immediate, the benefits are real (see Table 2.1).

A written plan can become a dust collector on your office bookshelf. Many times, business owners create a plan and then never look at it again. I highly recommend that you summarize your compensation plan on a couple of pages so you can easily refer to it (see Table 2.2).

Table 2.2   Benefits of Visualizing Your Plan

Using a visual framework helps you prioritize and focus.

You can map out and compare alternative scenarios.

You can see connections and sequencing of actions.

Deliverables and milestones become clear.

## A WRITTEN PLAN WILL HELP
## YOU BE CONSISTENT

Whatever you decide to do, it should be part of your plan and you should implement it consistently. Inconsistency or a failure to follow through will undermine the effectiveness of your incentive compensation plan in motivating employees.

## USING A CALENDAR TIME LINE

I like to use a time line to visualize my plan. With the time line framework, I can see the next 12 months at a glance. On the calendar, you can map out the annual patterns of your business: busy periods, slow periods, and key events such as trade shows or delivery deadlines. Then you can map out when you can realistically focus on reviewing your compensation and benefits and developing a plan. Once you schedule it, you are much more likely to make it happen. This will encourage you to focus on your task, gather information, and make decisions. It will enable you to implement your decisions in a coordinated manner. Further, it gives you a clear picture of what is going on. Of course, things change as the year unfolds. If changes need to be made, you can make them in the context of the overall plan. You can use Worksheet 2.3 to start your calendar time line.

In summary, the writing process helps you get your ideas out on paper, surface your assumptions, and invite other people to review your ideas and assumptions and provide feedback.

Planning begins by taking stock of your current situation:

- What is valued and rewarded in your company?
- What do you currently offer to employees and how much does it cost?

## WORKSHEET 2.3
### Plan Visual Calendar Timeline

| AREA | JAN | FEB | MAR | APR | MAY | JUN | JUL | AUG | SEP | OCT | NOV | DEC |
|------|-----|-----|-----|-----|-----|-----|-----|-----|-----|-----|-----|-----|
| B U S  D A T E S | | | | | | | | | | | | |
| O P E R A T I O N S | | | | | | | | | | | | |
| R E V I E W S  P L A N | | | | | | | | | | | | |

- What is the level of employee participation in the current programs?
- How do your compensation incentives and benefits compare with those of other employers?
- What is working well?
- What is not working well?
- What behaviors do you want to encourage?
- What behaviors do you want to discourage?
- What outcomes do you want to reward?

## NEXT, CREATE A VISUAL CALENDAR FRAMEWORK FOR YOUR PLANNING PROCESS

Mapping out your calendar lets you see your business year at a glance. With a visual framework, you can schedule your planning process as part of your business operations:

- Map out the key events of your business year.
- Map in a rough timetable for compensation and benefit review and planning.

With your planning framework, you can make some realistic choices about how you will develop your integrated compensation plan. Before you go too far into the specifics of your plan, try to get employee input.

## WHAT IS IMPORTANT TO EMPLOYEES?

Ultimately, the employees' reaction to your compensation plan will determine its effectiveness. Chapter 3 discusses how to ask employees what is important to them.

## PLANNING IS AN ONGOING PROCESS

Like an exercise program, planning only proves beneficial when it becomes a routine activity. Annual reviews are a relatively painless means of updating your compensation plan to reflect actual experience and changes in the business environment.

---

### COMMON MISTAKES AND TIPS TO GET A GOOD VALUE BENEFITS PLAN

Matt Hollister is the president of Business Benefits, which is located in Clinton, Massachusetts, and on the Internet at www.b-benefits.com. He shares his insights about common mistakes that business owners make, as well as tips for how business owners can get good value in their benefit plans.

Matt's firm is an insurance brokerage that helps companies find and implement group insurance benefits in the areas of health (medical, dental, vision) and welfare (life, accident, and disability) coverage.

According to Matt, these are common mistakes of business owners:

- Not reviewing their benefits on a regular basis to make sure that the coverage they have is appropriate and the price is competitive
- Being overly generous (such as paying 100 percent of the medical and dental coverage)
- Not offering adequate networks of care providers (such as too few options for doctors, hospitals)
- Not keeping their employee records up to date
- Not communicating clearly with employees about costs and need for changes in plans

- Not providing adequate coverage in key areas such as disability insurance (maximums may be too low)
- Not checking with employees about what they want and how satisfied they are with the company benefits

Matt recommends a "benefits audit" when you renew your benefit plans:

- Do you have the coverage that you think you have?
- Are your benefits on a par with the competition?
- Do you have adequate coverage in short- and long-term disability?
- What services do your vendors provide? (Do they advocate for employees when claims are denied?)
- What other options should you consider?

### Inexpensive Benefits for Employers

Matt suggests that employers consider offering Section 125 plans, which are simple to set up and usually pay for themselves. Section 125 plans allow employees to contribute pretax dollars to an account from which they get reimbursed for health and dependent care out-of-pocket expenses. This helps employees with little cost to the employer.

Matt also suggests offering voluntary plans. With optional extra coverage, employees can elect to pay for additional life and disability insurance from their compensation. This is a benefit to employees without cost to the employer. With coverage such as voluntary life and disability plans, employees have access to coverage that they may not be able to get elsewhere. Voluntary plans often come with some level of guaranteed coverage and will generally be better priced than individual policies. Also, voluntary disability plans purchased by employees with

*(continued)*

after-tax dollars pay a tax-free benefit, whereas with company-paid plans, disabled employees have to pay taxes on the benefit they receive.

### Second Opinion at Time of Renewal?

With the increasing costs of benefits (especially health care), it is more important than ever to be clear about your goals for benefits and your company's budget. Before you renew your plan, it is a sound business practice to get a second opinion. Finding a knowledgeable advisor is essential. You want more than just a sales quote; you want someone who can help you make informed choices for your business. Conscientious insurance brokers guide you in developing your benefit plans and work with you on an annual basis to make sure that you are happy with your coverage.

# 3

# WHAT IS IMPORTANT TO EMPLOYEES?

The information in this chapter was contributed by Bruce Katcher, Ph.D. Bruce has a wealth of knowledge and more than 20 years of experience in helping companies understand what is important to their employees and customers. Bruce's firm, The Discovery Group, is based in Sharon, Massachusetts, and is located on the Internet at www.discoverysurveys.com.

Bruce knows *how* to ask the right questions. How you ask is as important as *what* you ask. So, before plunging in and asking employees what they want, you need to understand how to ask questions that generate answers with useful information. Asking questions the wrong way can trigger a backlash of employee dissatisfaction. With Bruce's practical approach, you gain valuable insights.

## EMPLOYEE INPUT IS CRITICAL

Employee input is critical when designing a compensation and benefit program. A very rich program could turn into a total disaster if employees do not feel it is meeting their needs. You might create a 401(k) program with many investment choices and a large employer match and then find that few employees enroll in the program. Or you could build a day-care center but then discover that most of your employees have no interest in using it because they are satisfied with their present child-care arrangements.

It would be nice if your benefit program could delight everyone in your organization. After all, it represents a large ongoing financial outlay. However, our research in more than 40 organizations during the past 10 years shows that only 6 out of 10 employees feel that their organization's benefit program meets their needs and the needs of their family.

## RESEARCH SHOWS SOME REASONS
## FOR EMPLOYEE DISSATISFACTION

- *Show me the money.* Many employees, especially those paid on an hourly basis, would rather see more money in their paychecks than a rich benefit program.
- *I am covered by my spouse.* Some receive benefits from their spouse and would therefore prefer higher pay to benefits.
- *I am not thinking about retirement now.* Typically, younger employees are less concerned about long-term retirement programs than are older employees.
- *I am not going to be here that long.* Although pensions and annuities are rich benefits, most employees today realize that they are unlikely to stay with the company long enough to receive any payoff.
- *Other companies offer better benefits.* When evaluating their benefits, employees often compare the company's plan with the plans of larger and richer organizations instead of looking for organizations of a similar size in the same industry.

- *The one benefit I really want is not offered.* Employees often have specific needs that the benefit program does not meet, such as coverage for treatment by orthodontists, optometrists, or alternative medicine providers or the opportunity to allocate their 401(k) investments to a particular stock or fund.

## RESEARCH SHOWS WHAT EMPLOYEES TYPICALLY WANT

If a major objective of your compensation and benefit program is to provide employees with what is most important to them, our employee opinion survey research lends some valuable insights. Table 3.1 lists the factors that employees say are most important to them.

## IMPROVING *NONCOMPENSATION* ISSUES

Employees today want to enjoy the work they perform. For many, their allegiance to their profession and their actual day-to-day work takes higher priority than their allegiance to their organization. Employees also feel strongly that the company

Table 3.1　The Factors Most
Important to Current Employees
(Not Listed in Priority Order)

| |
|---|
| Enjoyment of the actual work |
| Adequate staffing levels |
| Amount of pay |
| Link between pay and performance |
| Work/life balance |

should have an adequate number of qualified employees to handle the workload in their area.

Complete the following checklist to see how your company is doing:

_____ We have met with all of our employees, one-on-one, to discuss whether they feel that they are using their skills and abilities on their job.

_____ We continually ask all employees if they are enjoying their work assignments.

_____ We provide all employees with the decision-making authority that they need to perform their job well.

_____ We have a system in place to continually monitor whether employees feel that they have received the training that they need to perform their jobs well.

_____ We provide the tools and equipment that employees need to perform their job well.

_____ We provide all employees with the opportunity to attend professional seminars and workshops to help them stay up-to-date with their professional skills.

_____ We provide the opportunity for employees to increase their job skills through additional training.

_____ We provide the opportunity for employees to increase their job skills through job rotation.

_____ We continually monitor all work areas and departments to ensure that there are enough qualified staff members to perform the job.

_____ We maintain a full complement of multiskilled workers so that we can provide additional support when increased staffing is required in specific areas due to increased workloads, vacation schedules, or absenteeism.

## IMPROVING *COMPENSATION* ISSUES

Pay is very important to employees at all levels of the organization. There are three major psychological components to employees' perceptions of any compensation package:

1. *Internal pay equity.* How fairly they are paid compared with others in your organization performing similar work.
2. *External pay equity.* How fairly they are paid compared with others performing similar work in similar organizations.
3. *Pay-performance linkage.* The connection between their job performance and their pay increases.

## HAS YOUR COMPANY DONE
## THE FOLLOWING?

_____ We have examined our internal pay structure to make certain that the salary ranges for positions are in appropriate balance.

_____ We have examined our internal pay structure to make certain that employees performing the same job are paid comparably.

_____ We have examined our internal pay structure to make certain that new hires are not paid more than current employees performing the same job.

_____ We have conducted or examined published salary surveys to learn the pay levels for other employees in similar organizations in our area.

_____ We have developed and communicated our pay philosophy to all employees (e.g., to pay all employees at

_____ the same level as the top-performing companies in our industry in our area).

_____ We have trained our supervisors and managers what to say to employees about our pay philosophy, pay levels, and pay increases.

_____ We make certain that the pay increases or bonuses for our best-performing employees are better than those we give to employees who do not perform as well.

_____ We have disciplined, retrained, or dismissed all poor performers in our organization.

### IMPROVING BENEFITS

Work/life balance is very important to employees. The problem is that "balance" means different things to different employees. It can mean:

- Not having to worry about work when I am at home
- Having a flexible work schedule so that I can come in late or leave early when I need to do so
- Setting my own work schedule each week
- Leaving work promptly at 4:30 P.M. every day so that I can pick up my children at day care
- Having enough sick and personal days so that I can take time off when my children need me
- Working part time
- Working from home some or all of the time
- Taking more than four weeks' vacation each year

In addition to determining what balance means for employees, you must recognize that there are several reasons you cannot always give employees everything that they want:

- What employees want is too expensive.
- What employees want will negatively impact customer satisfaction.
- Although you might be able to provide some of the desired flexibility to salaried workers, you cannot do the same for customer service or manufacturing employees since they are needed in their work areas at certain times of the day.
- Different employees want different things making it impossible to maintain internal equity in the organization.

## HOW TO ASSESS WHAT *YOUR* EMPLOYEES REALLY WANT

The key is first to understand what employees want and what is important to them. Combining this information with the practical realities of your business, as well as the estimated cost, will help you determine what you can and cannot provide to employees.

A survey of employees can provide you with this information. Here are some important dos and don'ts when conducting an employee benefit survey.

## BENEFIT SURVEY DOS AND DON'TS

1. *Make certain that the survey is completely confidential and anonymous.* If employees feel that their personal preferences will become public knowledge within the company, they will be very reluctant to participate.
2. *Use a benefit survey professional.* Keeping the survey anonymous may require you to use a consultant who

can design, analyze, and interpret the results for you. Be certain to use a survey research consultant, not a benefit consultant who will try to sell a particular benefit program to you.

3. *Do your homework first.* It is better to have a general idea of what benefit and work/family options might be available to employees before you construct the survey. Ask employees what specific trade-offs they would be willing to make regarding health care deductible amounts, required copayments, and the amount of money that would be taken out of their paychecks to help pay for the plan.

4. *Try to get input from all employees.* If only half or fewer respond to the survey, you will not be able to rely on the results. You still will not really know how employees feel about their benefits and what is most important to them.

5. *Do not just develop a list of possible benefits and ask employees if they are interested in any of them.* Virtually all employees will say that they want all of the possible benefits that you have listed. This will not be very helpful.

6. *Ask how well employees understand their current benefits.* This information is often confusing to employees. By asking them how well they understand any documents or memos they have received, you can learn how best to improve your communications.

7. *Ask employees how satisfied they are with their current benefits.* Table 3.2 shows an example of a simple questionnaire that will provide the answer when you collate the results of all of your employees' responses.

Table 3.2    Benefit Satisfaction Questionnaire

Please circle the number that best expresses your satisfaction/dissatisfaction with each benefit:

| Insurance | Very Dissatisfied | Dissatisfied | Partly Satisfied/ Dissatisfied | Satisfied | Very Satisfied |
|-----------|-------------------|--------------|-------------------------------|-----------|----------------|
| Medical   | 1                 | 2            | 3                             | 4         | 5              |
| Dental    | 1                 | 2            | 3                             | 4         | 5              |
| Life      | 1                 | 2            | 3                             | 4         | 5              |

8. *Ask employees what benefit is most important to them.* Use ranking items to determine employees' preferences. For example:

  Please circle the *one* benefit below that is most important to you and your family:
  a. Medical insurance
  b. The 401(k) plan
  c. The bonus plan

9. *Include demographic items.* When designing a benefit plan, you need to know how different categories of employees feel about the current benefits and what changes they would like to see. Therefore, ask employees to indicate sex, age, full or part time, family income, dependents, salaried versus hourly, and whether they are covered under a spouse's plan.

10. *Include items that require employees to make choices.* Such items can provide valuable information that will help you make intelligent decisions when designing a benefit plan. For example:

If necessary, I would be willing to pay more out of my paycheck to receive, or to receive an increase in:

a. Medical insurance
b. Dental insurance
c. Life insurance
d. Prescription drug coverage
e. Vision care

Please circle the *one* most important change that you would like to see made to our medical plan:

a. Reduce the medical insurance required copayment when I receive services
b. Increase the types of coverage provided in the plan
c. Allow me to visit any doctor
d. Reduce the amount of money I contribute toward the cost of the plan

## CONCLUSIONS

- Employee input must be taken into account when designing or improving employee benefit and compensation plans.
- Trying to make everyone in the organization happy with the benefit and compensation plan is an unrealistic goal.
- The most important issues to employees today are pay, pay-performance linkage, adequate staffing, enjoyment of their work, and work/family balance.
- An employee benefit survey can help you identify what is most important to your employees.

# 4

# WHAT IS THE CURRENT EMPLOYEE PICTURE?

Almost invariably, business owners are surprised by the actual information about their employees. They are surprised that one employee's salary is so high and another's salary is so low. Sometimes they learn that a key person (one who really helps the company make those critical deadlines) has been overlooked and has not received a bonus in years.

## GETTING AN INTEGRATED
## PICTURE OF THE WORKFORCE

Worksheet 4.1 on page 36 provides a framework for pulling together information about employees, their compensation, benefits, performance assessment, and developmental needs. It is a framework for analyzing the components of the compensation plan in an integrated way.

**WORKSHEET 4.1**
**Employee Data Table—**
**Compensation and Performance Information**

| Employee Name | Date of Birth | Date of Hire | Position | Hours | Base Pay | Benefits | Performance Assessment? Developmental Needs? |
|---|---|---|---|---|---|---|---|
|  |  |  |  |  |  |  |  |
|  |  |  |  |  |  |  |  |
|  |  |  |  |  |  |  |  |
|  |  |  |  |  |  |  |  |

## INFORMED DECISION MAKING

With integrated information about your employees, you can get a better picture of your overall workforce. You can make informed decisions about whom you want to reward and whether your compensation is fair and equitable relative to work performance. This is also a tool for identifying high-performing employees—their strengths and developmental needs. You can make evaluations about which employees need training or a new assignment.

Within this framework, you can adjust compensation to reward the strong performers. You can adjust compensation to ensure pay equity among workers who are doing similar work. It is a sound business practice to review whether women or minorities are being paid fairly relative to compensation paid to white men for similar work. This reduces the risk of litigation for discriminatory employment practices.

## CONCLUSION

Aggregating employee information in an integrated framework will help you evaluate alternatives for establishing a retirement plan for your company and enable you to make informed decisions about your compensation plan.

# 5

# FAMILY BUSINESS?

Family relationships add complexity to running a business. Successful family businesses that stand the test of time find ways to resolve disputes and rivalries among family members and ensure that the leadership of the company is in capable hands. Sometimes this means finding nonfamily hands.

Compensation planning is especially important in family businesses. Frequently, the extended family depends heavily, sometimes exclusively, on profits from the business to maintain their way of life. To develop an effective compensation plan for a family business requires addressing all the issues discussed in Chapters 1 through 4 as well as dealing with the family dynamics.

## RECURRING PATTERNS OF FAMILY DYNAMICS

Although each family business has unique characteristics, there are recurring patterns that affect compensation planning. These include sibling rivalry, unwillingness of younger family members to take over, nonproductive family members, and the classic parent's reluctance to "let go."

The successful transition of ownership and management of a family business is fraught with problems, and the statistics are not encouraging. An article by John Bedosky in *Trusts & Estates* (April 2002), titled "Family Conflict, Not the Taxman, Is the Biggest Obstacle to Passing the Business to Successors," states: "Often because of inadequate succession planning, less than 13 percent of today's family businesses stay within a family for more than 60 years."

Succession planning is a complex process, especially in families with multiple siblings and spouses. Suggested background reading includes *Working with the Ones You Love: Conflict Resolution and Problem Solving Strategies for a Successful Family Business*, by Dennis T. Jaffee (Conari Press, 1990), and *Passing the Torch,* by Mike Cohn (The Cohn Financial Group, 1992). Online resources such as the Family Business Magazine web site (http://www.familybusinessmagazine .com) provide a broad range of useful family business background information. NetMarquee's Family Business NetCenter (http://nmq.com/fambiz.nc) includes 28 university-based family business programs, plus articles on succession planning.

## SUCCESSION PLANNING 1-2-3

Planning ahead is the best way to achieve your goals and a smooth transition of management and ownership of the business. To achieve a successful family business succession, I recommend the 1-2-3 approach:

1. Assess the current situation.
2. Articulate your long-term goals.
3. Develop a written plan.

## Step 1.  Assess the Current Situation

**Objectively Assess Family Members' Roles in the Business.**
Being objective about family members is difficult to impossible. Many family business owners find it helpful to have outside advisors assist them on this process. To get a picture of family roles in the business, Worksheet 5.1 expands Worksheet 4.1 to include a family role. Completing the worksheet will give you a picture of the current situation.

With this information, you can look for the answers to some critical questions:

- Do family members have clear roles and responsibilities?
- How can I objectively evaluate the performance of family members?

---

**WORKSHEET 5.1**
**Employee Data Table—**
**Compensation and Performance Information**

| Employee Name | Date of Birth | Date of Hire | Position and Family Role | Hours | Base Pay | Benefits | Performance Assessment?<br><br>Developmental Needs? |
|---|---|---|---|---|---|---|---|
| | | | | | | | |
| | | | | | | | |
| | | | | | | | |
| | | | | | | | |

- Do nonfamily members respect family members for their contribution to the business?
- Are there conflicts among family members that affect the business?
- Do family members feel fairly treated?
- Are family members fairly compensated for their contributions to the business?
- How does family compensation compare with nonfamily employee compensation?

**Assess Whether Family Members Can Successfully Run the Business.**   Based on your answers to the preceding questions, you can make an informed judgment about whether it is realistic to transfer management to family members. No matter whether you plan to transfer ownership to family members, it is critical to develop a succession plan. Without a plan, a smooth transition is unlikely. In the worst scenario, it can severely disrupt business operations and even result in a serious legal battle.

### Step 2.  Articulate Your Long-Term Goals

Planning for your succession is never easy. Your goals should drive the planning process. Hence, articulating your long-term goals is a critical step in the planning process. Answering the following questions will help you establish a framework for planning:

- Do you plan to retire? At what age?
- Do you plan to transfer ownership and/or management within the family?
- Do you plan to transfer ownership and/or management to employees?
- Do you plan to sell the business?

## Step 3. Develop a Written Plan

A written succession plan provides for the orderly transition of ownership and management of your company. The plan can be reviewed, discussed, and revised over time. It is essential to put the plan in writing because people have selective memories and memory fades with time. The importance of communication, and more communication, about the plan among family members cannot be overstated.

The written plan becomes a road map for the parties and can be invaluable in the event of a crisis such as owner illness or death. The absence of a plan can be a financial disaster for your business and your survivors. So, think of your succession plan as a critical element of your estate planning. It is truly a kindness to your survivors to lay out a plan that minimizes disruption to the business, their primary source of income.

**Use Experts for Legal and Tax Advice.**   There are many ways to structure your succession plan. The company can redeem (buy back) your stock over time giving you a nice retirement income. Or, there can be a buyout by others, family members, employees, or a third party. You can transfer ownership, but retain control by using nonvoting stock. Because of complex tax and legal issues, expert advisors should assist in developing the succession plan.

**Use Compensation as a Tool to Achieve Your Goals.**   Compensation is a key tool to developing and retaining key employees, both family and nonfamily. Taking another look at Worksheet 5.1, what compensation changes are needed? Which employees are critical to retain? What is the mix of family and nonfamily employees? What incentives do you want to put in place?

## SPECIAL CONSIDERATIONS IN EVALUATING
## OPTIONS FOR A FAMILY BUSINESS

The options for deferred compensation and retirement plans, discussed in Chapter 6, need to be evaluated from the perspective of the mix of family and nonfamily employees in the business. Retirement plans that require *employer funding*—which small business owners usually view negatively, since they are paying for employees' retirement—can actually be an upside for family businesses. If most or all of the employees are family members, the business is able to obtain tax deductions (reduce current taxes) to fund the retirement of family members.

### If Most Employees Are Family Members

If most or all the employees are family members, a SEP (Simplified Employee Pension Plan) is an easy choice. SEPs are fully funded by the employer up to 25 percent of income to a maximum of $40,000 per year. With SEPs, employers are not locked into an annual funding commitment and decide each year what amount (percentage of compensation) they want to fund (up to the maximum), and they can even skip a year. In funding SEPs, employers cannot discriminate in favor of themselves or highly compensated employees. This can work well for a family business, if you are funding the retirement of family members.

### If Key Employees Are Nonfamily Members

If key employees are nonfamily members, the choices are more complicated.

The range of *qualified plans* (such as the defined contribution, 401(k)s, and defined benefit plans discussed in Chapter 6) offer some good choices but require satisfying the *discrimination* tests. The discrimination tests apply to all employees, so you cannot favor family members in funding retirement plans.

*Nonqualified plans* limit coverage to selected key employees. With nonqualified deferred compensation plans, you can put more money away and select the employees who are covered. Nonqualified plans can focus exclusively on the business owner and/or key employees (and exclude most other employees). Nonqualified plans can be implemented in addition to qualified plans.

Forfeiture provisions of nonqualified plans are an effective way to retain key employees. Forfeiture provisions also mean the employer does not have to pay employees who leave the company.

## Avoiding Older Generation's Dependence on Younger Generation

It is much easier for the older generation to "let go" if their retirement income stream is secure, separate, and apart from the future performance of the business. That way, their retirement income is not dependent on how well the kids or successor managers run the business. A carefully designed retirement plan can secure a retirement income, apart from the business.

Special considerations apply to the development of compensation and retirement plans for a family business. Recognizing family dynamics and retaining key nonfamily employees are essential factors. Using business planning methodologies and advisors can help to make the planning process more objective and reduce the emotional fallout. Experience confirms that you cannot please everyone and that some family members will not like the plan.

Even though you cannot make everyone happy, it is critical to have a written succession plan. The absence of a plan can spell disaster for your business. Within the framework of a succession plan, compensation and retirement plans are tools to accomplish your goals.

Owners of family businesses need to carefully analyze the options discussed in Chapter 6. Life insurance, discussed in Chapter 7, can be an important part of your financial security as well as a tool for equalizing interests among family members. Instead of leaving the business in equal shares to your survivors, you can provide for nonworking family members through life insurance and leave the business to the family members who are employees.

# 6

# WHAT ARE
# THE OPTIONS?

## PART 1—EASY AND INEXPENSIVE OPTIONS

Because cost and complexity are major considerations in choosing a retirement plan, it makes sense to look at the options in terms of those criteria. In discussing alternatives, we examine cost and complexity of administration from three perspectives: (1) inexpensive and simple, (2) more costly and complicated, and (3) complex and expensive. This framework will help you evaluate the pros and cons and make a choice that is a good fit for your business (see Table 6.1).

Table 6.1  Options Framework by Complexity
and Cost of Administration

| Easy/Inexpensive | More Complicated/Costly | Complex/Expensive |
| --- | --- | --- |
| **Bonus** | 401(k) | Stock options |
| SEP | Defined contribution | Nonqualified plans |
| SIMPLE | Defined benefit | ESOP |

## Bonus Program

The easiest and least expensive incentive is a bonus program. You decide each year what you can afford and then pay it out as part of W-2 compensation. There is no annual commitment or complicated administration. There are different ways to calculate and distribute bonuses.

It is important for employees to view bonuses as a reward and *not as an entitlement.* So, even if you have been giving bonuses for years, take the time to rethink what you are rewarding. Look at Worksheet 2.2 (Chapter 2): What behaviors and outcomes do you what to reward?

**Bonus Pool?**   Some companies calculate a "bonus pool" each year (funds available for bonuses based on the performance of the company that year) and then allocate the funds to employees based on specific criteria. The more objective the criteria, the better.

**Milestone Bonus?**   Another approach is to reward specific milestones, for example, shipping of new product, achieving ISO 9000 certification, or achieving revenue and profit targets. In determining these milestones, be careful to plan the reward so that employees work for the good of the company. While some competition among employees is healthy, a poorly structured reward can lead to backstabbing and cut-throat behaviors.

**Spot Bonus?**   Employees love to receive recognition for doing something positive in the workplace. So, if an employee does something extraordinary, acknowledge it with an "on-the-spot bonus" of a small amount of money or a gift certificate.

## Use a Bonus Program to Reward
## Desired Behavior

Sounds easy. You should structure your bonus plan to reward and reinforce desired behaviors. A word of caution, however. Employees are smart as well as sensitive, and dislike being manipulated. So think through your rewards, and use them in a small-scale test to confirm that they will be well received. The reward also needs to fit your style. An incentive plan may backfire and produce negative behaviors if the reward is not credible to employees.

If teamwork is critical to your business operations, rewarding team members requires special awareness. Employees can become extremely resentful if they feel burdened with unproductive workers on their team who share equally in team rewards. Hence, balancing individual and team accomplishments is important. Employees, more than managers, frequently know who is really deserving of a reward. Having employees participate on a compensation committee or in the decision-making process can assure that rewards recognize and reinforce the high achievers in your company.

### Be Consistent

Whatever you decide to do, it should be part of your plan and you should implement it consistently. Inconsistency or a

Table 6.2   Highlights of Bonus Program

| Pros | Cons |
| --- | --- |
| Reward selected employees. | Need to establish reward criteria. |
| Costs are low. | Can become employee entitlement. |
| Amounts are flexible. | |

failure to follow through will undermine the effectiveness of your incentive compensation plan in motivating employees (see Table 6.2). Figure 6.1 provides an example of a bonus program.

If you want to offer more than a bonus program and put money away for retirement in a tax-deferred way, the Simplified Employee Pension (SEP) plan is an alternative that is easy to set up and administer (see Table 6.3).

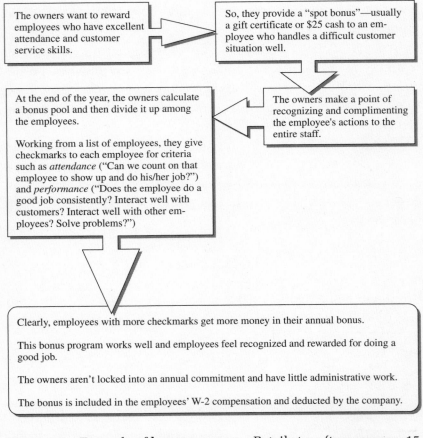

Figure 6.1   Example of **bonus** program—Retail store (two owners, 15 part-time employees).

Table 6.3  Options Framework by Complexity
and Cost of Administration

| Easy/Inexpensive | More Complicated/Costly | Complex/Expensive |
|---|---|---|
| Bonus | 401(k) | Stock options |
| **SEP** | Defined contribution | Nonqualified plans |
| SIMPLE | Defined benefit | ESOP |

## Simplified Employee Pension

A SEP plan operates like a super-IRA (Individual Retirement Account). It is easy to set up and has few administrative requirements. Employers essentially establish individual accounts for themselves and their eligible employees using IRS Form 5305-SEP.

SEPs work well for sole proprietors without any employees. A business owner can contribute (in 2002) up to 25 percent of self-employment income to a maximum of $40,000 per year.

SEPs also work well for companies with 10 or fewer employees. Employers must offer SEP contributions to all employees who are at least 21 years of age, have been employed by the business for 3 of the previous 5 years, and earn at least $450 per year. Employees set up an IRA to receive the employer's contributions.

Employers fund the SEP accounts, and employees own them. Employers are not locked into an annual funding commitment. Employers decide each year what amount (percentage of compensation) they want to fund (up to the maximum) and can even skip a year. In funding SEPs, employers cannot discriminate in favor of themselves or highly compensated employees. Since employees own their SEP account and employer contributions are 100 percent vested immediately,

Table 6.4   Highlights of SEP Plans

| Pros | Cons |
|---|---|
| Easy to set up and administer. | Employer funds, vests 100 percent. |
| No annual commitment to fund. | |
| Okay to skip a year. | Employees can walk away. |
| Contributions are tax deductible. | No flexibility in eligibility or vesting. |

employees who leave take their SEP with them (see Tables 6.4, 6.5, and 6.6).

A SIMPLE (Savings Incentive Match Plans for Employers) plan is another option that is relatively easy to set up and administer.

Table 6.5   Examples of SEPs

Consulting/professional service firms often use SEPs (financial, medical, legal professionals and consultants).

Sole Proprietor (No Employees)

According to Paul J. Brennan, Actuary, and owner of Boston Benefits Consulting in Concord, MA, a SEP (Simplified Employee Pension) is a good choice for a sole proprietor or company without employees. SEPs allow the owner to contribute up to 25 percent of self-employment income up to $40,000.

Corporation or LLC Firm (with Employees)

The SEP is also a good choice when there are 10 or fewer employees and the employer wants to pay the full amount of the employees' pension contribution. The employer determines the percentage of compensation to contribute and pays the money, understanding that the employees own it and can walk away with their money. A 401(k) plan is another choice that should be considered (see discussion later in this chapter).

Table 6.6    Options Framework by Complexity
and Cost of Administration

| Easy/Inexpensive | More Complicated/Costly | Complex/Expensive |
| --- | --- | --- |
| Bonus | 401(k) | Stock options |
| SEP | Defined contribution | Nonqualified plans |
| **SIMPLE** | Defined benefit | ESOP |

## Savings Incentive Match Plans for Employers

With SIMPLE plans, employers do not pay the entire amount. Instead, they match employee contributions up to certain limits. Employees may elect to contribute up to $7,000 of their annual pretax pay (in 2002). The maximum contribution amount increases $1,000 per year to a maximum of $10,000 (in 2005).

The employer match is calculated using one of two formulas:

1. *Matching contribution formula.* Match dollar for dollar up to three percent of employee's compensation 1-3% for the year, or at a lower rate not less than one percent of employee compensation.                    > d.f. ?
2. *Alternative formula.* Match two percent of compensation for each eligible employee earning at least $5,000 per year.

SIMPLE plans work like payroll deduction IRAs. They are established by using IRS FORM 5304-SIMPLE or 5305-SIMPLE.

Numerous other rules make so-called SIMPLE plans, not so simple. Employers cannot have any other qualified plan when they have a SIMPLE plan. Further, employees who withdraw contributions within the first two years face a 25 percent penalty (see Tables 6.7 and 6.8).

The SEP and SIMPLE plans enable an employer to offer a retirement plan to employees with minimal administrative

Table 6.7   Highlights of SIMPLE Plans

| Pros | Cons |
| --- | --- |
| Easy to set up and administer. | Owner max contribution $7,000. |
| Employer does not fund 100 percent. | Cannot have any other qualified plan. |
| Employees decide their contribution. | Employer must match. |
| No annual commitment to fund. | Employees can walk away. |
| Contributions are tax deductible. | Penalties for early withdrawal. ✓ |

*- can they leave it there?*

expense and hassle. For companies that want to put higher amounts into their retirement plans, there are additional options, called "defined contribution" (DC) and "defined benefit" (DB) plans. The DC and DB plans are more complicated and costly to administer, but they allow larger current tax deductions and employees can put away larger amounts for retirement.

Table 6.8   Example of SIMPLE Plan—Professional
Services Consulting Firm

The SIMPLE plan limits the owner to contributing $7,000 ($7,500 if over age 50).

Company cannot have any other qualified plan. ✓

There is little administrative hassle.

Employees can elect to participate or not. ✓ *- will they still get match?*

The owner decides what level of match to provide, between 1 and 3 percent of employee compensation.

The business claims the tax deduction and the employer's match contribution is included in the respective employee's W-2. No additional tax return or reporting is required.

## PART 2—MORE COMPLICATED AND COSTLY PLANS

The next stage of "qualified" plans (meaning contributions are currently tax deductible) comprises the defined contribution and defined benefit plans. Defined contribution plans are ones in which you specify how much you will *contribute.* Defined benefit plans are ones in which you specify how much you want to *receive* at retirement (e.g., 50 percent of pay). The required amount of contributions is calculated to achieve that payout.

The DB and DC plans are more complicated to establish and more costly to administer than the SEP and SIMPLE plans. The 401(k) is the best-known DC plan (see Table 6.9).

### 401(k) Plans

Under Section 401(k) of the Internal Revenue Code, employees *may choose to* contribute up to 15 percent of annual pretax compensation up to a maximum $11,000 in 2002. In 2006, the maximum employee contribution increases to $15,000 of pretax pay. The maximum for employer and employee contributions combined is 25 percent of compensation up to a maximum of $40,000 in 2002. Similar plans for nonprofits are called "403 (b) plans."

Table 6.9   Options Framework by Complexity
and Cost of Administration

| Easy/Inexpensive | More Complicated/Costly | Complex/Expensive |
| --- | --- | --- |
| Bonus | Defined contribution | Stock options |
| SEP | **401(k)** | Nonqualified plans |
| SIMPLE | Defined benefit | ESOP |

It sounds like a win-win choice for employers and employees. Employees benefit by reducing current income taxes and receiving tax deferral on the earnings in the plan. The employer benefits because employees are funding their own retirement plans and the employer (and highly compensated employees) can put away up to $40,000 on a tax-deferred basis.

There is a catch: 401(k)s are costly to set up and administer.

## Cost of Setup

Setting up a 401(k) is more difficult than starting a SEP or SIMPLE. You will need to work with a financial institution or advisor to establish a plan. You can sign up over the Internet, but carefully check out the company before you start sending in money. Working with a well-known institution is preferable, especially when you are dealing with retirement funds. Setup fees vary, but beware of "no fee" claims. You need to identify the cost because the fees may be hidden.

## Complexity of Administration

*Employee participation is a critical element in 401(k) plans.* To ensure that they are not favoring highly compensated employees, the plans must meet nondiscrimination tests. You will need an actuary to determine whether you meet the complex test criteria. Discrimination testing is a costly annual process. If the tests show that lower-paid employee participation is not sufficient to justify contributions by highly compensated employees, the excess contributions have to be refunded to maintain plan compliance. This can be a big hassle for all involved.

A key challenge for business owners is getting lower-paid employees to participate in the 401(k) plan. Although employers

are not required to contribute to 401(k) plans for their employ- ✓
ees, it may make sense. Employers can elect to make matching
contributions up to a certain amount of employee contributions.
Employer matches are discretionary and can be changed from
year to year. Employer matching contributions encourage employee participation.

## Safe Harbors—Employers Match
## Employee Contributions

Employers can avoid the discrimination testing process by
complying with the "safe harbor" provisions. Employers can
elect to:

- Match all employee contributions up to three percent of
  compensation.
- Contribute two percent on behalf of all eligible employees.

Employer match contributions can vest over time (graded
vesting can be up to seven years depending on the plan). So,
departing employees cannot walk away with employer contributions.

By electing to meet the safe harbor match requirements,
owners and highly compensated individuals can contribute
more to their own accounts and avoid the discrimination testing process (see Table 6.10).

## Fiduciary Responsibility

Another aspect of 401(k) plans is the employer's "fiduciary"
responsibility to act "prudently." Some plans allow participants to direct their own investments. Whether your plan is
assigned to a company officer for management or participants

Table 6.10   Evaluating Whether a 401(k) Is a Good Choice

---

How many employees will participate?

How will you educate employees about the plan?

What investment choices (choice of funds) will you offer?

Will you match employee contributions to obtain safe harbor status?

How much will it cost annually for administration, record keeping, and tax reporting?

---

manage their own investments, this is a risky area. Fiduciaries face a potential personal liability for investment decisions, especially in down markets. It is important to establish prudent investment policies and monitor investment choices and performance. This responsibility should not be casually assigned to an overworked member of your management team. It is safer to hire a firm qualified in administering 401(k) plans.

## Catch-Up Provisions

If you are 50 or older, the law now allows you to make "catch-up" contributions. This means that you can increase the amount of pretax elective deferrals to 401(k) plans, SEP, or SIMPLE plans as shown in Table 6.11.

Table 6.11   Catch-Up Limits—Additional Contributions
for Plan Participants Age 50 or Older

|      | 401(k) and SEP ($) | SIMPLE ($) |
|------|--------------------|------------|
| 2002 | 1,000              | 500        |
| 2003 | 2,000              | 1,000      |
| 2004 | 3,000              | 1,500      |
| 2005 | 4,000              | 2,000      |
| 2006 | 5,000              | 2,500      |

Employers who want to allow catch-up contributions must amend their plans and notify participants of their ability to make the additional contributions. Anyone who turns 50 *at any time* during the plan year is eligible to make catch-up contributions. This is another area in which it is wise to get local expert advice. Since the states have not uniformly adopted these provisions, the state tax treatment may differ from federal tax treatment.

Employers need to be careful to remit amounts deducted from employees' paychecks in a timely manner. The funds deducted from employee paychecks become "plan assets" and must be transferred to the mutual fund company *before* the 15th day of the month *following* the month in which the deduction was made. Fines and penalties, including criminal penalties, can result if the payments are not made in a timely manner (see Tables 6.12 and 6.13).

Sounds good, but is a 401(k) worth the hassle? Cynthia Sechrest, CPA, thought otherwise (see Table 6.14).

A 401(k) makes sense for companies in which a large percentage of employees (especially lower-paid employees) are likely to participate. The 401(k) works well for large companies that want to encourage employee savings, minimize employer contributions, and are willing to spend thousands of dollars a

Table 6.12    Highlights of 401(k) Plans

| Pros | Cons |
| --- | --- |
| Funded by employees | Discrimination tests |
| Larger employer contributions | Cost of administration |
| Safe harbors | Record keeping |
| Employer match vests over time | Compliance and tax reporting |
| Catch-up provisions for age 50+ | Fiduciary responsibility |

**Table 6.13  Example of 401(k) Plan—Does a 401(k) Plan Make Sense in This Situation?**

---

### Professional Services/Consulting Firm
### (One Owner, Two Salaried, and Three Hourly Employees)

---

One-owner firm employs two full-time highly compensated employees (each earning $65,000 per year as base salary) and support staff of three hourly paid workers (each earning less than $40,000 per year). Owner compensation is usually in excess of $100,000 per year. Owner is age 50 and wants to establish a retirement plan to maximize benefits for him. Firm is organized as an S-Corporation and turnover is extremely low. Employees range in age from 25 to 55.

Paul J. Brennan, Actuary, and owner of Boston Benefits Consulting in Concord, Massachusetts, makes two suggesitons:

1. *401(k) Plan with No Employer Contribution*

   Each employee would be able to contribute up to $11,000 (plus another $1,000 if age 50 or over in 2002). These amounts will each increase by $1,000 until 2006 when the limits will be $15,000 plus an additional $5,000 if age 50 or over. The owner will probably be able to contribute about 2 percent more than the average percentage that the employees contribute.

2. *401(k) Plan with Employer Match*

   If a small number of employees contribute or if the 401(k) employee contributions are low (average only 2 percent to 3 percent of compensation), then the owner might consider using the 401(k) Safe Harbor Matching formula. This matching contribution would be 100 percent of amounts each employee contributes up to 3 percent of compensation plus 50 percent of contributions from 3 percent to 5 percent of compensation (a maximum matching contribution of 4 percent of compensation).

   Providing this Safe Harbor Matching contribution would allow the owner to contribute $12,000 in 2002, increasing $2,000 per year up to $20,000 in 2006. In addition, the owner would receive a matching contribution of 4 percent of compensation.

---

Table 6.14    CPA Firm Prefers SIMPLE to 401(k)

---

Cynthia Sechrest, CPA, is the owner of Sechrest & Associates CPAs, a five-employee firm, in Acton, Massachusetts. Cynthia says that a SIMPLE plan is cost-effective for her firm. She tried a 401(k) plan and found that it was expensive to set up and employee participation was low. As a result, she had complicated end-of-year adjustments to meet the 401(k) participation and discrimination tests. So, she canceled the 401(k) and set up a SIMPLE plan. Now, she just decides on the match that she will offer, puts her own $7,000 away each year, and takes the tax deduction. She can offer a plan to her employees without an administrative hassle.

---

year on the administrative and compliance issues. (The so-called "Single K" which is beneficial for the self-employed or small business owner who employs only family members, is discussed in Chapter 12.)

## Annual Financial Commitment?

Before committing to a plan, make sure that you understand the magnitude of the annual financial commitment. One benefit of a 401(k) plan is that the contributions come mostly from employees. Employers have flexibility about the amount they choose to match and are not locked into an annual contribution. But they *are* locked into the annual cost of administration.

In evaluating the best fit for your business, consider how much of an *annual* commitment you can afford to make to the plan.

## Volatile versus Stable Profits?

How predictable are your profits? Does your business have up years and down years? Or, is profitability stable from year-to-year? This factor makes a significant difference in what type of plan is right for your business.

In businesses with volatile profits, flexibility is important. You may need to skip making contributions for a year to fund operations. Defined contribution profit-sharing plans give you flexibility.

In businesses with stable profits, annual financial commitments make more sense. Defined benefit pension plans allow you to put more money away but lock you into a fixed annual contribution commitment.

### Defined Contribution Profit-Sharing Plans

A profit-sharing plan gives you the flexibility to decide on an annual basis how much you will contribute. In 2002, employer contributions could not exceed 25 percent of total compensation of participating employees. Employer contributions can vary from year to year, and to retain qualified status must be *substantial and recurring.*

Table 6.15   Example of Defined Contribution Profit-Sharing Plan

- Company A has $20,000 in profits to distribute among participants.
- Allocation based on salary as a percentage of total salary.

|  | Salary ($) | Salary (%) | Contribution ($) |
|---|---|---|---|
| Owner | 100,000 | 50 | 10,000 |
| Employee 1 | 50,000 | 25 | 5,000 |
| Employee 2 | 30,000 | 15 | 3,000 |
| Employee 3 | 20,000 | 10 | 2,000 |
| Total | 200,000 | 100 | 20,000 |

Table 6.16    Example of Defined Contribution Profit-Sharing Plan

- Company A has $20,000 in profits to distribute among participants.
- Allocation based on age.

|  | Salary ($) | Salary (%) | Age | Contribution ($) |
|---|---|---|---|---|
| Owner | 100,000 | 50 | 55 | 15,150 |
| Employee 1 | 50,000 | 25 | 45 | 3,350 |
| Employee 2 | 30,000 | 15 | 35 | 900 |
| Employee 3 | 20,000 | 10 | 25 | 600 |
| Total | 200,000 | 100 | 160 | 20,000 |

With a profit-sharing plan, you specify how the contributions will be allocated among employees, usually based on salary, service, age, or a combination of factors (see Table 6.15).

With the allocation based on salary as a percentage of total salary, the owner receives 50 percent of the contribution. If the allocation includes age as well as salary, the owner receives a significantly higher portion of the amount contributed to the plan (see Table 6.16).

## Vesting

With a profit-sharing plan, the employer can establish a vesting schedule. This means that employees who leave prior to vesting forfeit their accounts.

There are three vesting options:

1. *Cliff.* Employee benefits vest after five years of service.
2. *Graded.* Employee vests gradually, for example, 20 percent per year.

Table 6.17    Highlights of Defined Contribution Profit Sharing

| Pros | Cons |
| --- | --- |
| Contributions are discretionary. | Offered to all employees. |
| Flexible allocations (age, salary). | Discrimination tests. |
| Vesting. | Cost of administration. |
| Forfeitures reallocated to plan. | Record keeping. |
| | Contributions are discretionary. |
| | Fiduciary responsibility. |

3. *Immediate.* For plans requiring two years of service for participation, employee benefits vest immediately.

Cliff vesting is a good choice for companies with high employee turnover. With gradual vesting, employees who leave when partially vested forfeit the unvested portion of the benefit. Forfeitures are reallocated among plan participants based on salary and/or service, and hence tend to benefit the owner over time (see Table 6.17).

The DC profit-sharing plan is a good choice for business owners with volatile revenues because contributions are flexible and can be adjusted to the business results on an annual basis. Further, this plan works well for businesses with high employee turnover because the forfeitures benefit the long-term plan participants—the owner and key employees.

### Defined Benefit Pension Plan

For the small business owner, defined benefit (DB) plans are like traditional pension plans; you know the specific amount you will receive when you retire. The contributions are calculated to achieve the desired payout.

#### Table 6.18 Example of Defined Benefit Plan

Plan promises 60 percent of pay at retirement at age 65.

Amount of contribution is determined by *amount of benefit* promised.

Participant earning $100,000 per year before retirement is entitled to receive $60,000 per year.

The contribution needed to fund this payout is calculated by an actuary based on several factors including the employee's age, date of retirement, and financial assumptions about interest rates.

For companies with owners and key employees who are 50 or older, who want to retire in 10 years or less, DB plans are an attractive choice. If you are an older business owner, this is a great way to catch up because you can contribute (and tax-deduct) as much as necessary for an annual retirement payout

#### Table 6.19 Example of Defined Benefit Pension Plan

| Name | Age | Service | Compensation ($) | Defined Benefit Contribution ($) |
|---|---|---|---|---|
| Owner | 53 | 20 | 200,000 | 137,113 |
| Owner's spouse | 53 | 20 | 52,000 | 29,357 |
| Employee 1 | 38 | 8 | 36,000 | 5,388 |
| Employee 2 | 25 | 3 | 20,000 | 1,208 |
| Employee 3 | 42 | 4 | 36,000 | 5,543 |
| Employee 4 | 31 | 3 | 32,000 | 2,891 |
| Employee 5 | 41 | 7 | 28,000 | 4,636 |
| Employee 6 | 29 | 5 | 26,000 | 2,049 |
| Employee 7 | 35 | 2 | 21,000 | 2,280 |
| Employee 8 | 44 | 10 | 48,000 | 10,215 |
| Total | | | 499,000 | 200,000 |

age - years & service.

of 100 percent of pay up to $140,000 per year (see Tables 6.18 and 6.19 on page 65).

### Defined Benefit Plan Funding Requirements

The funding requirements for DB plans are complex. Minimum funding standards are required to ensure that the funds will be there to pay the benefits promised. Compliance is a complex and costly annual process. It is critical for your company to maintain a cash flow that can handle the annual financial commitment. Waiver of the annual financial payment for hardship reasons is possible but difficult to obtain (see Table 6.20).

### Is One of These Qualified Plans the Right Fit for Your Company?

*401(k)*

- Uses employee funds
- High cost of administration, compliance
- Internet options

Table 6.20    Highlights of Defined Benefit Plan

| Pros | Cons |
| --- | --- |
| Fixed benefit established | High annual commitment |
| Great catch-up for older owner | Highly complex calculations |
| Rewards long service employees | Discrimination tests |
| Vesting | Cost of administration |
| Forfeitures reallocated to plan | Risks of underfunding |
| | Compliance and tax reporting |
| | Fiduciary responsibility |

*Defined Contribution—Profit Sharing*

- Flexible contributions, can skip a year
- Allocations based on age, salary

*Defined Benefit—Pension (Fixed Payout)*

- Great catch-up for older employees
- Complex calculations, costly to administer
- Fixed annual financial commitment

## Discrimination Tests of Qualified Plans

In considering a qualified plan, remember the discrimination tests. To qualify for a tax deduction, you must show that your plan does not discriminate in favor of *highly compensated employees* (usually the owner and key employees). Highly compensated employees are defined as owners of 5 percent or more of the company, are in the *top-paid group* (the top 20 percent of employees), or receive annual compensation of $85,000 or more. (This amount is indexed as 50 percent of the maximum defined benefit limit, which was $170,000 in 2000.)

## Highlights of the Nondiscrimination Tests

- *Percentage test.* At least 70 percent of all NON-highly-compensated employees must benefit from the plan.
- *Ratio test.* The ratio of NON-highly-compensated employees to highly compensated employees must be at least 70 percent.
- *Average benefits test.* It considers the economic value of all benefits and is extremely complicated.

A qualified plan requires compliance with the discrimination tests. If you really want to pick and choose which

Table 6.21   Options Framework by Complexity
and Cost of Administration

| Easy/Inexpensive | More Complicated/Costly | Complex/Expensive |
| --- | --- | --- |
| Bonus | Defined contribution | **Stock options** |
| SEP | 401(k) | Nonqualified plans |
| SIMPLE | Defined benefit | ESOP |

employees will benefit, then a nonqualified plan may be a better choice. Nonqualified plans allow you many choices including shared ownership with employees. Nonqualified
plans are not eligible for current tax deductions and are the
most complex and expensive to administer (see Table 6.21).


## PART 3—COMPLEX AND EXPENSIVE PLANS

This section describes the complex and expensive-to-administer
choices for deferred, incentive compensation, and retirement
plans for small business (see Table 6.22).


### Stock Options—Do They Make
### Sense for a Small Business?

Stock options are a way of creating an employee incentive
program. Stock options grant the right to purchase stock in

Table 6.22   Complexity and Cost of Administration

| Easy/Inexpensive | More Complicated/Costly | Complex/Expensive |
| --- | --- | --- |
| Bonus | Defined contribution | **Stock options** |
| SEP | 401(k) | Nonqualified Plans |
| SIMPLE | Defined benefit | ESOP |

## AVOIDING COMMON MISTAKES IN
## RETIREMENT PLANS

Paul J. Brennan is president of Boston Benefits Consulting, located in Concord, Massachusetts. An actuary by training, Paul performs the complex calculations required to analyze different retirement plan options as well as the actuarial analysis to ensure compliance with ERISA and the Tax Code.

In Paul's experience, business owners considering retirement plans fall into two basic categories: (1) Those who want a retirement plan but cannot afford costly setup and administrative fees; and (2) those who are willing to spend several thousand dollars for up-front design and annual administrative costs. There are pitfalls in both categories:

**1.** Business owners using low-cost "off-the-shelf" plans

SEP or SIMPLE plans can be a good choice, depending on the employee situation. A 401(k) plan can be expensive to administer. Internet-based 401(k) plans are providing more cost-effective options for employers willing to do everything online with little support.

Common mistakes include:

**a.** Rushing to implement a plan

Business owners rush at year-end to implement a retirement plan to reduce current tax liability. To get a plan in place quickly, and at what appears to be low cost, the business owners implement plans offered by financial institutions.

Business owners need to be aware that financial institutions use retirement plans as a "wrapper" for their investment products. Financial institutions focus on investments and charge service fees that may not be clear to the business owner. Such fees include "loads" and service charges.

*(continued)*

While these plans can work, often they are not the best choice for the business owner's situation. Financial institutions tend neither to ask detailed questions about the employee picture nor to provide the required follow-up, such as updating plan documents, preparing tax filings, and monitoring compliance.

**b.** Not making required contributions for employees

The IRS estimates that there are thousands of SEP plans in which the employer is not making the required contributions on behalf of employees. With both SEP and SIMPLE plans, business owners must make contributions for eligible employees. Failure to do so allows the IRS to invalidate the plan and disallow the tax deductions.

As businesses grow and change, the employee picture changes. Hence, owners should review the plan periodically to ensure that all the requirements are being met.

**2.** Business owners willing to pay up-front design fees and annual administrative fees for retirement plans designed to maximize their benefit

A 401(k) plan with a profit-sharing component can be a good choice. With this approach, the 401(k) plan has four "buckets"—the employee contribution, the employer match, rollovers, and a "profit-sharing bucket." The amount contributed to the profit-sharing bucket can be allocated based on age so that older, more senior people can receive a significantly larger portion of the contribution, up to the maximum of $40,000.

Defined benefit plans are a great way for older employers to put away sufficient funds to achieve their target retirement income. With a defined benefit plan, a 50 plus-year-old business owner can contribute and get a tax deduction for $100,000 to $150,000 annually. Defined benefit plans work well when there are few employees and sustained profitability.

Common mistakes include:

**a.** Implementing 401(k) profit-sharing plans without sufficient fund assets

It may not be cost-effective to design and implement a 401(k) profit-sharing plan for payrolls below $500,000.

**b.** Implementing a defined benefit plan with too many employees or without sustained profitability

With defined benefit plans, the obligations to employees are fixed. So, if the fund balance declines, or profits decline, the business owner might be committed to funding a plan that benefits the employees, not the business owner.

Paul says that there is a "Grand Canyon" between the retirement plan options available to the business owner with payroll over $500,000 (who is willing to pay for plan design and administration) compared with the options for the business owner whose payroll is under $500,000. Whether the payroll is large or small, pitfalls exist. To get the right plan for their situation, business owners need to be clear about objectives and realistic about costs.

the company at a specific price and under specific circumstances. In theory, stock options create an ownership mentality among employees and motivate them to help the company grow and prosper.

Young and growing companies that cannot afford to pay high salaries use stock options to attract and retain key employees. Stock options are particularly attractive for public companies or companies that *intend* to go public because there will be a market for the stock.

Stock options are somewhat problematic in small businesses because there is limited ability to sell the shares. So employee shareholders cannot cash out or sell their stock unless and until there is a liquidity event such as the sale of the business.

## Employee Shareholders Have Rights

Before granting rights to buy stock in your company, carefully consider the implications. Employee shareholders have rights, and you can experience major problems if you are remiss in handling stock options and stock ownership. Your shareholder agreement should specify how the shares of departing or deceased employees are to be valued and transferred so that you do not find yourself with unwanted shareholders. Sometimes the company buys back the shares at a stated amount, or alternatively, the other shareholders may buy the departing shareholder's shares. Having this kind of agreement can help you avoid legal battles. Without a shareholder agreement, you may find yourself with disgruntled former employees or the heirs of your deceased partner as shareholders in your business.

There are two types of stock options: *qualified* incentive stock options (ISOs) and *nonqualified* restricted options (NQSOs). The tax treatment is complex and different for the employer and the employee.

## Qualified Incentive Stock Options

To be qualified, the options must meet the requirements of the Internal Revenue Service concerning option price (at fair market value) and exercise period (no longer than 10 years).

When exercising the option, employees are subject to the Alternative Minimum Tax (AMT) on the difference between the option price and the then fair market value. The AMT is up to 28 percent and is essentially a prepaid tax. When selling the stock, employees may have ordinary income or capital gain depending on how long they held it. The gain may be capital gain if the employee held the stock for at least two years after the date of grant or one year from the exercise date. Otherwise, the gain is taxed as ordinary income. The real disadvantage of ISOs occurs when the stock goes down in value. In a down market, employees who exercised at a higher value can have stock that is now worth much less than they owe in taxes.

Employers do not get a tax deduction when they grant an ISO. If the employee selling the stock pays ordinary income tax on the gain, the employer can deduct as compensation the amount included in the employee's income.

## Nonqualified Restricted Stock Options

There are no restrictions on the option price or exercise period. Hence, employers can offer a low option strike price (pennies per share) and specify vesting events (such as sale of business).

When the stock vests, employees have a taxable event of ordinary income, based on the difference between the option price and the present fair market value of the stock. They have not received any cash, and yet they have taxable ordinary income. By filing an 83(b) election with the Internal Revenue Service (IRS) within 30 days of issuance of the restricted stock, employees can defer the taxable income until they sell the stock. Usually, when employees exercise nonqualified options, they sell enough of the stock to pay the tax.

The employer has a tax deduction for the amount considered income for the employees (see Table 6.23).

Table 6.23    Example of Qualified versus
Nonqualified Stock Options

|  | 10,000 Shares | |
| --- | --- | --- |
|  | ISO | NQSO |
| Option price | $10 per share | 10 cents per share |
| Vesting | 1 year | 1 year |
| FMV at vesting | $25 | $25 |

Qualified Incentive Stock Option (ISO)

- Employee pays no money up front for stock.
- Employee is liable for Alternative Minimum Tax (AMT) at exercise, approximately $42,000.
- Employee is also liable for tax when stock is ultimately sold, which can be at capital gain or ordinary income rates, depending on how long stock is held.
- Employer tax deduction is available when and if taxed as ordinary income to employee.

Nonqualified Restricted Stock Option (NQSO)

- Employee spends $1,000 up front to acquire shares.
- If employee makes 83(b) election, and holds at least one year, taxed as capital gain.
- If employee does not make 83(b) election, and/or sells less than one year later, taxed as ordinary income.
- Employer tax deduction is available when and if taxed as ordinary income to employee.

## TAX CONSEQUENCES—INCENTIVE STOCK OPTIONS

### What Are the Tax Consequences for Employees?

The tax consequences depend on when the employee sells the stock:

1. An employee who meets the holding requirements for the ISO can sell the stock and receive preferential long-term capital gain rates. The shares must be held for at least two years from the date of the option grant and at least one year from the date of option exercise.

    When exercising (buying) the options, the employee may be liable for the AMT at 28 percent.

    Using the example in Table 6.23, the following simplified calculation shows how to estimate the tax that would be due: Calculate the difference between the fair market value of the stock at the time of exercise and the price paid (the spread at exercise) and multiply by 28 percent.

$$(\$25 - \$10) \times 10{,}000 \text{ shares} = \$150{,}000$$
$$\times 28 \text{ percent} = \$42{,}000$$

    Any AMT paid generates a credit that may be used to offset the gain when the stock is sold or at other times when the taxable income exceeds the alternative minimum taxable income.

2. An employee who does not meet the holding requirements for the ISO and sells the stock has a disqualifying disposition. The AMT no longer applies. The employee has to report compensation income equal to the lesser of (a) the spread at exercise or (b) the excess of the sales price over the exercise price.

## What Are the Tax Consequences for the Employer?

The employer obtains a tax deduction for ISOs only if the employee engages in a "disqualifying disposition" and if the company successfully tracks these disqualifying dispositions.

The employer does not receive a tax deduction if the ISOs are qualifying transactions.

## TAX CONSEQUENCES—NONQUALIFIED STOCK OPTIONS

### What Are the Tax Consequences for Employees?

When employees exercise a NQSO, they recognize compensation income equal to the difference in the exercise price and the market price at the time of exercise (the spread).

Using the same example:

$(25 - 0.10) \times 10,000 = \$249,000$ of compensation income will be reported

### What Are the Tax Consequences for the Employer?

The employer will have a tax deduction for the compensation income recognized by the employee. The employer will pay payroll employer taxes on the compensation (FICA, Medicare, federal and state unemployment taxes), and these taxes are deductible by the employer.

Independent contractors can receive NQSOs. In that case, they receive a 1099 for the spread (the difference between the option price and the fair market value).

### Nonqualified Stock Options That Vest When the Business Is Sold

An effective approach in small business is to use NQSOs that vest on the sale of the business. This allows the employer to

Table 6.24    Highlights of Stock Option Program

| Pros | Cons |
| --- | --- |
| Attracts employees | Loss of ownership control |
| Motivates employees (ownership mentality) | Complex tax issues |
| Low up-front cost | No current tax deduction |
| NQSOs vest on sale of business | Risk of unwanted shareholders |

retain control of the business and still motivate employees, who will share in the growth of the business when it is sold (see Table 6.24).

Stock-based compensation has benefits, including the ability to attract and motivate employees at relatively low up-front cost. Still, it is important to recognize the complex tax issues as well as the risks of having minority shareholders in terms of losing ownership and control your business. Further, the employer does not receive a current tax deduction (current tax savings) from stock options. An effective use of stock options for a small business is to have them vest on the sale of the business.

If you do not want to share stock ownership with employees, consider a deferred compensation plan.

## Nonqualified Deferred Compensation Plans

With nonqualified deferred compensation plans, you can put more money away and select whom you will cover. Nonqualified plans can focus exclusively on the business owner and/or key employees (and exclude most employees). Nonqualified plans can be implemented in addition to qualified plans (see Table 6.25).

Table 6.25   Options Framework by Complexity
and Cost of Administration

| Easy/Inexpensive | More Complicated/Costly | Complex/Expensive |
| --- | --- | --- |
| Bonus | Defined contribution | Stock options |
| SEP | 401(k) | **Nonqualified plans** |
| SIMPLE | Defined benefit | ESOP |

Owners and employees who want to defer more income than is allowed under qualified plans such as the 401(k) can consider a plan in which a portion of the employee's current salary is deferred and the employer promises to pay that amount in the future. To avoid paying income tax currently, the employee must not have "constructive receipt" or the ability to access and control the funds. To avoid current taxation, there must be a *substantial risk of forfeiture.* The goal is to delay paying the income until the employee is in a lower tax bracket, usually in retirement. The business owner does not receive a deduction for the deferred compensation until the employee recognizes the income.

## Forfeiture Provisions

With nonqualified deferred compensation plans, there are no required vesting schedules and there must be forfeiture provisions to obtain tax deferral. Forfeiture provisions mean that employees have a substantial risk of losing the deferred compensation. Examples of forfeiture provisions include leaving the company, working for a competitor, conviction of a crime, or loss of license.

Forfeiture provisions are effective in retaining key employees. Forfeiture provisions also mean the employer does not have to pay employees who leave the company.

*funded - taxable to ee*
*unfunded - risk want be there*
*Life Ins - way to informally fund*

Tax Consequences—Nonqualified Stock Options        79

## Funded or Unfunded Plan?

With a funded plan, the employer transfers the deferred compensation money to an irrevocable trust. This assures that the
funds are set aside to pay the deferred compensation and are
protected from claims of creditors of the company. The risk
with a funded plan is that the IRS may decide that the funds
have become *substantially vested* and the income will be taxable to the employee currently.

In unfunded plans, the employer has access to the deferred
compensation funds, and they are subject to the claims of creditors. The risk is that the funds will not be available when the
employee retires. Life insurance can be used as an informal
funding mechanism to assure the employee that the funds will
be there in the event of the employee's death.

## IRS Scrutiny

The Internal Revenue Service scrutinizes these plans. The IRS
can find that deferred compensation payment for the owner is
really a "disguised dividend" and should be taxable currently.
Further, the IRS may find that the substantial risk of forfeiture
is not credible and hence the funds should be taxable as current income (see Table 6.26).

Table 6.26   Highlights of Nonqualified
Deferred Compensation Plans

| Pros | Cons |
| --- | --- |
| More income tax deferred | Employer tax deduction delayed |
| Selected employees | Funded versus unfunded issues |
| Forfeiture provisions | IRS scrutiny |

*Nonqualified deferred compensation* plans offer the mechanism to defer more current income—above and beyond the limits of qualified plans—for selected employees without the entanglement of employee shareholders. The forfeiture provisions are effective in retaining key employees.

The downside is that the employer does not receive a tax deduction until the funds are paid, and there are complex issues and risks around funding the plans. Further, IRS scrutiny of nonqualified plans can result in large tax liabilities. When properly designed and implemented, deferred compensation plans can be a highly effective incentive for retaining key employees and providing a more generous retirement than is possible with qualified plans.

### Retirement Is Succession Planning

For the small business owner, retirement planning is also succession planning. Who will run the business when you retire? Some business owners want their employees to buy the business. With *Employee Stock Ownership Plans* (ESOPs), the tax laws provide a complicated but highly tax-advantaged way for owners to get the value out of a business and transfer ownership to employees (see Table 6.27).

ESOPs are *qualified* retirement plans with many tax and compliance requirements. Unlike most retirement plans, ESOPs

Table 6.27   Options Framework by Complexity
and Cost of Administration

| Easy/Inexpensive | More Complicated/Costly | Complex/Expensive |
| --- | --- | --- |
| Bonus | Defined contribution | Stock options |
| SEP | 401(k) | Nonqualified plans |
| SIMPLE | Defined benefit | **ESOP** |

invest primarily in the employer's stock. With an ESOP, the employer makes annual contributions of stock and/or funds. The contributions (fair market value of the stock) are fully tax deductible to the company as long as it meets all the requirements. Participating employees have accounts in the ESOP, and the allocation of individual shares is usually based on compensation. Employees are not taxed on the contributions to the ESOP.

ESOPs can also borrow money to purchase stock from the employer (called a *leveraged* ESOP). This is a way for employers to get cash out of their business in a tax-advantageous manner because the principal and interest on the loan are both tax deductible to the company. *And,* business owners do not recognize or pay tax on the gain (difference in their basis and the value at the time of transfer) when the stock is transferred to the ESOP. They can effectively roll over their company stock (tax-free) into a diversified mix of blue chip investments. This is a huge benefit for owners.

### Employee Buyout

ESOPs also enable employees to buy a business that they could not afford to buy outright. For the right group of employees, ESOPs are a wonderful means of achieving ownership. The success of an ESOP depends on the continuation of effective management of the company.

In an employee buyout, it is important to verify that the employee group is committed to acquiring the business and is capable of managing it. Usually, the employee group forms a company and purchases the stock (or assets) using a combination of personal and borrowed funds. The borrowed funds are repaid from the cash flow generated by the business. Sometimes this cash flow covers the entire purchase price.

It requires significant time and expense to set up this buy-out process and document the agreement. Numerous tax and accounting issues must be addressed as well. Before you start down the ESOP path, you want to be sure that the employees are capable of managing the company.

## Assessing Employees' Capability

The following questions can help you assess whether employees will be able to manage the company:

1. What are the employee group's motives for buying the business? Can they define their objectives for acquisition?
2. Is the employee group prepared to make a full commitment of its collective time, energy, and resources? As you know, operating a business requires a tremendous amount of time and total dedication.
3. Are the members of the employee group financially committed and aware of the financial risks?

## Establish a Leadership Committee or Team

Before proceeding with an ESOP, take time to carefully assess the employee group's motivation, competence, and commitment. One approach is to form a *Leadership Committee* or team of selected employees to participate in the planning and operations for the coming year. With this approach, the selected employees will gain experience in actually running the business and you will be able to assess whether they can follow through and perform the expanded responsibilities of management (see Table 6.28).

Although ESOPs sound great, they are complicated and expensive to administer. If the rules are not followed precisely,

Table 6.28   Highlights of Employee
Stock Ownership Plans (ESOPs)

| Pros | Cons |
| --- | --- |
| Owners get wealth out tax-free. | Cost and complexity. |
| Employees become owners. | Annual appraisal requirement. |
| Employee management (strong). | Employee management (weak). |

the result is disqualification and significant tax liabilities. An annual appraisal is required, which is an expensive process. Success depends on having an employee management team that can run the company successfully.

For many small businesses, nonqualified plans provide a more realistic way to provide for a secure retirement.

---

**SUPPLEMENT RETIREMENT INCOME USING NONQUALIFIED PLANS FOR THE BUSINESS OWNER AND KEY EMPLOYEES**

Thomas Bishop, CLU, CFP, and senior vice president of USI Consulting Group works with business owners who want to put more money aside for retirement than is possible with qualified plans (such as 401(k)s and profit-sharing plans). USI Consulting Group specializes in the design, implementation, and administration of executive compensation and benefit programs. USI has offices in Atlanta, New York, and the Boston area, and is located on the Internet at www.uscigepb.com.

According to Tom, studies indicate that about 70 to 80 percent of preretirement income is needed to maintain current lifestyle. For highly paid people, this is hard to accomplish with

*(continued)*

qualified retirement plans. In many cases, the combination of Social Security and qualified retirement plans will replace only about 25 percent of preretirement income.

To bridge the gap, nonqualified plans can be an effective tool.

For example, a business owner aged 55 earning $220,000 per year who wants to retire at age 65 with 75 percent of preretirement income will need about $165,000 per year after retirement. Analysis of his current plans shows that Social Security and 401(k) plans will produce about $57,000 per year. Hence, the business owner has a retirement income shortfall of $108,000 per year.

| | |
|---|---|
| Current Salary | $220,000 |
| Retirement Target Percentage | 75% |
| Target Retirement Income/year | $165,000 |
| Projected Income 401(k) and Social Security | $ 57,000 |
| Shortfall or Gap | $108,000 |

A nonqualified retirement plan can be designed to bridge the income gap. Funds contributed to a nonqualified plan are after-tax dollars. That means there is no current tax deduction for the contributions. However, withdrawals are tax-free if the plan is designed correctly. Insurance contracts are one way to fund these plans.

Common mistakes that Tom sees are:

**1.** Underestimating the amount of income needed in retirement

The business owner who has lived on an annual salary of $220,000 and is suddenly cut to $57,000 per year will have to drastically readjust his lifestyle. From Tom's experience, this is not easy to do and can result in dire economic and emotional consequences.

**2.** Putting a plan in place and then not reviewing it on a regular basis

A plan is designed using assumptions, such as age, projected date of retirement, profitability of the business, and number of employees. Business conditions and personal circumstances change. The plan should be reviewed on an annual basis and adjusted for changes in the company or personal circumstances of the business owner.

**3.** Tying retirement security to the successor management (or next generation)

Nonqualified plans can be a highly effective means of providing retirement income security to the outgoing generation. This is segregated money that secures retirement income separate from the business. So, Mom and Dad are not dependent for their retirement income on how successfully the kids run the business.

**4.** Not ensuring continuity in the management team

Nonqualified retirement plans can be used to retain key employees and ensure continuity in the management team. This can significantly enhance the value of a business to a prospective buyer. This also helps ensure a smooth transition when the business owner retires.

**5.** Working with a "pseudo" insurance broker instead of a "true" insurance broker

Most insurance agents will tell you that they are brokers. A true broker has no affiliation with any insurance company. A pseudo broker is affiliated with a primary insurance company such as Metropolitan Life, Guardian, or Northwestern Mutual Life. Pseudo brokers will push you toward their

*(continued)*

primary company instead of objectively assessing the best choice in the marketplace for your circumstances.

6. Mistaking a brand-name insurance company for a quality, cost-effective product

Buying the insurance from a well-known company does not assure that the insurance product is the best, most cost-effective choice for your situation. It is especially important to check out alternatives if there are any health problems or unusual circumstances. For example, Security Life of Denver, Colorado, a subsidiary of ING, provided excellent coverage and an affordable premium for a pilot of experimental airplanes. Jefferson Pilot of North Carolina provided an affordable premium for an 80-year-old with major heart problems. In both cases, big-name insurers either declined coverage entirely or priced it out of reach.

Tom recommends developing a plan to supplement your retirement income. Tom also recommends using what he calls the "Warren Buffet approach" when selecting an advisor. Work with someone you like, trust, and respect. Ask about the person's experience, affiliations, and ongoing back-office support. Beware of someone who is pushing the product sale. You want to know that you are working with someone who is not just selling products but is designing, implementing, and administering your plan to achieve your goals.

# 7

# WHAT DO YOU REALLY NEED TO KNOW ABOUT BUYING LIFE INSURANCE?

This chapter provides background information and suggests questions you should ask to obtain the best buys in life insurance. The information in this chapter was contributed by David M. Isaacson, a principal of First Financial Resources, a national firm providing *independent* insurance and financial services to companies of all sizes. David is located in Waltham, Massachusetts, and on the Internet at david@ffr-mass.com.

## WHY BUY LIFE INSURANCE?

Small business owners buy life insurance for five primary reasons:

1. Repaying creditors and investors
2. Funding a buy-sell agreement
3. Covering key employees

4. Providing employee benefits
5. Providing for family members

## Repaying Creditors and Investors

Many business owners go into debt to start or maintain their business. Many loans call for business owners to sign both individually and as the president of their company. Frequently, bank loans call for the business owner to have life insurance that names the bank as a "collateral assignee." This means that if you die prematurely, the bank will collect their outstanding balance before your family sees any life insurance benefits. Similarly, life insurance provides assurance to investors that they will recover their investment.

## Funding a Buy-Sell Agreement

To avoid finding yourself in business with the spouse or children of your deceased business partner, you need to have an agreement that deals with death and other matters. This legal document is called a "buy-sell" or "stock redemption" agreement. It states that the deceased agrees to sell his or her stock or ownership interest back to the firm or the partners as long as the deceased's family receives an appropriate cash settlement.

Life insurance assures that the funds will be available to purchase the deceased owner's interest. Buying life insurance that equals or exceeds the value of the business is called "funding the agreement." The value of the business (and the amount of insurance) should be updated from year to year. Without the insurance, the heirs are usually bought out over time from the future revenues of the business (e.g., $100,000 a year for 10 years). This situation creates stress on the surviving partners and drains the resources of the company. It also creates uncertainty for the heirs.

## Covering Key Employees

Most firms insure their cars, building, and equipment as a natural course of business. But it is the key *people* who truly generate the revenue and are responsible for the profits of the business. Whether that key person is an owner or not, it is reasonable to insure his or her life in the event of death or disability. The amount of insurance needs to reflect the profits, deals, and resources that would be lost if this person should suddenly be gone from the company. The loss of a key person can cause stock values to tumble and loans to be called. In determining the amount of life insurance to buy, it is important to consider the disruption to the business and the cost of searching for and hiring a replacement.

## Providing Employee Benefits

Group life insurance is a staple of today's benefit packages. Once you begin hiring staff, your company should consider offering this benefit, even if employees are asked to pay a portion of the monthly premium. It is a low-cost and easy-to-obtain benefit for most companies. Firms of two to nine employees can obtain "package plans" and groups over 10 employees can have "true group" options.

The amount of the death benefit varies from industry to industry and in different parts of the country. The most common approaches call for either a flat dollar amount for all employees or a multiple of their salary (e.g., two times annual salary to a maximum of $300,000). The cost for employees' insurance is tax deductible to the company. Employees with more than $50,000 of coverage may have their W-2 forms adjusted at year-end to reflect a small additional phantom income that is determined by IRS tables and is taxable to the employee.

Built-in benefits of group life insurance include a "Waiver of Premium" provision that says there will be no cost for employees who are disabled beyond a stated waiting period such as four or six months. Even if the firm cancels the master contract, the "free" insurance will continue until recovery or a stated age such as 65. The life insurance death benefit amount is typically matched by a benefit that pays in the event of accidental death or disability. This is called "AD&D" insurance and only costs a few cents per month for each $1,000 of life insurance in force.

Finally, departing employees may take their insurance with them if they are willing to convert it to a permanent form of insurance within 30 days of leaving the company. This is generally not a good buy unless the person is in particularly poor health.

### Providing for Family Members

Life insurance can make a big difference in the quality of life for your survivors. Providing funds for children's education and money to pay off a mortgage are important benefits of life insurance. You may not need life insurance if your liquid assets are equal to six or seven times your annual income.

## OVERVIEW OF THE LIFE INSURANCE
## BUYING PROCESS

Buying life insurance is a complex and confusing process. Over the years, there have been numerous class action suits against top insurance companies by people who felt they were misled about the life insurance products that they purchased. Insurance products are regulated by state and federal insurance laws and, in some cases, by the Securities and Exchange Commission.

Figure 7.1 provides a diagram of the Life Insurance Buying Process.

## The Products

There are over 1,700 insurance companies selling more than 5,700 different life insurance policy variations in the United States. Competition is fierce. The industry is in the midst of a massive and ongoing consolidation in which the larger companies are buying out or absorbing the smaller ones. Private companies (called mutual companies) have been "going public" to obtain the financing they need for massive overhauls of internal systems and to create more competitive products and services. Metropolitan Life and Sun Life are just two such companies.

The way you buy life insurance has gone from a simple to a complex model. Prior to the 1990s, most people bought life insurance directly from an agent or representative of a specific insurance company or they bought it through a broker who represented the client's interest and could place business with multiple insurance companies.

Now, you can buy life insurance from your banker, your accountant, your securities broker, or the traditional life insurance agents and brokers. With these new players, the level of training and competence in representing insurance products varies dramatically. As a result, there has been a significant increase in consumer confusion about life insurance products.

## The Applications

Table 7.1 summarizes the reasons that people buy life insurance. In addition to the reasons discussed earlier (repaying creditors and investors, funding a buy-sell agreement, covering key employees, providing employee benefits, and providing

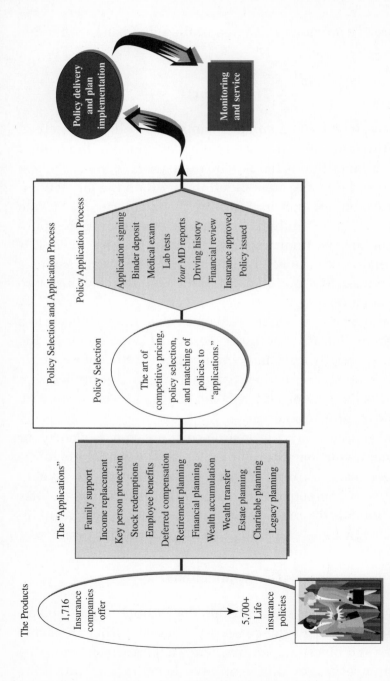

The Products

The "Applications"

Policy Selection and Application Process

Policy Selection

Policy Application Process

1,716 Insurance companies offer

5,700+ Life insurance policies

Family support
Income replacement
Key person protection
Stock redemptions
Employee benefits
Deferred compensation
Retirement planning
Financial planning
Wealth accumulation
Wealth transfer
Estate planning
Charitable planning
Legacy planning

The art of competitive pricing, policy selection, and matching of policies to "applications."

Application signing
Binder deposit
Medical exam
Lab tests
Your MD reports
Driving history
Financial review
Insurance approved
Policy issued

Policy delivery and plan implementation

Monitoring and service

Your Broker/Advisor

Figure 7.1    Life insurance buying process: How to get the most for your money.

92

Table 7.1  Rule of Thumb

| Uses of Life Insurance | Trigger Condition(s) | Why | When | Stumbling Points | Remarks |
|---|---|---|---|---|---|
| Family support | Married with children. | To replace your lost income earmarked to support your family. | Prior to or at the birth of your children. | Health | Low-cost term insurance at a minimum. |
| Investor/creditor protection | Your firm owes money. | Desirable, maybe mandatory. | Prior to or during loan application. | Health | Not deductible. |
| Buy-sell or stock redemption | You have a business partner. | So the survivor retains control and the deceased partners' heirs are fairly paid. | When the fair market value (or debt) is significant to you. | Establish stock's value<br>Health<br>Financial underwriting<br>Terms of agreement | Corporate or personal premium payments affect long-term tax treatment of stock. |
| Group life and ADD | You have nonowner employees. | Low cost tax, effective traditional benefit. | Current or pending employees want it. | Group size<br>Desired limits | Company's cost generally tax deductible.<br>Employees taxed on benefits over $50K. |
| Group supplemental life insurance | You have ≥10 employees who want more insurance. | A cost-free and employee-friendly benefit. | When there are enough employees who want it and will pay for it. | Group carrier's limitations and guidelines | Individual policies may be less expensive if employee is in good health and wants pure term insurance. |

*(continued)*

93

Table 7.1  *Continued*

| Uses of Life Insurance | Trigger Condition(s) | Why | When | Stumbling Points | Remarks |
|---|---|---|---|---|---|
| Payroll deducted life insurance | You have ≥10 employees who want more insurance. | A cost- and employee-friendly benefit. | When there are enough employees who want it and will pay for it. | Too few sign up. | Common in blue-collar firms ($3 to $12/week). |
| Group travel accident | You have ≥5 employees and travel is significant. | Low cost, employee friendly plan and/or key person protection. | Anytime. | Certain foreign travel, private pilots. | Can provide business only or 24-hour coverage (deductible). |
| Key man replacement | You identify ≥1 employees whose loss could cripple the business. | To replace lost profits and cost to replace key person. | Anytime. | Health. Financial justification. | Nondeductible, but often tax-free when received. |
| Key man bonus | Golden handcuffs desirable. | Motivate key people. | When business will last, > 5 to 10 years. | Health, agreements, and taxes. | Death benefit and cash equity both based on performance and longevity. |

94

| | | | | | |
|---|---|---|---|---|---|
| In retirement plans | Not usually recommended except for special conditions. | Cost of individuals insurance is tax deductible. | Profit sharing or deferred benefit plans are established. | Health and IRS regulations. Also some tax to employee. | Either a plan investment or to provide a "completion feature" for employees' retirement. |
| Supplemental executive retirement plans (SERPS) | Discriminating retirement plans needed. | Qualified plan inadequate for key people. | High-income key people need strong incentive. | Health, agreements funding, and administration options. | Assets may be subject to firm's creditors. |
| Estate tax relief | You have children and an estate tax liability. | Usually cheaper to buy insurance than to self-insure. | You are ready to begin organizing your affairs to minimize your estate taxes and probate costs. | Health age, procrastination, family "issues." | Husband and wife apply for insurance via an irrevocable trust. Policy pays at the death of the second insured. |

for family members), life insurance can fund retirement plans, deferred compensation, and estate planning, and can be useful for equalizing interests when transferring a family business.

## Policy Selection

You want to be certain the insurance company is strong and is going to be around to pay claims. Because of some spectacular insurance company failures, including Mutual Benefit Life, Confederation Life, and Executive Life, there has been renewed emphasis on independent agencies that review and evaluate insurance companies for "safety and strength." Ratings are provided by Standard & Poor's, A.M. Best, Moody's, Fitch Ratings, and Weiss Ratings.

Ratings and company valuations focus on things other than the quality or competitiveness of the products themselves. There is a strange trade-off in that the strongest companies may offer higher priced products to ensure they retain their standing as a "safe" company. Sometimes the best buys can be found at niche companies that are well rated but are not household names.

## The Application Process

The application process starts with basic data collection—your personal data, including date of birth, Social Security number, address, the amount of insurance you are applying for, and the type of policy. The owner and the beneficiary will be specified as well as the premium payment schedule. Finally, your travel and certain hobbies will be listed if they are likely to affect the cost of the insurance. The insurance company usually will schedule a medical exam by a doctor (other than your own), and the paramedic or doctor will come to your home or place of business for this brief exam. A blood test and urine sample will also be taken, and an EKG may be required for larger amounts and/or older applicants.

Virtually all life insurance applications include a reference to the Medical Information Bureau (MIB). Your signature on the form allows the underwriters to check to see when and to whom you have applied for life insurance over the past few years. There are also codes that indicate certain general information and some details such as whether you reported being a smoker or not.

Once the application and exam report have been completed, the insurance company may ask to see your own doctor's records of your medical history. Your driving records will be accessed to look for excessive tickets, speeding, or drunk driving. For large policies, the insurance company or an outside agency will also complete an "Inspection Report" that will involve calling you to confirm and clarify certain data on your application.

The underwriting department at the insurance company then reviews all the information, and you will be assigned a health classification. It may be a standard or preferred rate category or it may be discounted for especially good health. It can also be a "rated" offer, which means you are being assessed a surcharge due to some aspect of your situation.

The policy will be sent to you or your broker for your final acceptance and payment of any premium balance that may be due. You have 10 days from receipt of the contract to return it for a full refund if you are not satisfied for any reason.

## WHAT TO DO IF YOU ARE IN POOR HEALTH

Most everyone is able to obtain life insurance at some price! Your objective is to get it at the lowest price possible given your age, health, and circumstances. The very best way to make this happen is to work with an experienced broker who has access to multiple carriers.

The broker will evaluate your health records and personal situation before selecting which insurance companies to talk to on your behalf. Confidential discussions with home office underwriters may result in several different offers from various insurance companies. Your broker is your advocate and should include a cover letter introducing you and explaining any special circumstances with every submission for evaluation.

Some policies are specifically designed for people in very poor health. They may have a graded or limited death benefit, but they can be purchased from various companies and can add up to $100,000 or more on top of any group benefits that you can obtain without having to go through the underwriting process.

The timing of your application can also be important. At the end of the business year, some insurance carriers relax their underwriting standards to put more policies and premiums on their books.

## TAX ISSUES

Life insurance premiums are usually not tax deductible, but the death proceeds are generally received free of corporate or personal income taxes. Many owners feel it is easier to use the business checking account to pay for the insurance. This is acceptable, but partnerships and S-corporations will find that the cost of the insurance falls through to them as taxable income in a percentage equal to their percentage ownership in the firm.

C-corporations may own and pay for life insurance. If the firm is the beneficiary, it can use the funds to buy back the ownership interest of the deceased. When there are many owners, this may be the only practical approach. It is called a "stock redemption" agreement. In this case, the surviving owners receive no step-up in their cost basis and will have to pay taxes accordingly if and when the company is sold in the future.

If the C-corporation pays the premium and calls it a tax-deductible bonus to the stockholder, the owner can buy life insurance on a partner(s) life with a contractual agreement that directs the death benefit to be paid to the owner personally. The arrangement, called a "cross purchase" agreement, then calls for the survivor to use the funds to personally buy the stock of the deceased. This *does* create an increase in the survivor's cost basis and may ultimately be the most tax-wise option. All firms that are not C-corporations can also use this technique, but it always becomes a complex transaction as the number of owners increases from two or three if each has to own life insurance on the lives of all other partners.

## TIPS FOR GETTING THE BEST TERMS

While an insurance broker may print out a cost-and-benefit illustration using insurance company software, the final cost will depend on the company's review of your total application package.

Every permanent life insurance sales illustration is created with certain inherent assumptions. What you see is not what you will get, but merely an indication of what would happen if interest rates and internal costs were to remain at current levels. Therefore, it is appropriate to ask to see how the policy would perform if interest rates fall by one or two percent. And, what is the worst possible performance? What are the minimum guarantees if I continue to pay the premiums I agreed to pay?

If you already own a cash value life insurance policy, you should call your broker or the insurance company's policy-holder service department to ask for an "in force illustration," which will lay out where you are and what it may look like to age 100.

You should also ask what actions by you or by the insurance company could void your policy guarantees. For example, sometimes an underpayment can be made up and retain the policy guarantees—and sometimes it cannot. Sometimes a loan or death benefit reduction will void guarantees. None of these policies comes with a very user-friendly owner's manual.

Some insurance companies charge you based on your actual age, and some look at your age as of your nearest birthday. Life insurance contracts can be legally backdated up to 6 months. So ask, "What would the cost be if you backdated the application to save my earlier age?"

Term insurance policies can be paid on an annual basis or they can be financed. Although the insurance companies do not use that word, they generally charge an internal interest rate that can range from 12 to 24 percent. Nevertheless, your circumstances may call for payments other than annually.

"Table ratings" that are designated alphabetically or numerically (e.g., Table B or Table 2) reflect extra cost for extra risks. On a cash value policy, you may ask if they can convert the table rating to a "flat extra charge."

Each insurance policy has an annual charge for billing and administration. The charge may range from $25 to $150. In addition, there are often discounts at certain "volume bands." Therefore, it is usually cheaper to buy one large policy than several smaller ones.

## Table 7.2 Comparison of Life Insurance Contracts

| Types of Life Insurance Policies | Key Features | Caveats | Comments |
|---|---|---|---|
| Term (nongroup) | Pure protection with no equity buildup. Level death benefits and level premium payments for 1 to 30 years. Usually, convertible to a permanent policy regardless of your future health. | Some term policies refer to a level premium, but the real guarantee may be for just 5 or 10 years. Prices skyrocket after the guarantee period. Smokers pay about twice the cost of non-smokers. | It pays to shop around. A company offering the best conversion rights may not be the lowest cost term policy. The maze of "good health discounts" make it hard to predetermine who is going to offer the lowest cost. |
| Whole Life | The most conservative and least flexible plan of permanent life insurance. It has fixed costs and fixed death benefits; it often pays dividends and includes cash value* build up. | Guarantees will be weakened by adding nonguaranteed term insurance riders or unreasonable reliance on future, nonguaranteed dividends. Missed premiums create interest bearing loans. | Death benefit may be level or increasing. Premiums must be paid each year for life. Dividends can be used to reduce cost. Surrender charges not disclosed. |
| Universal Life | The most flexible permanent insurance. It allows changes of premiums and death benefit amounts while (usually) building cash value.* All internal costs and earnings are reported annually. | Reduced investment earnings or underpaying premiums may cause the policy to terminate earlier than expected. In return for lower and flexible premium payments, it is best for owners to monitor it periodically. | Death benefit may be level or increasing. There are no dividends. Unlike Whole Life, surrender penalties are disclosed. They may last from 0 to 20 years. |

*Unlike traditional cash value policies where equity growth is based on the insurance company's bond portfolio, "variable life" policies shift the investment risk to policy owners who can invest their premium payments into mutual fund type sub-accounts inside whole life or universal life policies.

## BEST BUYS IN LIFE INSURANCE

Life insurance is a complex financial tool. The glossy presentations and illustrations are difficult to understand. To avoid the common mistakes and ensure that you get the best buy possible for your situation, work with an *independent* insurance advisor (see Table 7.2 on page 101).

---

### AVOIDING COMMON MISTAKES IN BUYING INSURANCE

David Isaacson, the contributor of this chapter, has developed a program called Insurance Advocate. This is an independent insurance advisory service that includes:

- Analyzing the needs of the business owner
- "Stress testing" current plans to evaluate the cost, coverage, and quality
- Providing personalized, specialized services to negotiate favorable pricing and terms for specific situations

This section highlights how to avoid eight common mistakes that small business owners make:

**1.** Not having a buy-sell agreement

A buy-sell agreement is critical to provide for the transfer of ownership of the company in the event of death or disability of a business owner. "It's a disaster in the making," according to David, "if there's no agreement in place, because the surviving spouse and/or children will inherit the deceased owner's interest in the business." This can lead to a nasty legal battle that could be avoided with a buy-sell agreement.

---

**2.** Not funding the buy-sell agreement with insurance

Life and disability insurance provide the funds to either buy out or redeem the ownership interest of a deceased or disabled business owner. If there is no insurance, the drain on the cash resources of the company can impair the future of the business.

**3.** Not buying *key man* insurance

The loss of a key person can significantly impair any business. Key man insurance provides funds to reassure customers, investors, and creditors that the business can weather the untimely death of a key employee. Insurance proceeds will make up for lost profits and increased expenses while the firm locates and hires a replacement.

**4.** Getting rejected for insurance

Business owners are pushed to buy insurance by their investors or lenders who want to recover their investment in case something should happen to the business owner. If the business owner has any health issues or adverse medical history, it is wise to go through an informal review process before applying. Different companies use different criteria. So, what may be an unacceptable risk for one company is acceptable for another. An official rejection may make it much more difficult to obtain insurance in the future. Honesty really is the best policy. Do not let the insurance company discover something you did not first bring to your broker's attention—or worse, misrepresented.

**5.** Answering ads for super-low-cost term insurance

Many of the ads are really "bait and switch" advertising. Eligibility for the low prices is limited, and usually not clearly disclosed. So, you are unlikely to get the lowest price when you

*(continued)*

apply. Work with an experienced broker who can show you, in advance, the requirements for these low rates. That way you can avoid disappointment and/or switch to a more flexible insurance carrier.

**6.** Waiting too long

When you are young and healthy, insurance is easy to get. When you are 50 years old and have a history of medical problems, it is more complicated and expensive to get affordable insurance. Your doctor, who may consider your health "fine," has the implicit right to revise that diagnosis over time. The medical department at an insurance company takes account of many trends and factors, and then has to assign you a risk class with no chance to change it over the years ahead. And they really do have to "put their money where their mouth is"!

**7.** Making special deals to hire key employees

To attract a key employee, the business owner may offer to pay 100 percent of insurance or other benefits. This can be a problem down the road in implementing group coverage for employees. Qualified plans require meeting discrimination tests so that you are not favoring owners and highly compensated employees over other employees.

**8.** Carrying nonworking family members on the books as employees

Although it is tempting to cover family members, company employment records should only include actual employees. Carrying nonworking family members can jeopardize the status of your plan and lead to disqualification and tax penalties. It may also be disruptive to relations with employees. In a small company, never assume that secrets, shortcuts, and infractions will go unnoticed.

## CONCLUSION

Insurance is a complex subject. It is important to shop carefully, using knowledgeable people you trust. Too many people skip the analysis phase and go directly to buying a policy. This chapter has provided a broad overview of the benefits of insurance and how to make good choices for your situation.

# 8

# CASE STUDIES THAT ILLUSTRATE ALTERNATIVES

This chapter was contributed by David P. Gerstenblatt, Chairman of Pension Service Consultants, Inc. David is a Certified Financial Planner (CFP), a Certified Life Underwriter (CLU), and a Chartered Financial Consultant (ChFC). He has many years of experience creating wealth for clients through innovative tax reduction strategies with retirement plans. His firm is located in Newton, Massachusetts. Qualified retirement plans are a smart use of business dollars by the small business owner. Not only do you save money on taxes (the contributions are tax deductible and grow on a tax-deferred basis), qualified retirement plans also help attract and retain high-quality employees. At the same time, they provide for a comfortable retirement for you and your employees.

With some basic information, you can begin the search for a retirement plan that is a good fit for your situation. You will need the following information:

- Your date of birth
- Your employees' dates of birth and employment dates

- The number of hours worked by employees who work less than 1,000 hours per year
- Approximate or actual earnings of each employee
- Estimated budget for the amount the company could afford to put into the plan

You also need to identify what phase your business is in. The age of your business, its stage of development, and its profitability are key factors in choosing the right retirement plan for your company.

Admittedly, retirement planning can be confusing. So, if you are able to retain only one concept from this chapter, remember that different retirement plans make sense at different stages of your company's growth. Consider the following phases:

    Phase 1. Start-ups and the early years
    Phase 2. Continuing to grow
    Phase 3. Becoming more profitable
    Phase 4. Success! And your retirement approaches

Retirement plans need to change as your company, your goals, and your objectives evolve over time. The following case studies illustrate how small business owners selected a retirement plan that made sense for the phase that their business was in.

## PHASE 1. START-UPS AND THE EARLY YEARS

### Individual Retirement Account (IRA)

Richard, a software engineer in his 20s is beginning a consulting company. He is his company's only employee. While he scrambles for clients during the first few years of his business, his income is low and there is very little extra money. Saving for retirement and reducing taxes are low priorities for Richard right now. His accountant recommends that he place the maximum contribution allowed into a traditional Individual Retirement Account (IRA). He can contribute the lesser of $3,000 or 100 percent of his compensation. He opts to place $3,000 each year in an IRA while his business is still in its infancy.

## Simplified Employee Pension Plan (SEP-IRA)

Tired of being on his own, Richard took on Ellen as a business partner in the growing company. As the company builds accounts, it is able to pay Richard and Ellen salaries. Richard's previous $3,000 IRA contributions look small compared with his current income. He wants to increase his retirement savings and, at the same time, reduce his taxes. As a partner, Ellen is looking for equal treatment in a retirement plan. The two opt to use a Simplified Employee Pension Plan (SEP-IRA) for several reasons.

The SEP-IRA is very easy to set up and there are no administrative costs. It also allows their business to vary the contributions from year to year, depending on the economic health of the company. This flexibility is critical when their business is still young and its future is uncertain. Since they are the only two employees, they are not concerned that SEP-IRAs require including all employees (within certain guidelines). Both partners like being 100 percent vested immediately.

With a SEP-IRA, their business can contribute up to 25 percent of Richard and Ellen's compensation. Contributions, however, are limited to a $40,000 maximum so when either of their incomes approaches $160,000, the business may need to search for new retirement plan options.

They may also need to explore other retirement plans if their employee picture changes. Since they do not have any employees at this time, the SEP-IRA works well. Because employers must fund SEP-IRAs for their employees in the same percentage of compensation as they do for themselves, the SEP-IRA may become less attractive if they hire employees. Fortunately, other retirement plan alternatives are available.

## PHASE 2. CONTINUING TO GROW

### Savings Incentive Match Plan for Employees (SIMPLE IRA)

Warren is the president of a small retail business he started. Initially, he did not draw a salary, but now he does. He employs his wife, his son, and a few other people in important, but low-paid positions, so he needs to provide some retirement benefits. The company also uses part-time help. Although Warren's salary is the highest in the company, it is still modest. Warren needs a retirement plan that will provide for his own retirement while allowing other employees to participate.

The SIMPLE IRA that Warren selects has low administration costs and is less expensive than other plans such as traditional 401(k)s. However, the company is precluded from participating in any additional retirement plans while the SIMPLE IRA plan is in effect.

To be eligible for the plan, an employee must earn or be expected to earn at least $5,000 per year. This means that most of his part-time workers will not qualify and Warren's company will not need to contribute to the plan on their behalf.

All eligible employees in a SIMPLE IRA are immediately 100 percent vested—an attractive feature for Warren, his wife, and his son, who want to keep their retirement funds should any of them leave the company. In addition, the SIM-PLE IRA allows individual employees such as Warren and his full-time clerks to also make voluntary, tax-deferred contributions of up to 100 percent of their compensation or $7,000, whichever is less.

Under a SIMPLE IRA plan, Warren's company, as the employer, has two options:

1.  Make a mandatory two percent (of compensation) contribution for all eligible employees whether they put their own money into the plan or not.
2.  Match up to three percent of the voluntary contributions made by each employee.

In either scenario, the maximum employer contribution is $8,000 (for 2003). For employees aged 50 and older, an additional $1,000 catch-up contribution (in 2003) may be made. Warren, who is over age 50, can reach the annual maximum of $17,000 with his own $8,000 deferral, the company's matching contribution of $8,000, and the $1,000 catch-up provision.

### Simple 401(k)

The Greene Agency is a small, private, family-owned business with just a few employees, including Andrew and his wife Joan. Andrew is the primary wage earner for the family, and Joan works only a few hours a week. They selected a Simple 401(k) because it has no administrative costs and allows each employee to contribute up to 100 percent of his or her pay up to $7,000.

Andrew and Joan realize that using a Simple 401(k) precludes them from participating in any other retirement plan during those years the Simple 401(k) is in effect. This is not a problem because neither anticipates being financially able to contribute more than $7,000 each year. For Joan, who is concerned about falling behind in retirement savings while she raises their family, the Simple 401(k) offers her the opportunity to contribute 100 percent of her salary.

There is some flexibility for the Greene Agency, as the employer, but in general, it must match up to 100 percent of the contributions of all participating employees (up to 3 percent of salary) or provide 2 percent to all employees, even those who opt not to participate. The Greene Agency's matching employer contributions are tax deductible and all participants are immediately vested 100 percent.

Other retirement plans offer more flexibility and higher contribution limits than the Simple 401(k). The Greene Agency should consider investigating other plans that will allow them to accomplish their goals.

## PHASE 3. BECOMING MORE PROFITABLE

### Qualified Plans

Before looking at the business owners who selected qualified plans, it is helpful to review a few general rules that apply to qualified plans:

- Eligibility is generally limited to employees who work over 1,000 hours a year, who are over age 21, and who have been with the company for one year.
- A minimum of 70 percent of the non-highly-compensated must be in the plan if they are eligible.

- If two qualified plans share any one specific individual, there is a limit to the amount that can be placed in the two plans. The total of the two plans cannot exceed 25 percent of the total compensation.
- If you own more than one entity, you need to be aware of the control group and affiliated service group rules, which may require you to bring all your entities into the plan.

A 401(k) component can be integrated into any of the profit-sharing plans so that employees may defer income tax-free.

Keep in mind that a 401(k) plan can be stand-alone or used in combination with a profit-sharing plan. With a 401(k) plan, $12,000 can be deferred. With a profit-sharing component, the company can put more money into the plan.

## Traditional Profit-Sharing Plans

When Nicole, a business owner and company vice president with seven employees came to me for a retirement plan, she wanted plenty of flexibility. Her business had experienced some phenomenally profitable years and other years when revenues had dropped. She needed a plan that could accommodate the ups and downs of her industry.

At "40-something," Nicole had plenty of time to accumulate retirement funds and was not motivated to provide employees with the opportunity to contribute their own pretax dollars into a retirement plan. The business paid Nicole a high salary that allowed her to meet her living expenses plus more, and still the business had additional profits.

A profit-sharing plan offered Nicole built-in flexibility in making contributions. Under such a plan, the employer decides annually if a contribution will be made and in what amount. Previously, contributions were limited to up to 15 percent, but since 2002, businesses have been allowed up to 25 percent of the covered payroll (up to $40,000 for any one individual).

As shown in Table 8.1, Nicole's company is contributing 15 percent. A traditional profit-sharing plan also allows the higher paid employees to receive a slightly larger percentage in certain situations. This arrangement is called "integration" or "permitted disparity."

Notice in Table 8.1 that the key employees (President and VP) receive 76 percent of the company's total contribution to the plan. As VP, Nicole receives a smaller contribution, but she can accumulate $1.2 million over the 25 years she will participate in the plan. Table 8.2 summarizes the tax savings achieved with this plan.

When Nicole's company becomes even more profitable, it will probably make sense for her to review and reassess her present plans.

Table 8.1   Contributions to a Profit-Sharing Plan

|  | Age | Salary ($) | Annual Contribution ($) | Total Contribution (%) | Accumulation at Age 65* ($) |
|---|---|---|---|---|---|
| President | 55 | 150,000 | 24,309 | 43 | 359,375 |
| VP | 40 | 120,000 | 18,814 | 33 | 1,273,265 |
| A | 33 | 45,000 | 5,677 | 10 | 669,508 |
| B | 28 | 25,000 | 3,154 | 6 | 541,103 |
| C | 25 | 20,000 | 2,523 | 4 | 538,937 |
| D | 22 | 20,000 | 2,523 | 4 | 668,900 |
| Total |  | 380,000 | 57,000 |  |  |

*Assumes seven percent interest rate. This is an integrated plan. Actual accumulations depend on the amounts deposited and investment experience.

Table 8.2   Traditional Profit-Sharing
Summary after Taxes

| Employer Tax Bracket | 39% |
| --- | --- |
| Total contribution | $57,000 |
| Less tax savings | 22,230 |
| Net after tax outlay | 34,770 |
| Deposit for owner/employees and executives | 43,123 |
| Net gain or cost (–) | $ 8,353 |

## 401(k) Profit-Sharing Plan

Greg's company opted to establish a 401(k) profit-sharing plan. The company's employees like being able to defer money on their own behalf, using pretax dollars. Under a 401(k) plan, employees may be able to contribute up to $12,000 in 2003 ($13,000 if age 50 or over) on a pretax basis.

As the company's owner, Greg appreciates the plan's flexibility. The company may elect to match a percentage of the employees' deferrals and/or to make discretionary contributions on an annual basis. Such discretionary matches can generate goodwill and loyalty from employees by rewarding them for "a job well done" in years of greater profits. But even if Greg does not match or make discretionary contributions, employees still benefit from being able to save for retirement while deferring taxes on both their contributions and the fund's growth.

Table 8.3 shows how a 401(k) is a tactical strategy for Greg's company. The contributions to the plan only total $52,320—a savings over the $57,000 required to fund Nicole's company's

Table 8.3   Contributions to 401(k) Profit-Sharing Plan

| | Age | Salary ($) | Annual Corporate Contribution ($) | Total Corporate Contribution (%) | Annual Employee Contribution ($) | Accumulation at Age 65[a] ($) |
|---|---|---|---|---|---|---|
| President | 55 | 150,000 | 37,500 | 71.9 | | 554,385 |
| VP | 40 | 120,000 | 8,880 | 17 | | 600,967 |
| A | 33 | 45,000 | 2,430 | 4.6 | | 286,578 |
| B | 28 | 25,000 | 1,350 | 2.5 | | 231,607 |
| C | 25 | 20,000 | 1,080 | 2.0 | | 230,698 |
| D | 22 | 20,000 | 1,080 | 2.0 | | 286,331 |
| Total | | 380,000 | 52,320[b] | | 14,520 | |

[a] Assumes seven percent interest rate. Actual accumulations depend on the amounts deposited and investment experience.

[b] Employee deferrals are $14,520/Net employer cost is $37,800. Employer's contribution is based on age-based, profit-sharing allocation.

traditional profit-sharing plan (Table 8.1). Greg, the president, receives 71 percent of the total contribution or $37,500 while the president in Nicole's company receives 43 percent or $24,309.

The 401(k) plan also permits highly compensated employees like Greg to defer two percent more than the average percentage deferred by the other employees in the plan. If the eligible employees as a group defer an average of three percent of their compensation, Greg and the other highly compensated employees may defer up to five percent of salary.

Since the 401(k) allows employees to contribute, the total annual contribution is actually a sum of the employee and employer contributions. In this example, the $52,320 is a sum of $14,520 from employee pretax contributions and the employer's cost of $37,800. Compare that $37,800 with the $57,000 employer cost in Nicole's traditional profit-sharing plan, and it is easy to see why 401(k) plans are so popular. Table 8.4 summarizes the tax results for Greg's company.

Table 8.4    401(k) Profit-Sharing
Summary after Taxes

| Employer Tax Bracket | 39% |
| --- | --- |
| Total contribution | $52,320 |
| Less tax savings | 20,404 |
| Net after tax outlay | 31,916 |
| Deposit for owner/employees and executives | 46,380 |
| Net gain or cost (−) | $14,464 |

## PHASE 4. SUCCESS! AND YOUR
## RETIREMENT APPROACHES

### Age-Based Profit Sharing

An older business owner like Douglas (age 55) with less than 10 years to retire needs a plan that accelerates his contributions so that he can reach his objectives in the not-so-distant retirement future. While Douglas wants to reward younger employees with a retirement plan, his primary objective is to provide for himself.

Douglas can also set up a vesting schedule so that the business owner does not lose significant contributions to employees who leave the company after only a few years of service. The vesting will apply to the employer's contributions only.

Age-based profit sharing offers all the advantages of a traditional profit-sharing plan, but has a unique feature: Employer contributions are apportioned based on compensation levels and age. Table 8.5 shows how a smaller $40,505 total annual contribution by Douglas's company results in a greater accumulation for Douglas, the president ($443,508),

Table 8.5    Age-Based Profit Sharing

|  | Age | Salary ($) | Annual Contribution ($) | Total Contribution (%) | Accumulation at Age 65 ($) |
|---|---|---|---|---|---|
| President | 55 | 150,000 | 30,000 | 74 | 443,508 |
| VP | 40 | 120,000 | 7,059 | 17 | 477,728 |
| A | 33 | 45,000 | 1,496 | 4 | 176,429 |
| B | 28 | 25,000 | 750 | 2 | 128,671 |
| C | 25 | 20,000 | 600 | 1.5 | 128,166 |
| D | 22 | 20,000 | 600 | 1.5 | 159,073 |
| Total |  | 380,000 | 40,505 |  |  |

Table 8.6    Age-Based Profit-Sharing Summary
after Taxes

| Employer Tax Bracket | 39% |
|---|---|
| Total contribution | $40,505 |
| Less tax savings | 15,796 |
| Net after tax outlay | 24,709 |
| Deposit for owner/employees and executives | 37,059 |
| Net gain or cost (−) | $12,350 |

than under the traditional profit-sharing plan described for Nicole's company. The tax results appear in Table 8.6.

## CROSS-TESTED PROFIT-SHARING 401A(4)

Lee, a company president and owner wants a much higher percentage of retirement monies to be contributed for himself and the other highly compensated employees than for the other staff at his company. For that reason, he selected a cross-tested profit-sharing plan.

As shown in Table 8.7, the cross-tested plan will work well for Lee because his company is small and the key employees are older than the other employees. In a cross-tested plan, larger contributions are made for older employees who have fewer years before retiring. Younger employees receive smaller contributions because they have more time for their benefits to accumulate. At retirement, the benefits for both older and younger employees will be in the same proportion to their salaries.

Table 8.7  Contributions for Cross-Tested Profit-Sharing 401A(4)

| | Age | Salary ($) | Total Contribution ($) | Total Contribution (%) | Accumulation at Age 65 ($) | Individual's Monthly Pension ($) |
|---|---|---|---|---|---|---|
| President | 55 | 150,000 | 40,000 | 50.46 | 448,762 | 4,563 |
| VP | 40 | 120,000 | 32,000 | 40.37 | 1,833,291 | 18,641 |
| A | 33 | 45,000 | 2,975 | 3.75 | 297,694 | 3,027 |
| B | 28 | 25,000 | 1,652 | 2.08 | 244,212 | 2,483 |
| C | 25 | 20,000 | 1,322 | 1.67 | 246,483 | 2,506 |
| D | 22 | 20,000 | 1,322 | 1.67 | 310,303 | 3,155 |
| Total | | 380,000 | 79,271 | 100 | 3,380,745 | |

Table 8.8    Cross-Tested Summary after Taxes

| Employer Tax Bracket | 39% |
| --- | --- |
| Total contribution | $79,271.00 |
| Less tax savings | 30,915.69 |
| Net after tax outlay | 48,355.31 |
| Deposit for stockholders and executives | 72,000.00 |
| Net gain or cost (−) | $23,644.69 |

By establishing the cross-tested plan, each year Lee can decide how much money he wants to put into it and where it should be allocated based on the plan and the formula. The plan is "cross-tested" because special assessments are necessary to determine whether it falls within the correct formulas. Lee's employees will not be able to defer their own income into this plan unless a 401(k) component is added. Table 8.8 presents the tax consequences.

There are two other plans that basically make little sense to use anymore: a target plan and a money purchase pension. With the advent of the cross-tested and age-weighted profit-sharing plans, employers have more flexibility than they can achieve with a target plan. And now that profit sharing has been increased to a maximum of 25 percent of compensation, there is no need for a money purchase pension.

## DEFINED BENEFIT PLANS

Defined benefit plans are a form of a pension plan. Instead of saving a percentage of salary for retirement, a defined benefit plan provides for individual employees to retire with a certain percentage of their salaries set aside for them (e.g., retiring with guaranteed payment of 60 percent of pay). In such a plan, the employer and the employee are both counting on there being sufficient money in the plan to fund each eligible person's retirement at the levels specified in the plan.

Changes in the Economic Growth and Tax Relief Act of 2001, which took effect in January 2002, have made defined benefit plans more attractive than ever before.

## Traditional Defined Benefit Plans

Kevin has spent most of his career as the owner of a company with primarily younger employees. With retirement rapidly approaching, Kevin is looking for a plan that provides more rewards for the oldest, long-term employees like him. He realizes that he wants to be guaranteed a specific pension. Fortunately, his company can afford a continuing fixed commitment to substantial, tax-deductible contributions. This traditional defined benefit plan also can provide Kevin with death benefits.

Kevin understands that the contribution must be made regardless of his company's profitability in any given year. He knows that the maximum dollar benefit that can be guaranteed at retirement (as indexed) is the lower of $160,000 or 100 percent of his average compensation for the last 3 years he works. As a long-term employee, he does not need to be concerned with the plan's reduction in contributions for employees with less than 10 years of service (see Tables 8.9 and 8.10).

Kevin can increase his contribution into his defined benefit plan by adding life insurance. While the plan's accumulation at age 65 remains the same, if he fails to live to retirement, his family will get the death benefit from the life insurance. By adding the life insurance component to his defined benefit plan, Kevin

Table 8.9  Defined Benefit Plan without Insurance

| | Age | Salary ($) | Investment Fund Contributions ($) | Insurance Premium ($) | Total Contribution ($) | Total Contribution (%) | Accumulation at Age 65 ($) | Individual's Monthly Pension ($) |
|---|---|---|---|---|---|---|---|---|
| President | 55 | 150,000 | 143,787 | 0 | 143,787 | 77 | 1,279,339 | 9,333.33 |
| VP | 40 | 120,000 | 29,801 | 0 | 29,801 | 16 | 1,370,721 | 10,000.00 |
| A | 33 | 45,000 | 6,585 | 0 | 6,585 | 4 | 514,020 | 3,750.00 |
| B | 28 | 25,000 | 2,586 | 0 | 2,586 | 1 | 285,566 | 2,083.33 |
| C | 25 | 20,000 | 1,692 | 0 | 1,692 | 1 | 228,454 | 1,666.67 |
| D | 22 | 20,000 | 1,393 | 0 | 1,393 | 1 | 228,454 | 1,666.67 |
| Total | | 380,000 | 185,844 | 0 | 185,844 | 100 | 3,906,554 | |

Table 8.10   Defined Benefit Plan
Summary after Taxes

| Employer Tax Bracket | 39% |
|---|---|
| Total contribution | $185,844 |
| Less tax savings | 72,479 |
| Net after tax outlay | 113,365 |
| Deposit for owner/employees and executives | 173,588 |
| Net gain or cost (–) | $ 60,223 |

makes certain that whether he lives or dies, a substantial benefit will be paid (see Tables 8.11 and 8.12).

### Defined Benefit Plans 412(i)

Joe is a 55-year-old successful business owner with a traditional defined benefit plan, but now he would like to guarantee an even higher retirement benefit for himself. The 412(i) Plan is a great solution for Joe. A variation of the traditional defined benefit plan, a 412(i) uses only insurance products that are guaranteed for the lifetime of the plan. If the plan earns more than the amount guaranteed in any given year, the excess is used to reduce future years' contributions.

Joe likes the 412(i) because, as shown in Tables 8.13 and 8.14, it provides much higher tax-deductible contributions, especially for older employees like him, who have less time for the contributions to earn interest. The 412(i) also lets Joe's plan earnings accumulate tax deferred. He understands that in the early years of the 412(i), the guaranteed retirement benefit is lower, but at age 55 he is not planning on retiring in those early years, so that is not a concern for him. He is attracted to

Table 8.11  Defined Benefit Plan with Insurance

| | Age | Salary ($) | Total Contribution to Investment Fund plus Insurance Premium ($) | Total Contribution (%) | Accumulation at Age 65 ($) | Cash Value* ($) | Initial Death Benefit ($) | Individual's Monthly Pension ($) |
|---|---|---|---|---|---|---|---|---|
| President | 55 | 150,000 | 159,813 | 75 | 1,279,339 | 120,064 | 933,333 | 9,333.33 |
| VP | 40 | 120,000 | 36,606 | 17 | 1,370,721 | 354,470 | 1,000,000 | 10,000.00 |
| A | 33 | 45,000 | 8,576 | 4 | 514,020 | 152,261 | 375,000 | 3,750.00 |
| B | 28 | 25,000 | 3,542 | 2 | 285,566 | 90,167 | 208,333 | 2,083.33 |
| C | 25 | 20,000 | 2,411 | 1 | 228,454 | 74,275 | 166,667 | 1,666.67 |
| D | 22 | 20,000 | 2,071 | 1 | 228,454 | 76,075 | 166,667 | 1,666.67 |
| Total | | 380,000 | 213,019 | | 3,906,554 | | | |

*Cash values shown are only if all premiums have been paid.

Table 8.12   Defined Benefit Plan
Summary after Taxes

| Employer Tax Bracket | 39% |
| --- | --- |
| Total contributions | $213,019 |
| Less tax savings | 83,077 |
| Net after tax outlay | 129,942 |
| Deposit for owner/employees and executives | 196,419 |
| Net gain or cost (−) | $ 66,477 |

the 412(i)'s substantially higher guarantees that will be there for him when he reaches age 65.

## CONTRIBUTIONS: COMPARING APPLES WITH APPLES

Your head may be swimming with all the details of so many retirement plans and their rules. Table 8.15 compares the more sophisticated qualified retirement plans previously discussed. It can help you decipher the differences between the plans in terms of what matters most to you—contributions, death benefits, accumulations, and so on.

## NONQUALIFIED PLANS

A handful of "nonqualified" retirement plans for executives can be useful for supplementing qualified plans. Each of these nonqualified plans allows companies to be selective in eligibility; for example, not all highly compensated employees have to be included.

Table 8.13   Contributions to 412(i) Defined Benefit Plan

| | Age | Salary ($) | Annuity Deposit ($) | Insurance Premium ($) | Total Contribution of Annuity Deposit and Insurance Premium ($) | Total Contribution (%) | Accumulation at Age 65[a] ($) | Initial Death Benefit ($) | Individual's Monthly Pension[b] ($) |
|---|---|---|---|---|---|---|---|---|---|
| President | 55 | 150,000 | 171,084 | 161,273 | 332,357 | 75.28 | 2,007,168 | 5,117,267 | 9,333 |
| VP | 40 | 120,000 | 34,329 | 39,849 | 74,179 | 16.80 | 2,150,538 | 2,758,327 | 10,000 |
| A | 33 | 45,000 | 8,148 | 9,663 | 17,811 | 4.03 | 806,452 | 928,855 | 3,750 |
| B | 28 | 25,000 | 3,443 | 4,070 | 7,513 | 1.70 | 448,028 | 485,187 | 2,083 |
| C | 25 | 20,000 | 2,381 | 2,784 | 5,165 | 1.17 | 358,424 | 374,012 | 1,667 |
| D | 22 | 20,000 | 2,077 | 2,394 | 4,470 | 1.01 | 358,424 | 359,829 | 1,667 |

[a]Total cash value of insurance and annuity.
[b]Instead of a monthly pension, the employee would most likely take a lump sum and purchase an annuity with a much higher rate of return than the monthly pension would provide.

Table 8.14   412(i) Defined Benefit Plan
Summary after Taxes

| Employer Tax Bracket | 39% |
| --- | --- |
| Total contribution | $441,494.47 |
| Less tax savings | 172,182.84 |
| Net after tax outlay | 269,311.63 |
| Deposit for owner/employees and executives | 406,535.58 |
| Net gain or cost (−) | $137,223.95 |

In most nonqualified plans, the employer contributions are not tax deductible. Companies and executives look to insurance products to augment their qualified retirement plans because of their unique ability to grow tax-free and, with a correct method of withdrawal, provide tax-free distributions as well.

## Deferred Compensation

Deferred Compensation is an unfunded promise to pay, and it cannot be secured by anything.

Jim, the owner of the Applegate Corporation, decided that one of his employees, Sam, is extremely valuable to his company. Jim wanted to create a strong incentive for Sam to stay with the company until he retires.

Applegate executed an agreement with Sam stating that, starting at age 65, Sam would get—for 20 years—100 percent of the average of his last 3 years' salary on the condition that Sam did not leave the company before age 65. In addition, the corporation promised Sam that if he died, the corporation would pay his heirs $100,000 per year for 10 years.

Table 8.15  Comparison of Contributions across Several Retirement Plans

| | Age | Annual Compensation ($) | 25 Percent Profit-Sharing Plan ($) | Cross-Tested Plan Contribution ($) | Defined Benefit Plan Contribution with Insurance ($) | 412(i) Plan Contribution ($) |
|---|---|---|---|---|---|---|
| Owner | 50 | 200,000.00 | 40,000.00 | 40,000.00 | 138,628.72 | 805,120.00 |
| A | 50 | 37,000.00 | 9,250.00 | 1,890.70 | 12,284.39 | 11,677.00 |
| B | 33 | 35,000.00 | 8,750.00 | 1,788.50 | 6,933.12 | 29,895.00 |
| C | 25 | 20,000.00 | 5,000.00 | 1,022.00 | 2,350.92 | 39,069.00 |
| Total | | | 63,000.00 | 44,701.20 | 160,197.15 | 885,761.00 |

The corporation decided to prefund this agreement because they wanted to make sure that money would be available at age 65 to pay the benefit. To accomplish this, the corporation purchased an insurance policy on Sam's life.

Insurance has some unique characteristics. It provides money in the form of a death benefit if Sam dies and the cash value, which accumulates tax-free, will be available to either fully or partially fund the retirement benefit.

However, the deferred compensation benefit due from the corporation cannot be secured or connected *in any way* to the insurance policy. The policy is simply an informal funding of the deferred compensation benefit. As long as there is no connection between the insurance policy and the agreement between Sam and his employer, there should be no "constructive receipt" and Sam should not have to pay taxes on that deferred compensation now.

*tax free w/o and tax deduction by co*

In addition, if Sam dies, the corporation, as agreed, will pay his beneficiaries $100,000 per year for 10 years. When the corporation pays this deferred compensation to Jim's beneficiaries, it will be able to deduct those expenses.

A potential problem with this plan is that the deferred compensation is considered an asset of the corporation. In a bankruptcy, the reserve in the cash value of the policy could go to creditors. Even a "Rabbi Trust," as it is known to financial planners, does not protect against bankruptcy, although it does provide some limited creditor protection.

### Executive Bonus Plan

Companies use executive bonus plans to reward key employees. Bonuses that are paid in cash to an employee are deductible to the corporation and are currently taxable to the individual. Colleen's company opted for an alternative plan. It used her bonus money to purchase a permanent life insurance policy for her. The unique characteristics of the insurance policy are that it can grow tax-free and come out tax-free. If Colleen withdraws the money properly, she can receive it tax-free as well. This bonus plan, with insurance funding, also provides a death benefit to Colleen's beneficiaries. Executive bonus plans work well in both small and large companies.

## CONCLUSION

As these case studies show, many choices are available for business owners who want to reduce taxes and save for retirement. Planners tend to make four common mistakes that can easily be avoided.

### Only Looking at a Few Choices

Frequently, business owners do not see the full spectrum of choices. A financial advisor may jump to a conclusion and recommend a plan without presenting the full range of possibilities. Ask to see alternative plans and decide for yourself whether they make sense for your company.

### Sticking Too Long with One Plan

You need to review plans on a regular basis, at least every couple of years, to ensure that they are still a good fit for your objectives. The plan may need to be updated, amended, or redesigned to reflect changes in the employee census, changes in the law, or even changes in business conditions or goals.

## Thinking a 401(k) Plan Will Fund Your Retirement

The 401(k) plans help the rank and file, but do not allow business owners to shelter enough money to fund a comfortable retirement. As a successful business owner, you need to think beyond 401(k)s.

## Excluding Defined Benefit Plans

The defined benefit plans intimidate many business owners because of the perceived "lock-in" to a large annual funding commitment. Defined benefit plans can be a good fit for situations in which the business owner is over 50 and has few highly paid employees.

Wherever you are in your business development, there is a retirement plan that fits your circumstances. The more successful you are, the more important it is to take advantage of the sophisticated plan alternatives that save taxes and enable you to put money away for a comfortable retirement.

# 9

# REQUESTING PROPOSALS

To realistically assess your alternatives, you need to receive proposals tailored to your situation. The proposals should show the costs and benefits of the different options. Drawing from the information presented in the previous chapters, you can pull together a request for proposal (RFP) and submit it to pension consultants and financial advisors. By requesting several proposals, you ensure that you will receive a broad range of options.

Seek recommendations from pension consultants, Certified Financial Planners, and financial advisors affiliated with financial institutions. Make certain that you understand whether they are independent or affiliated with a financial institution or insurance company.

Make a preliminary contact by telephone and confirm that they are interested in talking with you. Then send a letter confirming that you are seeking their advice and recommendations for a retirement plan for yourself and your company. If you already have a retirement plan, indicate that you want them to review it and advise you. Be certain to find out what fees, if any, are involved in this review process. Your request should include basic information about your company, including your employees' ages and length of service, your age and expected retirement date, and how much you feel you can commit to funding a plan. Highlighting your key goals is also helpful:

- Reduce taxes currently
- Maximize contributions for principals
- Minimize administrative cost
- Fund retirement of owners in _____ (how many) years

Figure 9.1 shows an example of a request for proposal.

---

Dear Pension Consultant,

   This letter is intended to follow up on our conversation concerning the retirement plan for Company X. As we discussed, we currently have a 401(k) plan in place, but the participation rate by our employees has been low so we are interested in re-evaluating our alternatives.

   The following table summarizes our current employee situation:

   Name       Age       Date of Hire       Salary

The company is organized as an S-corporation, owned by 3 principals, all in their mid-50s, who want to retire at age 65. The primary goals are to reduce taxes and maximize retirement income for the principals. Based on prior earnings and projected cash flow, the company can afford an annual funding commitment of $100,000.

   We would like to see proposals for both Defined Contribution and Defined Benefit Plans that compare and contrast the costs and benefits of the different plans.

   We look forward to receiving your proposals.

                          Sincerely,


                          President, Company X

---

Figure 9.1   Sample Request for Proposal Letter

Choosing a retirement plan is an important business decision, so do not rush to accept the first proposal that sounds promising. Consider several options and ask questions. Which recommendations do you want to explore in greater depth? You can ask the advisor who provided each proposal to help you understand why that proposal is the best fit for the business owner and company's situation.

Using this approach will generate multiple proposals tailored to your company's situation and goals. With more information presented in a way that focuses on your goals and business situation, you will be better able to make an informed decision.

# 10

# IMPLEMENTING YOUR PLAN

Business owners often think their job is finished when they select the plan. This is just not correct. Successful implementation requires commitment and follow-through. To achieve the benefits of the plan, you need to assure appropriate employee participation and compliance with the legal requirements.

Implementing your plan has two major phases: (1) introducing the plan to employees; (2) staying in compliance with the law.

## PHASE 1.  INTRODUCING THE PLAN TO EMPLOYEES

In prior chapters, we have looked carefully at the plan from the business owner's perspective. You should have a clear picture of the benefits for you: tax deductions, deferred compensation, retention of key employees. Now, using familiar, nontechnical terms that everyone can understand, you need to communicate the benefits that are available for your employees. This is really critical to the success of the program.

Occasionally, business owners go through the whole process of selecting a plan that they really intend to benefit the rank-and-file employees only to find that employee participation is too low to make the plan viable.

It is helpful to prepare educational materials and hold information meetings with employees. You need to be proactive about encouraging employees to sign up. Do not assume that all the employees will understand the benefits immediately. Some employees will be eager to sign up, and others will not. Some companies have found that asking employees "opt out" as opposed to "opt in" is an effective technique for encouraging participation.

## PHASE 2.  STAYING IN COMPLIANCE WITH THE LAW

The Internal Revenue Service (IRS) and the Department of Labor (DOL) review plans for compliance with the law. If your plan is found to be out of compliance, the consequences can be invalidation, disallowance of the deductions, and the imposition of penalties. It is much better to stay in compliance than to have to rectify a problem found in an audit.

Problem areas include:

- *Participation: not allowing all eligible employees to participate in the plan.* A common misconception is that part-time employees can be excluded because they do not qualify for benefits. In fact, part-time employees who are 21 years old, have 1 year of service, and work 1,000 hours per year should be included in the plan.
- *Vesting: not complying with the vesting requirements.* Whether you choose immediate, or 7-year graded, or 5-year cliff vesting, it is important to implement vesting

consistently. In plans that delay employee eligibility for participation until the completion of 2 years of service (the maximum allowed), vesting is 100 percent.

- *Nondiscrimination: not complying with the discrimination tests.* Unless your plan is in a safe harbor, you need to check each year to ensure that you are in compliance with the discrimination requirements. Even law and accounting firms, knowledgeable about these requirements, have unexpectedly found themselves to be out of compliance with these rules.
- *Prohibited transactions: violations of the rules.* Issues arise because of distributions or loans that are not in compliance with the requirements.
- *Minimum funding: not meeting the minimum funding requirements.* If a business begins to have cash flow difficulties, it is critical to pay attention to funding requirements. By not taking action early to provide notice and amend a plan, a company can find itself locked into a funding commitment that it can ill afford in a difficult economy.

### Establishing a Compliance Process and Calendar

Jim Simons, is Principal of Compensation and Benefits Solutions, a consulting firm specializing in assuring compliance of compensation and benefits plans with federal and state laws. He recommends establishing a "process" and a "calendar" to make compliance easy to administer. In this section, Jim shares some of his insights from his work with a broad range of companies in helping them realize the full benefit of their compensation programs. Jim is located in Newton, Massachusetts, and on the Internet at cabsolutions@rcn.com.

While qualified retirement plans provide an excellent method for employers to extend retirement benefits to their employees, these plans are subject to extremely technical rules and regulations of the IRS, the DOL, and other agencies. The combination of highly technical rules (subject to frequent change) and rigorous government scrutiny means that an employer must establish a process to maintain compliance. An effective compliance process is a system that administers plans fairly, limits administrative complexity, and provides solid benefits to both the business owner and the employees.

## Compliance Process

Compliance requirements are not limited to qualified retirement plans. Employers are required to comply with a broad range of federal and state laws concerning all aspects of employment compensation and benefits. Tables 10.1, 10.2, and

Table 10.1    Minimum Number of Employees for Benefit Plan Requirements—Federal Law

| Law | Eligible Employee Minimum* |
| --- | --- |
| Age Discrimination in Employment Act | 20 |
| Americans with Disability Act | 15 |
| Civil Rights Act, Title VII | 15 |
| COBRA | 20 |
| ERISA (qualified retirement, health, and welfare) | 1 |
| Family and Medical Leave Act | 50 |
| HIPAA (participants) | 2 |
| Mental Health Parity Act | 50 |
| Newborn and Mothers Health Protection Act | 50 |
| Pregnancy Discrimination Act | 15 |

*Part time employees are generally counted as regular employees. Active employees not eligible for COBRA are counted as fractional employees based on scheduled hours. Federal law applies unless state law benefit is more generous.

## Table 10.2 Employee Retirement Income Security Act (ERISA) Compliance

| Requirement | Purpose | Disclosure | Comments |
|---|---|---|---|
| Document Disclosure | Provide plans documents to participants on request | • COBRA<br>• Contracts, agreements<br>• ERISA disclosure (SPD)<br>• HIPAA coverage<br>• Summary Annual Report<br>• Mental Health Parity (SPD)<br>• Newborn Mothers and Health Protection (SPD)<br>• Plan document<br>• Qualified Medical Child Support Order (SPD)<br>• Summary plan description<br>• Trust agreements<br>• Women's Health and Cancer Rights Acts | Provide on demand:<br>• WHCRA<br>• HIPAA certificate<br>• Contracts, agreements<br><br>Provide upon plan eligibility:<br>• SPD<br><br>Provide upon coverage loss:<br>• HIPAA certificate<br>• COBRA<br><br>Provide annually:<br>• SAR<br>• WHCRA<br><br>Provide upon change:<br>• SMM<br>• SPD |
| Form 5500 | A summary of plan expenses, eligibility, and enrollment to the IRS | Complete Form 5500 for all applicable plans including pension, profit sharing, stock ownership, medical, dental, and insured disability. | Certain unfunded or uninsured plans with less than 100 participants can avoid filing the Form 5500. |
| Summary Annual Report | Basic financial information to participants for the plan period described in a manner the average participant can understand | Must contain information from the Form 5500 filing to IRS. | Certain unfunded or uninsured plans with less than 100 participants can avoid issuing the SMM. |

*(continued)*

Table 10.2 *Continued*

| Requirement | Purpose | Disclosure | Comments |
|---|---|---|---|
| Summary of Material Modifications (SMM) | A written summary of changes to participants described in a manner the average participant can understand | Changes to:<br>• Plan sponsor or administrator<br>• Collective bargaining agreement<br>• Eligibility<br>• Vesting<br>• Break-in-service<br>• Benefits<br>• Plan year<br>• Claim procedures | Disclose to all participants within 210 days following the end of the plan year.<br><br>Group health plans must disclose within 60 days of a "material reduction in benefits." |
| Summary Plan Description (SPD) | Plan information to participants described in a manner the average participant can understand | Effective the first day of the second plan year beginning on or after January 22, 2001 (for calendar year plan that is 1/1/03):<br><br>*Group Health Plans*<br>• Cost sharing<br>• Lifetime benefit caps<br>• Preventive services provided<br>• Drug coverage<br>• Medical tests, devices, and procedures<br>• In and out-of-network use, coverage and providers<br>• COBRA rights<br><br>*All Plans*<br>• Authority to terminate, amend, or eliminate the plan<br>• Participant rights; obligations<br>• Model pension plan statement<br>• ERISA rights<br>• Plan type administered | Disclose within 90 days of plan eligibility; within 30 days of request.<br><br>Provide to all eligible employees every 5 years if revised or at least every 10 years if no changes.<br><br>Employee handbook does not take the place of plan description. |

Table 10.3   Record-Keeping Requirements—Select Statutes

| Statute | Records | Retention Period |
| --- | --- | --- |
| Age Discrimination in Employment | Payroll records | Payroll: one year |
| | Employee records including employment, job applications, promotions, demotions, layoff | Employee: three years |
| | | Benefits, and so on: full period plan(s) is in effect plus one year |
| | Benefit plans, seniority, or merit rating system | |
| Americans with Disabilities Act | Any employment record made or kept by employer | Employment: One year from date record was created or action taken whichever is later |
| | Records relevant to discrimination charge | Discrimination: until final disposition of charge |
| | EEO-1 report (100 or more employees) | EEO-1: keep copy of most recent file for each reporting unit |
| Davis-Bacon Act (public contracts) | Payroll records including name, address, pay rate, hours worked, deductions, and wages paid | Three years from date of contract completion |
| Employee Polygraph Protection Act | Copy of statement to employee setting forth incident | Three years from date of polygraph test |
| | Copy of opinions, reports, charts, and so on related to polygraph test | |
| Employee Retirement Income Security Act (ERISA) | Plan descriptions and other records necessary to certify information | Descriptions: Not less than six years after filing date of documents based on information contained |
| | Employee records to determine benefits | Employee records: As long as relevant |

*(continued)*

Table 10.3   *Continued*

| Statute | Records | Retention Period |
| --- | --- | --- |
| Fair Labor Standards Act | Basic employment and payroll records | Basic: three years |
| | | Supplementary: two years |
| | Supplementary records | Certificates: until termination of employment |
| | Certificates of age | |
| | Written training agreements | Training: duration of program |

10.3 provide a quick reference guide for many ongoing legal compliance requirements. While each employer's requirements will differ, the process to comply is similar.

## Compliance Calendar

Preparing a compliance calendar for the year helps business owners stay ahead of the compliance requirements. The calendar should include a start date with enough lead time to prepare and review results. Templates are available for certain communications in addition to required forms. The DOL web site www.dol.gov is a good source for background information.

## Compliance Requirements for Compensation Plans

A common problem for business owners is compliance with the Fair Labor Standards Act (FLSA) with respect to employee eligibility for overtime pay after 40 hours worked. A compliance program should include a periodic review of jobs as performed to ensure job incumbents are properly categorized for this purpose. This requires determining whether jobs meet the overtime requirement as described in the FLSA. The Wage and Hour Division of the DOL actively enforces the FLSA.

## CONCLUSION

Maintaining compliance is much better than correcting defects. Establishing a compliance process and calendar helps ensure that you maintain compliance with the laws and regulations. The consequences of being out of compliance for a qualified plan include disallowance of employer deductions, taxable income to participants, return of pretax contributions, and disallowance of rollovers. Plan defects should be corrected ahead of an audit to avoid possible plan disqualification and fines.

Here are three effective business practices:

1. *Review your plan(s) on a regular basis.* A comprehensive assessment of your plan(s) is recommended at least every couple of years. Plans should be amended and updated as appropriate to keep current with changing business conditions and legal requirements. If audited, you will need to produce current and amended plan and trust documents.
2. *Maintain good records.* Payroll records and records of plan activity are critical. You should be able to show administrative procedures, "testing" analysis, and documentation of distributions.
3. *Establish a compliance process and calendar.* Maintaining compliance is an ongoing process. Stay ahead of the requirements by establishing a compliance process and calendar.

# 11

# TIPS FROM EXPERTS TO AVOID COMMON MISTAKES IN RETIREMENT PLANS

Because cost, complexity, and compliance are major consider-ations in choosing and successfully implementing a retirement plan, it makes sense to learn from the experience of experts and avoid common mistakes. The following interviews repre-sent a broad spectrum of experience and expertise. These nut-shell summaries can shorten your learning curve and help you navigate around the most common mistakes. For example, you will learn how to avoid choosing the wrong plan, "back load" fees, "discrimination tests," and record keeping problems.

With these expert perspectives, you will better understand the questions to ask and how to avoid common mistakes. It is not feasible to address all possible mistakes, and this is not a substitute for independent advice on your specific situation. The first mistake to avoid is choosing the wrong plan.

## Avoid Common Mistakes by Careful Plan Design and Selection of Retirement Plans

### Carol C. Brown, Esq.

Carol C. Brown, Esq., concentrates her practice exclusively in employee benefits law, including ERISA (the federal statute that governs employee benefit plans) and executive compensation. Carol's firm, Parker & Brown, P.C., is located in Boston, Massachusetts, and on the Internet at www.parkerbrown.com.

Carol works with businesses and nonprofit organizations to achieve their objectives and keep their plans in compliance with ERISA and the tax code. In avoiding problems, Carol's approach is to *minimize the downside* and *maximize the upside.*

### Downside: Two Reasons That Problems Arise

**1.** Choosing the wrong plan

Business owners often adopt a prototype retirement plan without thoroughly considering what kind of retirement plan they want. They go to their local financial advisor and get into a "one size fits all" plan, often in insurance-based products where everyone gets the same benefit. Although they may need a different type of plan if their primary objective is to maximize the benefits for the owners, getting out of a plan can be complicated and expensive.

Nonprofits need to be especially careful in selecting their plans. For one thing, nonprofits have limited ability to offer "nonqualified" deferred compensation plans to attract top talent such as for a university president or hospital CEO. Their plans need to be carefully tailored to comply with the rules. On the other hand, some nonprofits have additional choices of plans not available to other employers. Nonprofits that are tax exempt under IRC Section 501(c)(3) can offer a 403(b) plan (alternative to the 401(k) without the special 401(k) discrimination rules).

**2.** Sloppy implementation and operation

Business owners can find themselves with an invalid plan if they begin making contributions and collecting dollars from employees before finalizing their documents. This includes formally signing the documents and having minutes of a board of directors meeting to adopt the plan. If the plan is found to be invalid, the business owner may have to return the money, unwind the plan, and deal with penalties from the IRS. A really late adoption may cause the employer to lose a valuable tax deduction for its contributions to the plan.

Sloppy record keeping is another common problem for business owners. Business owners frequently underestimate the record-keeping requirements and find themselves unable to satisfy the nondiscrimination tests or make the required allocations and calculations. They may miscalculate contributions, inadvertently exclude employees, or fail IRS nondiscrimination rules. These things happen, Carol says, but the employer should try to minimize them. Sometimes business owners will go for plans that offer "bundled services" including record keeping, without realizing that they have signed up for insurance products with "back loads" (fees due upon sale) and termination charges. If a record-keeping problem develops, they may incur a substantial fee to change record keepers.

### Upside: Four Choices That Reflect Careful Plan Selection and Design

**1.** Defined benefit plans

Carol sees a big upside in defined benefit plans, especially for business owners over age 50. Defined benefit plans allow

*(continued)*

business owners to put away far more retirement dollars than any other retirement plan. Defined benefit plans work best when the owner is older than most of his or her employees. Many business owners are afraid of defined benefit plans because of the annual commitment to funding the plan. The annual funding commitment can be adjusted by amending the plan to change the benefit formula, changing the actuarial assumptions, and selecting actuarial funding methods that allow flexibility. So, it is really not as rigid a funding commitment as it appears.

There is even less of a financial commitment for a small professional services organization. There is an exemption from Title IV of ERISA for plans that cover professionals (e.g., doctors, lawyers, architects, accountants) that allows such plans to be terminated without being fully funded. So, the employer can terminate the plan and walk away.

**2.** New comparability plans

Carol sees a lot of small businesses adopting new comparability plans because they are flexible and focus on the owner. A new comparability plan is an aggressively discriminatory profit-sharing plan that allows an employer to contribute at a higher rate for the owner or highly compensated employees than for lower paid employees. Sometimes a new comparability plan goes so far as to specify individually the contribution level for each participant in the plan. A new comparability plan satisfies IRS rules that prohibit discrimination in favor of highly compensated employees by cross-testing, a technique that compares the amount of retirement benefit that will be payable at retirement instead of the amount of contribution that is made for each employee. A new comparability plan works best when the owner is older than the rest of the employees. Because a new comparability plan is a profit-sharing plan, it does not require the same level of commitment as a defined benefit plan. It can be terminated at any time and does not require a fixed level of funding each year. The downside is that the limits on contributions are much lower than under a defined benefit plan, especially for an older owner.

**3.** Age-weighted profit-sharing plans

Another popular type of plan, says Carol, is an age-weighted profit-sharing plan. This type of plan allocates employer contributions under a formula that is based in part on the age of the participant—the older the participant, the larger his or her contribution. Like a new comparability plan, an age-weighted profit-sharing plan favors an older owner and satisfies IRS nondiscrimination rules through cross-testing. An age-weighted profit-sharing plan does not require the same level of commitment as a defined benefit plan. It can be terminated at any time and does not require a fixed level of funding each year. Again, the downside is that the limits on contributions are much lower than for a defined benefit plan.

**4.** Design-based safe harbor 401(k) plans

Carol notes that small employers often have trouble offering a 401(k) plan. One reason is that under IRS rules the amount that the owner and other highly compensated employees can contribute depends on what lower paid employees contribute, and lower paid employees often contribute very little. A design-based safe harbor 401(k) plan avoids these problems, but retains the same advantages as a regular 401(k) plan, including allowing principals in the company to contribute different amounts to the plan.

More importantly, this plan eliminates the special nondiscrimination tests that apply to 401(k) plans at the cost of a

*(continued)*

modest employer contribution to the plan. Unlike a SIMPLE 401(k) plan or IRA, a design-based safe harbor 401(k) plan can permit deferrals up to the full IRS limit ($11,000 for 2002) and can include other discretionary employer contributions. A 401(k) feature can sometimes be combined effectively with either an age-weighted or new comparability profit-sharing contribution, or even with a defined benefit plan.

Occasionally, despite careful planning and monitoring, problems arise. These problems can usually be corrected. Carol says that while the IRS has programs for fixing broken plans, it is better to pick the right plan, implement it efficiently, and operate it carefully.

## AVOID COMMON MISTAKES BY UNDERSTANDING THE PROCESS AND FEE STRUCTURES IN RETIREMENT PLANS

### Robert (Bob) Hokanson

Robert (Bob) Hokanson is a Certified Life Underwriter (CLU) and a Life Underwriting Training Council Fellow (LUTCF) located in Boylston, Massachusetts, and on the Internet at rehfinancial@aol.com. Bob has more than 20 years' experience in financial services and holds a number of securities licenses including Series 7, 63, and 65.

In Bob's experience, small business owners tend to make mistakes because they do not understand the process and tend to "jump in" without carefully evaluating what is the best choice for their situation.

Business owners make four common mistakes:

**1.** Dealing with a "one-product" salesperson

Business owners should be wary of dealing with someone pushing one particular investment product. There are a broad range of choices for plans and investment vehicles. A client-oriented advisor will ask a series of questions to help determine whether a qualified retirement plan makes sense by evaluating the business owner's goals and the workforce characteristics (including ages and salaries). Only after completing this process will the advisor recommend particular investment vehicles.

**2.** Not understanding fee structures

Everyone involved in setting up and managing a retirement plan gets paid. There is a lot of confusion about how the fees are structured, and it is difficult to compare one plan with another. Some fees are on the front end and some are on the rear end. Business owners should be wary of "Contingent Deferred

*(continued)*

Sales Charges," which can amount to 5 percent of assets in the event the plan is terminated or rolled over into another plan. Sometimes the fees are negotiable. It is good business practice to ask questions about the fees and get a couple of opinions before jumping into a plan or a particular investment product.

**3.** Trying to manage employee funds in the plan

Business owners should be extremely careful about managing employee pension funds. Employers need to understand that they are held to the highest standards for investment decisions and can be sued if the retirement plan loses money. It is much better to hire an institutional money manager.

Employers should avoid having "unallocated" accounts, in which all the pension funds are in one large pool. It is preferable to use "allocated" accounts that segregate each employee's funds into a separate account, and the individual employee makes the investment choices.

**4.** Not choosing a "good fit" third-party administrator (TPA)

Third-party administrators (TPAs) can be a cost-effective way to manage your plan. They handle the record keeping, updating, and tax and compliance work. Picking a TPA that is set up to handle the type of plan and investment vehicles (e.g., specific mutual funds or group annuity insurance products) used in your plan is important. It is a good idea to solicit competitive proposals and ask, "Have you worked with plan/product X?" Fees will be higher if the TPA lacks experience with and is not set up to handle your type of plan.

Bob recommends that business owners take the time to understand the process before jumping in. He says, "It's like buying a car, once you understand the process you get a better deal." Working with an experienced advisor (not a one-product salesperson) can help you avoid the pitfalls and make a good choice for your situation.

### AVOID COMMON MISTAKES BY BEING REALISTIC AND GETTING INDEPENDENT ADVICE ABOUT RETIREMENT PLANS
#### Bob Miller

Bob Miller, Certified Financial Planner (CFP), is affiliated with Lexington Advisors, a registered investment advisory firm located in Lexington, Massachusetts. His e-mail address is rpmmjm@aol.com.

Bob works with small businesses, ranging from sole proprietors to companies with up to 100 employees. Since Bob was a small business owner before becoming a financial planner, he knows from firsthand experience the problems that the small business owner faces.

The reality is that small businesses, with 10 or fewer employees, have severely limited choices for retirement plans. Bob says that it is sort of like "getting into the real estate market"; you have to start with an "entry level plan." Usually this means an off-the-shelf insurance company plan, which is basically an annuity product. The small business owner gets penalized because the sales commissions on these plans are quite high. This approach, however, allows the business owner to get started. After building up some assets, the business owner can move up to the next level. The threshold is probably about $500,000 in plan assets before the small business owner has a broader range of options.

Bob describes five common mistakes of business owners:

**1.** Failing to think through their future employee situation

Business owners need to realistically assess their future employee situation. Sometimes, business owners put a plan in place when they have no employees without realizing that when they have employees they will have to make contributions

*(continued)*

for their employees (e.g., SEP and SIMPLE plans require employer contributions for employees).

By thinking through their future employee needs, business owners can select a plan tailored to their situation. For example, if there will be a high turnover workforce, a plan can be tailored to delay vesting of the employer contributions.

**2.** Being unwilling to contribute for employees

If the business owner is adamant about not paying for their employees' retirement, it is difficult to make a qualified retirement plan work. To comply with the requirements of tax-deductible retirement plans, some employer contribution is usually needed.

Business owners who want to minimize the amount they contribute on behalf of employees can use a 401(k) plan or other defined contribution plan that allows the employees to put money away pretax. This limits the amount the business owner can contribute because of discrimination testing and compliance requirements.

**3.** Having insufficient cash flows

Business owners need to be realistic about what they can afford to fund on an ongoing basis.

If their business is cyclical or cash flows are volatile, business owners should avoid retirement plans, such as defined benefit plans, with annual funding commitments.

**4.** Price shopping only on administrative cost

Smart business owners are cost conscious and shop carefully for good prices. Price shopping and comparison of fees for retirement plans are complicated. Business owners tend to focus on administrative costs. But the things that really make a difference in retirement plans are difficult to assess when you shop only on the basis of administrative cost. Attributes such as type of investment choices available, service level, and reporting level are difficult to quantify and can make a significant difference in the business owner's experience with the plan. Business owners who select package plans because they appear to have lower administrative charges can find themselves with a plan that limits their investment choices and has other significant shortcomings.

5. Assuming that the sale of their business will provide for their retirement

Sometimes business owners drain their resources to fund expansion, assuming that they will sell their business and retire on the proceeds. This is a risky retirement strategy. Unless there is substantial real estate, or it is a high-value niche business, it is unlikely to sell for what the business owner needs to fund a comfortable retirement.

Bob recommends that small business owners get started with a retirement plan that is affordable for their current situation. Although Bob feels that "some plan is better than no plan," he encourages business owners to pay for independent advice such as provided by a Certified Financial Planner. A CFP bases advice in terms of the best fit for the business owner's goals and situation.

### Avoid Common Mistakes by Integrating Business and Personal Financial Planning in Evaluating Retirement Plans

**Elaine Morgillo**

Elaine Morgillo, CFP, is President of Morgillo Financial Management, Inc., an investment advisory firm located in North Andover, Massachusetts, and on the Internet at www .morgillofinancial.com.

Elaine works with individuals and business owners to manage their investments and plan for a comfortable retirement. Elaine's approach is highly personalized. *She takes an integrated approach, looking at the big picture—the individual, the family, and the business.* Then, she works with other professionals to design and implement a financial and retirement plan specifically tailored to the individual's situation.

Waiting too long to start putting aside money for retirement is the most common mistake that Elaine sees. The reasons for waiting vary. Because funds in a retirement plan grow on a tax-deferred basis, the sooner the business owner starts, the better. The longer the business owner waits, the shorter the period for the funds to grow.

Elaine mentions five common reasons that business owners delay putting funds aside for retirement:

**1.** Not doing tax planning with their CPA

Business owners can be so totally focused on running their business that they do not take time to plan for the future. Some CPAs are proactive in helping business owners see the "big picture" and plan ahead by proposing strategies. If the company's CPA is not initiating a discussion about business and tax planning, the business owner should be asking questions and seeking advice.

**2.** Waiting until their kids graduate from college

Sometimes business owners feel that they cannot afford to put money aside for retirement until they have fulfilled financial obligations such as paying for their kids' college education. Paying for college is a major financial hurdle, and financial planning can help. Putting money in a retirement plan is still a good idea. The dollars that go into retirement accounts generate current tax deductions. Further, the dollars that are in retirement accounts do not reduce eligibility for financial aid.

**3.** Waiting until they are exhausted and near burnout

Small business owners work extremely hard. Sooner or later, they realize that they "can't continue to work like this forever." The business owner who waits until age 50+ to think about funding retirement has limited options. Funding a retirement plan at age 50+ has to be very aggressive to achieve a comfortable retirement at age 62 (or age 65 or your selected age for retirement). This is especially difficult if the business owner is really anxious to retire because of exhaustion or burnout.

**4.** Assuming their business is too small to have a retirement plan

Sometimes business owners assume that their business is too small to afford a retirement plan. Even a minimal retirement plan is better than none. Just getting started is important. Funding an IRA ($2,000 per year) is worth doing. SEP and SIMPLE plans (discussed in Chapter 6) are specifically designed to help small business owners establish a realistic retirement plan.

**5.** Having unrealistic expectations about their 401(k) plan

The funds in a 401(k) plan do not guarantee a specific payout at retirement. When the stock market is booming, 401(k)

*(continued)*

investments look great. In a market downturn, the value of the 401(k) plan can disappear rapidly. Business owners should not depend on a 401(k) plan as their primary source of retirement income.

Elaine recommends that business owners start by pulling together a personal financial plan. The basic principles of a solid financial plan are asset allocation and diversification. *Asset allocation* means not having all your "eggs" (i.e., your business) in one basket. It is beneficial to have a balanced mix of different asset categories such as real estate, the business, and stocks and bonds. *Diversification* means that the assets are not too heavily concentrated in one company, industry, or geography.

By starting a personal financial plan, business owners reduce their risk and have a foundation on which to select an appropriate retirement plan. The sooner business owners begin contributing to the retirement plan, the better. Funding retirement plans is tax efficient since the business owner gets current tax deductions and the plan assets grow on a tax-deferred basis.

## AVOID COMMON MISTAKES OF BEING TOO GENEROUS OR TOO RESTRICTIVE IN RETIREMENT PLANS

### Renee W. Senes

Renee W. Senes is an Investment Advisor Representative and Financial Consultant with Commonwealth Financial Network, Member NASD. Her office is located in Harvard, Massachusetts, and on the Internet at rsgold@bicnet.net.

Drawing from her prior experience in special education and in estate planning and administration, Renee's approach is to look at the whole person, their family situation, and their long-term objectives. In helping a business owner select an appropriate retirement plan, Renee feels that it is especially important to understand the business owner's whole situation, the employee picture, whether there are family relationships, and what is realistically affordable.

Renee says that she sees a couple of common mistakes:

**1.** Picking the wrong plan in a last-minute rush to reduce tax liability

Business owners wait until the last minute and act only after their accountant tells them that they made "a lot of money" and owe a large amount in taxes. Acting in haste to reduce their tax liability, business owners pick the wrong plan.

**2.** Being too generous or too restrictive in their plan

Making employees eligible for plan participation on the first day of employment is an example of a business owner being too generous. The business owner can find him/herself with administrative headaches if employee turnover is high.

On the other extreme, examples of a business owner being too restrictive include delaying eligibility for the plan for

*(continued)*

maximum allowed under the law (two full years) or by refusing to make any matching contribution to the employee
plan. Business owners can experience an employee backlash
from such actions. By refusing to make any matching contributions, business owners are missing the safe harbors that reduce risk and enable larger contributions for themselves as
well as their highly compensated employees.

A plan that functions and works smoothly for a company is
the goal.

A SIMPLE plan works well for many small businesses (with
100 employees or less). The business owner can put away
$7,000 plus up to three percent of salary to a maximum of
$14,000 in 2002. Employees can elect to participate. Employees
also elect the amount they wish to contribute up to $7,000
($7,500 if over age 50) of their pretax pay (in 2002). For partici-
pating employees, the business owner matches the employee's
contribution dollar for dollar up to three percent of compensation. The employer match can change from year to year. The
employer match can be one percent instead of three percent in
two out of five years.

Renee has seen the SIMPLE plan work well for a growing
business that is adding employees. Each participant's account
is an IRA and there is little additional work when employees
are added to the payroll. A critical issue is what date the employee is eligible to participate in the plan. Some business
owners choose to make employees eligible to participate after a
probationary period of several months. Others choose an eligibility date of the first anniversary of the date of hire.

Renee has also seen business owners who were unhappy
with the SIMPLE plan they put in place in haste because of
their extreme reluctance to fund the employer match.

There are restrictions in SIMPLE plans. The good news is
that the plans have no nondiscrimination rules. However, the

bad news is that business owners selecting a SIMPLE plan cannot have any other qualified retirement plan. In addition, there are severe penalties for a withdrawal before two years in the plan. So, a departing employee cannot simply roll over the IRA, and the business owner can be stuck with the small accounts hanging around for two years.

*including Roth?*

SEP plans, which are entirely employer funded, can be an excellent choice for a family business in which the employees are all family members.

Renee feels that picking the right plan is just the beginning of an ongoing process. She makes it her practice to schedule regular follow-up consultations, two to four times a year, with the business owner. She also makes herself available to the employees for consultations that can include family members. Retirement planning is not a one-step process. It requires ongoing education and checkups.

## AVOID COMMON MISTAKES BY MANAGING RISK IN RETIREMENT PLANS

### Robert (Bob) Cormier

Robert (Bob) Cormier is a Certified Financial Manager (CFM) and a Financial Advisor with Merrill Lynch located in Wellesley Hills, Massachusetts and on the Internet at Robert_Cormier@ML.com. Bob has a disciplined approach to financial planning.

Drawing from his military background (he received his BS from the U.S. Military Academy at West Point), Bob emphasizes the importance of having an operations plan before looking at investment choices. In helping business owners achieve their goals, Bob has found that it is more important to focus on managing risk than on "trying to beat the market" with aggressive investment strategies.

"Not shouldering the whole load," is another strategy that Bob says makes sense for some companies. With this approach, business owners can share the load of funding retirement plans with their employees by having a combination of plans, such as a 401(k) and a profit-sharing plan. The 401(k) plan is funded substantially from employee contributions. A profit-sharing plan allows the employer to share the good times with employees without being locked into contributions that can be difficult to afford in bad times. Other plan choices for business owners include the Simplified Employee Pension (SEP) and the Savings Incentive Match Plan for Employees (SIMPLE). The SEP plans may be preferable for businesses that are new or that have variable profits because the employer can choose whether to make contributions from year to year. SIMPLE plans may be more suitable for businesses with a stable income stream, since employer contributions are mandatory.

More information about retirement solutions for business owners can be found in Merrill Lynch's *Meeting Your Business Retirement Plan Needs.*

Here are three common mistakes that business owners make:

**1.** Unrealistic expectations

When the market was achieving double-digit returns in the late 1990s, almost every investment produced a positive return. This was followed by a severe decline in the market and high-profile corporate bankruptcies. Investment expectations should not be driven by the extremes of the market. *Before* choosing particular investments, it is important to work through the development of a plan. It should focus on achieving realistic returns and reducing risk through (1) proper asset allocation—investing in equities, fixed income, and cash; and (2) diversification across industry sectors, market capitalization, and investment styles.

**2.** "Do it yourselfers"

Some business owners want to "do it themselves." While there are business owners who understand and are committed to fulfilling their fiduciary responsibilities, including those under ERISA, most are simply too busy running their businesses to dedicate attention to all the details. Problems arise when business owners do not establish a prudent written investment policy, set up an investment committee, educate employees, keep adequate records, review performance, and make adjustments consistent with their investment policy. Business owners who do it themselves must devote significant efforts to staying up to date with changes in the market as well as the laws and regulations related to retirement plans. This means reviewing the plan and investments on a regular—at least, quarterly—basis.

*(continued)*

**3.** Not understanding "asset-based" fees

Asset-based administrative fees (a percentage of the funds under management) can seem to be low cost in the early days, but the costs escalate as the assets in the plan grow. How the fees are allocated among plan participants is another important consideration. Business owners need to be aware of the various implications of asset-based fees on their plan's portfolio.

Bob recommends that business owners take the time to develop a realistic plan to achieve their goals. An experienced financial advisor can help design and implement a plan that reduces risk and enables the business owner to stay "on top" of the plan.

# ══════12══════

# FINANCIAL HEALTH-CHECK: IS YOUR PLAN ON TRACK TO ACHIEVE YOUR GOALS?

Times change. The law changes. What made sense a couple of years ago may no longer be the best choice for you and your business. Recent changes in legislation have created many new opportunities for small business owners. For example, the recent advent of the "Single K" has made 401(k) plans a much more attractive option for many small businesses. A financial "health-check" can help assure that your plan is up to date and on track to achieve your goals.

According to Christopher J. (Chris) Williams, Senior Financial Consultant with Financial Network Investment Corporation, located at Clinton Savings Bank in Clinton, Massachusetts (cwilliams@clintonsavings.com), recent tax law changes have "leveled the playing field" for small businesses when it comes to employer-sponsored retirement plans. Many small business owners are not aware of the changes, nor do they have the time to devote to fully understanding their options. That is why Chris says his approach is "all about education, not sales."

## IS CURRENT FUNDING ADEQUATE
## FOR RETIREMENT NEEDS?

Chris talks with small business owners in plain, layperson language. He talks about getting from "point A" (where you are today) to "point B" (where you want to be at retirement age). Chris asks a few simple questions to understand the business owner's situation and current funding for retirement and then shows a visual illustration.

First question: What would you like to live on during your retirement years?

Suppose the business owner needs $5,000 a month to live comfortably in retirement.

Next question: What have you put aside for retirement?

Chris walks the business owner through a discussion as illustrated in Figure 12.1 on pages 170–175.
(This is only an illustration and is not intended to represent any investment.)
The first section is all about assumptions: how long until the business owner plans to retire; interest and inflation rates; and related matters. The second section is about retirement assets. This small business owner and his partner/spouse are each putting away about $3,000 per year. Based on this information, Chris generates an illustration about how much money they will have at retirement.
The illustration clearly shows a shortfall in funds for retirement. At the current funding level, the small business owner will run out of money after three years of retirement. So, how will he and his spouse cover the shortfall?

## FUNDING THE SHORTFALL

Sometimes, small business owners think that they will sell real estate, their business, or live off the revenue stream from an apartment building. Occasionally these strategies are realistic, but often they are just wishful thinking.

Funding the shortfall can be a difficult challenge. There is a strong tendency to shy away from setting aside money. It means taking cash out of pocket and curtailing current spending patterns. Business owners sometimes resist taking (e.g., $3,000 per month) cash out of current spending to fund their retirement plan. So, even if small business owners set up a plan, they may not fully fund it.

Convincing small business owners to actually fund their retirement plan is another educational process. At this stage, Chris is up front about the investment choices and fees (see Table 12.1). Chris "digs deep" to understand the small business owner's perspective on risk before discussing any investments. He also fully discloses the fee structures, with a simple,

Table 12.1    Fee Disclosure Framework Example[a]

| Mutual Fund Shares | Sales Charge | Annual Fees and Expenses (% of Assets under Management) |
|---|---|---|
| A | 5.75% Upfront | 0.50–1.50 |
| B | 0 Upfront<br>CDSC[b] 6 years | 1.25–2.25 |
| C | 0 Upfront<br>CDSC[b] 12 months | 1.25–2.25 |
| No load | 0 Upfront | 0.18–3.00 |

[a]These are examples and do not represent any particular mutual fund.
[b]CDSC = Contingent Deferred Sales Charge.

# Retirement Funding Needs Analysis

*Prepared for*

## John Doe

## Assumptions

| | |
|---|---|
| 65, 65 | Client, Partner Retirement Ages (Years: 2027, 2030) |
| 2027 | First Year of Retirement (Client 65, Partner 62) |
| $60,000 | Annual Retirement Spending Objective (Today's $) |
| $125,627 | Retirement Spending Objective (Future $) |
| 28 | Years of Life Expectancy after Retirement |
| 2054 | Final Year of Illustration |
| $0 | Desired Assets at Mortality (Today's $) |
| $0 | Desired Assets at Mortality (Future $) |
| $0 | Lump Sum Payout (Future $) in Year 2002 |

| | |
|---|---|
| 6.0% | Hypothetical Investment Return: Post-retirement |
| 3.0% | Assumed Rate Of Inflation |
| 2.0% | Social Security Growth Rate (COLA) |

## Current Retirement Assets

| | Current Balance | Annual Contribution | Increase Rate | Growth Rate | Retirement Value |
|---|---|---|---|---|---|
| Client - Qualified Retirement Plans | $5,000 | $3,000 | 2.0% | 8.0% | $315,467 |
| Partner - Qualified Retirement Plans | $5,000 | $3,000 | 2.0% | 8.0% | $315,467 |
| Other Retirement Assets (Non-Qualified) | $0 | $0 | 0.0% | 6.0% | $0 |
| Estimated Value Of Retirement Assets (at First Year of Retirement - 2027) | | | | | $630,935 |

170

## Estimated First Year Retirement Income (In Future $)

| | |
|---|---|
| Retirement Spending Objective | $125,627 |
| | |
| Income Potential of Estimated Retirement Assets (1) | $37,856 |
| Social Security | $28,197 |
| All Other income | $65,624 |
| **Total Income** | **$131,677** |
| | |
| **First Year Surplus (Shortage)** | **$6,051** |

## Estimate of Assets Needed at Retirement

| | |
|---|---|
| Capital Surplus (Shortage) at Retirement (Future $) <br> *(Adjusted for $0 remaining at mortality)* | ($684,889) |
| | |
| Capital Required to Fund Shortage (Today's $) | $159,578 |
| | |
| Level Monthly Savings Required to Meet Retirement Income Goals | $1,008 |
| | |
| Inflating Monthly Savings Required to Meet Retirement Income Goals (2) | $755 |

*These examples are hypothetical only and do not represent the actual performance of any particular investment.*
*(1) Represents the portfolio return from your retirement assets based on your hypothetical post-retirement return on investment*
*(2) Monthly savings assumed to increase by 3.0% each year*

*Christopher J. Williams*

*December 23, 2002*      *Financial Network Investment Corporation*

*This presentation must be accompanied by a cover and disclosure page*

Figure 12.1   Retirement fund needs analysis.

*(continued)*

# Retirement Funding Needs Analysis

*Prepared for*

## John Doe

**Post-Retirement Cash Flow**

*(in Future $)*

Start Year: 2027    End Year: 2054

| Year | Beginning Capital Pool | Capital Earnings | Retirement Expenses | SS Income | Other Incomes | Pension Income | Surplus/ (Shortage) |
|------|------|------|------|------|------|------|------|
| 2027 | $630,935 | $37,856 | $125,627 | $28,197 | $65,624 | $0 | $6,051 |
| 2028 | $636,985 | $38,219 | $129,395 | $28,761 | $66,937 | $0 | $4,521 |
| 2029 | $641,507 | $38,490 | $133,277 | $29,336 | $68,275 | $0 | $2,825 |
| 2030 | $644,332 | $38,660 | $137,276 | $58,593 | $0 | $0 | ($40,022) |
| 2031 | $604,309 | $36,259 | $141,394 | $59,765 | $0 | $0 | ($45,370) |
| 2032 | $558,939 | $33,536 | $145,636 | $60,961 | $0 | $0 | ($51,139) |
| 2033 | $507,800 | $30,468 | $150,005 | $62,180 | $0 | $0 | ($57,357) |
| 2034 | $450,443 | $27,027 | $154,505 | $63,423 | $0 | $0 | ($64,055) |
| 2035 | $386,388 | $23,183 | $159,140 | $64,692 | $0 | $0 | ($71,265) |
| 2036 | $315,123 | $18,907 | $163,914 | $65,986 | $0 | $0 | ($79,021) |
| 2037 | $236,102 | $14,166 | $168,832 | $67,305 | $0 | $0 | ($87,360) |
| 2038 | $148,742 | $8,925 | $173,897 | $68,652 | $0 | $0 | ($96,321) |
| 2039 | $52,421 | $3,145 | $179,114 | $70,025 | $0 | $0 | ($105,944) |
| 2040 | $0 | $0 | $184,487 | $71,425 | $0 | $0 | ($113,062) |
| 2041 | $0 | $0 | $190,022 | $72,854 | $0 | $0 | ($117,168) |

| Year | | | | | |
|---|---|---|---|---|---|
| 2042 | $0 | $195,722 | $74,311 | $0 | ($121,412) |
| 2043 | $0 | $201,594 | $75,797 | $0 | ($125,797) |
| 2044 | $0 | $207,642 | $77,313 | $0 | ($130,329) |
| 2045 | $0 | $213,871 | $78,859 | $0 | ($135,012) |
| 2046 | $0 | $220,287 | $80,436 | $0 | ($139,851) |
| 2047 | $0 | $226,896 | $82,045 | $0 | ($144,851) |
| 2048 | $0 | $233,703 | $83,686 | $0 | ($150,017) |
| 2049 | $0 | $240,714 | $85,360 | $0 | ($155,354) |
| 2050 | $0 | $247,935 | $87,067 | $0 | ($160,868) |
| 2051 | $0 | $255,373 | $88,808 | $0 | ($166,565) |
| 2052 | $0 | $263,034 | $90,584 | $0 | ($172,450) |
| 2053 | $0 | $270,925 | $48,244 | $0 | ($222,681) |
| 2054 | $0 | $279,053 | $49,209 | $0 | ($229,844) |

*This page illustrates your retirement cash flow position each year starting with the retirement date of the client and ending at the last mortality year. Your Retirement Capital Pool will grow or deplete each year depending on your yearly income vs. expenses situation.*

Christopher J. Williams

*December 23, 2002*                    Financial Network Investment Corporation

*This presentation must be accompanied by a cover and disclosure page*

Figure 12.1   Continued

*(continued)*

# *Retirement Funding Needs Analysis*

*Prepared for*

## John Doe

### Assumptions

| | |
|---|---|
| 65, 65 | Client, Partner Retirement Ages (Years: 2027, 2030) |
| 2027 | First Year of Retirement (Client 65, Partner 62) |
| $60,000 | Annual Retirement Spending Objective (Today's $) |
| $125,627 | Retirement Spending Objective (Future $) |
| 28 | Years of Life Expectancy after Retirement |
| 2054 | Final Year of Illustration |
| $0 | Desired Assets at Mortality (Today's $) |
| $0 | Desired Assets at Mortality (Future $) |
| $0 | Lump Sum Payout at Retirement (Future $) |

| | |
|---|---|
| 6.0% | Hypothetical Investment Return: Post-retirement |
| 3.0% | Assumed Rate Of Inflation |
| 2.0% | Social Security Growth Rate (COLA) |

## Assets Available

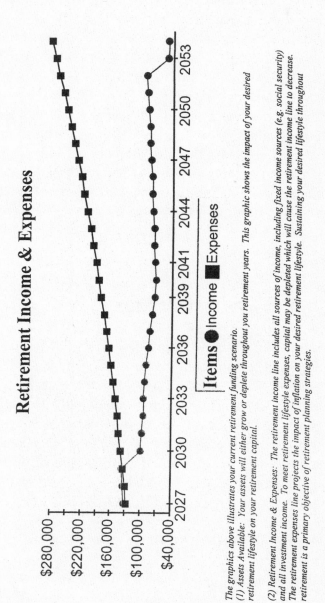

# Retirement Income & Expenses

**Items** ● Income ■ Expenses

*The graphics above illustrates your current retirement funding scenario.*
*(1) Assets Available: Your assets will either grow or deplete throughout you retirement years. This graphic shows the impact of your desired retirement lifestyle on your retirement capital.*

*(2) Retirement Income & Expenses: The retirement income line includes all sources of income, including fixed income sources (e.g. social security) and all investment income. To meet retirement lifestyle expenses, capital may be depleted which will cause the retirement income line to decrease. The retirement expenses line projects the impact of inflation on your desired retirement lifestyle. Sustaining your desired lifestyle throughout retirement is a primary objective of retirement planning strategies.*

*Christopher J. Williams*

*December 23, 2002*

*Financial Network Investment Corporation*

*This presentation must be accompanied by a cover and disclosure page*

Figure 12.1    Continued

(2)

175

easy-to-understand chart found in the "New Account Guide & Privacy Promise," and subtitled "Investing, What You Should Know" (available through Financial Network).

Chris talks candidly about fees. Financial advisors make the most money recommending "A" shares with their high up-front fees. The "B" shares are the next most profitable for financial advisors with long Contingent Deferred Sales Charges. Least profitable for financial advisors are the "C" shares. Chris does not steer his clients into any particular share class because he does not think "locking clients into investments with high up-front fees or long deferred sales charges is the right thing to do." He does not push particular products or investments because he does not have any sales quotas to meet. Whichever path the client wants to take, Chris strives to ensure that the business owner is fully informed.

### GET A SECOND OPINION

Chris's approach is like getting a "second opinion." When you have a clear picture of the options and the costs, you can make a more informed decision. For example, Chris says that the so-called Single K is really worth checking out (see Table 12.2). The Single K is a 401(k) for the self-employed or small business owner who only employs immediate family. It allows such business owners to put away an annual contribution of up to $40,000 ($41,000 if aged 50 or older in 2002).

### SCHEDULE A FINANCIAL HEALTH-CHECK

Staying up to date with all the changes is a formidable task for a small business owner who has a company to run. So, it is a

Table 12.2   Highlights of Single K

As discussed in Chapter 6, 401(k)'s historically have been too expensive and complicated for small businesses because of the administrative requirements. Recent changes in the law enable small business owners to shelter a larger amount of their income than is possible with SEP or SIMPLE plans. In Single K's, contributions of up to 25 percent of compensation, up to a maximum of $40,000, may be deducted by the employer as a business expense. Contributions and investment earnings grow tax deferred until withdrawal. Hardship withdrawals are available and discrimination testing is not required.

Single K's are not suitable for a business with rank and file employees. However, Single K's are attractive for small business owners who employ the owner and his or her family, or a few key employees, or part-time employees that can be excluded (less than 1,000 hours, less than one year of service, and under 21).

good business practice to schedule a regular review of your retirement plan.

An annual financial health-check, just like a regular health checkup, helps keep you and your business on track. You will learn about the latest changes in the law. Perhaps a new option is now available, such as the Single K, that is a good choice for your business. It also helps you confirm that you are current with your retirement planning goals. A financial health-check is the best way to monitor your progress toward achieving your retirement goals.

# 13

# AVOIDING CHAOS: ESTATE PLANNING AND RETIREMENT PLANNING

Estate planning and retirement planning are closely linked for the small business owner. If a small business owner dies without a proper estate plan, chaos occurs in the family and in the business. If the small business owner does not have a retirement plan, financial security for the later years of life is uncertain and remains tied to the business. Sometimes, fear of old age and death motivates small business owners to put retirement and estate plans in place. Other times, it is the desire to avoid a "fight among the kids."

There are many horror stories about family fights and legal battles when the beneficiaries of a small business owner try to divide up the estate. Businesses have been forced to sell property to pay taxes owed or close as a result. Many of these problems could have been avoided.

Estate planning for a small business is complicated and is beyond the scope of this book. This chapter is intended to highlight problems that have occurred that could have been prevented. Special thanks to John F. Shoro, Esq., a partner in the law firm of Bowditch & Dewey, LLP, located in Worcester,

Massachusetts, and on the Internet at jshoro@bowditch.com, for sharing his insights from many years of working with small business owners on estate and retirement planing. John's work often includes planning for succession or sale of the business. Retirement planning is a critical component of the planning process.

To avoid problems down the road, estate planning should be done with professional assistance. Do not just sign over property or give away stock. In an attempt to reduce estate taxes by making gifts, you may be unnecessarily increasing income taxes and putting your hard-earned property at risk. There are gifting and valuation techniques you can use to accomplish your objectives and reduce the taxes that you owe.

## SEVERE CONSEQUENCES OF DOING NOTHING

Business owners need to understand that there are severe consequences of doing nothing. Sometimes business owners think that the business will continue and fund their later years. For example, consider a family-owned business in which dad is the founder, mom and dad are the stockholders, and one of their two children is active in the business. The "Status Quo Retirement Plan," which is another way of saying "do nothing plan," is that after dad dies, mom continues to draw salary and take profit distributions as the sole or majority stockholder until her death in her late 80s. The parents really intended to leave the business property to their son who works in the business and leave other property to their daughter. Instead, mom dies with a simple will that leaves all of her property, including the stock in the business, in equal shares to her children. The kids then have a mess on their hands. The son has to grudgingly buy out his sister's interest in the business. It can be extremely difficult to achieve an equitable distribution of the estate, considering that the son has worked for years to make the business successful. The tax consequences can be severe and deductions for family-owned business interests can be lost. With planning, the family could have avoided this situation.

## Review Your Estate and Retirement Plans

If your will and estate planning documents were prepared years ago when the kids were little, as is frequently the case, they need to be reviewed and updated. If the small business owner's will or trust says, "equal shares to my children," there can be a disaster in the making.

To avoid the dreaded fight among the kids, family members who are active in the business should be treated differently from family members who are not participating in the business. There are ways to equalize the relative shares that each child receives while avoiding the potential for a power struggle in the business. For example, if one of your four children is active in the business and the other three are not, the one who is working in the business may take what the others consider to be an excessively high salary that reduces their share of the profits. A better scenario might be to give the business to the one who is working in the business and give real estate and other assets to the other children. If other assets are not available, insurance can be used to equalize distributions.

If the business owns real estate, it can make sense to separate the business and the real estate into different legal entities. The business can be transferred to the children working in the business and the real estate can be transferred to the children not participating in the business. The business can then pay fair rent to the real estate entity. This structure allocates assets and avoids a fight or power struggle between the children involved in the business and the nonparticipants.

Similarly, if you have put retirement and benefit plans in place over the years, it is important to review them from time to time. As discussed previously, the laws have changed and allow many more options for small business retirement plans. Having a professional financial planner review your plans will give you a clear understanding of what revenue stream you are likely to have in retirement. It also will give you an opportunity to take advantage of the recent changes in the law to put more money away for retirement in a tax-advantageous manner.

### Misconceptions about Retirement Planning

In John's experience, small business owners have many misconceptions about retirement planning:

- *"The cost is prohibitive."* Many business owners think that the cost to establish and maintain a retirement plan is prohibitive. In fact, there are several inexpensive and simple prototype plans that can work well.
- *"I'll be throwing away money on employees who leave."* Another concern is that employees will leave and take with them the money the business owner has just contributed to the plan on their behalf. In fact, there are ways to handle employee turnover. Gradual or "cliff" vesting schedules can ensure that only employees who stay the required minimum time periods are covered. Retirement plans can actually be an incentive for employees to stay.
- *"Compliance is complicated and tax penalties are draconian."* Small business owners fear that maintaining a retirement plan would be complicated and that draconian

tax penalties for noncompliance could put their own retirement money at risk.

Getting over the hurdle of complexity is the biggest issue.
John's firm tries to take the complexity out of the process. To
meet the needs of its clients, the firm has established a subsidiary called B&D Advisors, LLC, in which John is a principal.
B&D Advisors provides a "cohesive approach" to implementing
estate and retirement plans by coordinating services and working with investment providers. The firm is not affiliated with
any fund or security and hence is independent in advising
business owners.


## CONCLUSION

Chaos is almost guaranteed to occur unless you take steps
to put an estate plan in place. A comfortable retirement is
more likely with a retirement plan. Doing nothing can have
extremely severe and unintended consequences. Taking action before a crisis arises is much better than reacting under
stressful circumstances.

# ═══14═══

# RESOURCES AND
# REFERENCES

The goal of this book is to help small business owners make informed choices about compensation and retirement plans that are a good fit for their situation. By presenting information in clear jargon-free language, and by suggesting resources, this book provides guidance; it is not a replacement for professional advisors. After reading this book, you should be better able to evaluate your options and deal effectively with professional advisors.

The laws and regulations are complex and continually changing. As of this writing, legislation is pending in Congress to further expand the options. This chapter describes and provides some examples of additional resources. As time passes, the online information will be updated. With these references, you will have a road map of resources for the future. Many public (taxpayer-funded) resources as well as private companies provide information about compensation and retirement plans. Public resources include the Internal Revenue Service (IRS), Department of Labor (DOL), the Employee Benefits and Security Administration (EBSA), which was formerly named the Pension Welfare Benefits Administration (PWBA), and the *Federal Register.*

## INTERNAL REVENUE SERVICE

The IRS provides a wealth of information through its publications. Selected publications are:

- "Choosing a Retirement Solution for Your Small Business" (IRS Publication 3998)
- "Retirement Plans for Small Business (SEP, SIMPLE and Qualified Plans)" (IRS Publication 560)

For a complete listing, go to http://www.irs.gov/forms/pubs /index.html.

## DEPARTMENT OF LABOR (DOL) EMPLOYEE BENEFITS AND SECURITY ADMINISTRATION (EBSA)

This department of the DOL, formerly named the Pension Welfare Benefits Administration, can be found on the Internet at http://www.dol.gov/ebsa. Selected publications included here are:

- "Health Plans and Benefits"
- "Simple Retirement Solutions for Small Business"
- "A Look at 401(k) Plan Fees for Employers"
- "ABC PLAN 401(k) Plan Fee Disclosure Form"

Information is also available from nonprofit resources such as The Profit Sharing/401(k) Council of America (PSCA), which is a nonprofit association advocating increased retirement security through profit sharing, 401(k), and related defined contribution programs (www.pcsa.org; see, for example, "EGTRRA: Plan Amendment Primer").

Another source of information is the broad range of service providers. For example, Trustar Retirement Services (Wilmington, Delaware), provides record keeping, trustee, and retirement services for retirement plans. Included here, for example, is their newsletter, "Economic Growth and Tax Relief Reconciliation Act of 2001." This serves as a useful framework for understanding the key provisions.

Mutual funds, insurance companies, and investment advisors provide extensive information online. The following examples illustrate the range of information available online and are not intended to be an endorsement of any particular company:

- Connecticut General Life Insurance Company, a subsidiary of CIGNA Corporation, provides "CIGNA's Pension Analyst."
  http://www.cigna.com
- Oppenheimer Funds
  http://www.oppenheimerfunds.com/advisors
  /retirementplans/small_money.jhtml
- Raymond James
  http://www.raymondjames.com
- Merrill Lynch
  http://www.merrilllynch.com

An abundance of information is available—so much information that it is overwhelming. The challenge is figuring out what is the best fit for your business and situation. Returning to the framework provided in Chapter 6 provides a context for evaluating your choices. Once you position yourself in the framework, you can focus on a more limited set of options (see Table 14.1).

Table 14.1   Options Framework by Complexity
and Cost of Administration

| Easy/Inexpensive | More Complicated/Costly | Complex/Expensive |
| --- | --- | --- |
| Bonus | 401(k) | Stock options |
| SEP | Defined contribution | Nonqualified plans |
| SIMPLE | Defined benefit | ESOP |

Remember, your goals should drive the selection process. Financial advisors guide and advise. Some plans may sound great but are just too complicated and costly for you and your business. Other plans may not take full advantage of the options that are available to a company at your level of profitability. Using the "Options Framework by Complexity and Cost of Administration" can help you cut through the tangle of choices and enable you to make an informed decision.

# CHOOSING
## A RETIREMENT SOLUTION
*for Your Small Business*

Department of the Treasury
Internal Revenue Service
w w w . i r s . g o v
Publication 3998 (Rev. 7-2002)
Catalog Number 34066S

**SBA**
U.S. Small Business Administration

This pamphlet constitutes a small entity compliance guide for purposes of the Small Business Regulatory Enforcement Fairness Act of 1996. It does not constitute legal, accounting or other professional advice.

*Choosing A Retirement Solution for Your Small Business* is a joint project of the U.S. Department of Labor's Pension and Welfare Benefits Administration (PWBA), the Internal Revenue Service, the U.S. Small Business Administration, and the U.S. Chamber of Commerce. Its publication does not imply endorsement of any cosponsor's or participant's opinions, products or services.

This cosponsorship should not be construed either directly or indirectly as an endorsement or promotion of any products, services, activities or policies of any of the cosponsors by any of the other cosponsors. The material in this brochure is designed to provide accurate and authoritative information in regard to the subject matter covered. It is distributed with the understanding that the publisher is not engaged in rendering legal, accounting or other professional service. If legal advice or other expert assistance is required, the services of a competent professional should be sought. The cosponsors make no representations or warranties regarding this publication and in no event shall the cosponsors be liable for damages, including incidental or consequential damages, in connection with or arising out of the performance or use of this publication.

All programs of the Small Business Administration are provided to the public on a nondiscriminatory basis.

For a complete list of PWBA publications, call toll-free:
**1-866-275-7922**

This material is also available to sensory impaired individuals upon request.
Voice phone: 1-202-693-8664
TDD phone: 1-202-501-3911

This pamphlet is also available from the Internal Revenue Service at (please indicate Catalog Number when ordering):
**1-800-TAX-FORM (1-800-829-3676)**

**Starting a small business retirement savings plan can be easier than most business people think. What's more, there are a number of retirement programs that provide tax advantages to both employers and employees.**

## Why Save?

Experts estimate that Americans will need 60 to 80 percent of their pre-retirement income – lower income earners may need up to 90 percent – to maintain their current standard of living when they stop working. So, now is the time to look into retirement plan programs. As an employer, you have an important role to play in helping America's workers save.

By starting a retirement savings plan, you will help your employees save for the future. Retirement plans may also help you attract and retain qualified employees, and they offer tax savings to your business. You will help secure your own retirement as well. You can establish a plan even if you are self-employed. Better yet, you will join more than one million small businesses with 100 or fewer employees that offer workplace retirement savings plans.

## Any Tax Advantages?

A retirement plan has significant tax advantages:

- Contributions are deductible by the employer when contributed;
- Employer and employee contributions are not taxed until distributed to the employee; and
- Money in the retirement program grows tax-free.

## Any Other Incentives?

In addition to helping your business, your employees and yourself, recent tax law changes have made it easier than ever to establish a retirement plan. They include:

- Higher contribution limits so your employees (and you) can set aside larger amounts for retirement;
- "Catch-up" rules that allow employees aged 50 and over to set aside an additional $500 (or $1,000, depending on the type of plan) for 2002;
- Tax credit for small employers that would enable them to claim a tax credit for part of the ordinary and necessary costs of starting a SEP, SIMPLE, or certain other types of

plans (more on these later). The credit equals 50 percent of the cost to set up and administer the plan, up to a maximum of $500 per year for each of the first 3 years of the plan; and
- Tax credit for certain low- and moderate-income individuals (including self-employed) who make contributions to their plans ("Saver's tax credit"). The amount of the credit is based on the contributions participants make and their credit rate. The maximum contribution eligible for the credit is $2,000. The credit rate can be as low as 10 percent or as high as 50 percent, depending on the participant's adjusted gross income.

## A Few Retirement Plan Facts

Most private-sector retirement vehicles are either Individual Retirement Arrangements (IRAs), defined contribution (DC) plans, or defined benefit (DB) plans.

An IRA is the most basic sort of retirement arrangement. People tend to think of an IRA as something that individuals establish on their own, **but** an employer can help its employees set up and fund their IRAs. With an IRA, the amount that an individual receives at retirement depends on the funding of the IRA and the earnings (or income) on those funds.

Defined contribution plans are employer-established plans that do not promise a specific amount of benefit at retirement. Instead, employees or their employer (or both) contribute to employees' individual accounts under the plan, sometimes at a set rate (such as 5 percent of salary annually). At retirement, an employee receives the accumulated contributions plus earnings (or minus losses) on such invested contributions.

Defined benefit plans, on the other hand, promise a specified benefit at retirement – for example, $1,000 a month at retirement. The amount of the benefit is often based on a set percentage of pay multiplied by the number of years the employee worked for the employer offering the plan. Employer contributions must be sufficient to fund promised benefits.

Small businesses may choose to offer IRAs, DC plans or DB plans. Many financial institutions and pension practitioners make available one or more prototype retirement plans that have been pre-approved by the IRS.

*On the following two pages you will find a chart outlining the advantages of each of the most popular types of IRA-based and defined contribution plans and an overview of a defined benefit plan.*

191

| | Payroll Deduction IRA | SEP | SIMPLE IRA Plan |
|---|---|---|---|
| **Key Advantage** | Easy to set up and maintain. | Easy to set up and maintain. | Salary reduction plan with little administrative paperwork. |
| **Employer Eligibility** | Any employer with one or more employees. | Any employer with one or more employees. | Any employer with 100 or fewer employees that does not currently maintain another retirement plan. |
| **Employer's Role** | Arrange for employees to make payroll deduction contributions. Transmit contributions for employees to IRA. No annual filing requirement for employer. | Set up plan by completing IRS Form 5305-SEP. No annual filing requirement for employer. | Set up plan by completing IRS Form 5304-SIMPLE or IRS Form 5305-SIMPLE. No annual filing requirement for employer. Bank or financial institution processes most of the paperwork. |
| **Contributors To The Plan** | Employee contributions remitted through payroll deduction. | Employer contributions only. | Employee salary reduction contributions and employer contributions. |
| **Maximum Annual Contribution (Per participant)** | $3,000 for 2002 – 2004; $4,000 for 2005 – 2007; $5,000 for 2008. Additional contributions can be made by participants age 50 or over. | Up to 25% of compensation [1] or a maximum of $40,000. | Employee: Up to $7,000 (for 2002) with $1,000 annual incremental increases until the limit reaches $10,000 in 2005. Additional contributions can be made by participants age 50 or over. Employer: Either match employee contributions 100% of first 3% of compensation (can be reduced to as low as 1% in any 2 out of 5 yrs.); or contribute 2% of each eligible employee's compensation [2]. _up to 3 or 2 flat_ |
| **Contributor's Options** | Employee can decide how much to contribute at any time. | Employer can decide whether to make contributions year-to-year. | Employee can decide how much to contribute. Employer must make matching contributions or contribute 2% of each employee's compensation. [2] |
| **Minimum Employee Coverage Requirements** | Should be made available to all employees. | Must be offered to all employees who are at least 21 years of age, employed by the employer for 3 of the last 5 years and had earned income of $450 (for 2002). | Must be offered to all employees who have earned income of at least $5,000 in any prior 2 years, and are reasonably expected to earn at least $5,000 in the current year. |
| **Withdrawals, Loans and Payments** | Withdrawals permitted anytime subject to Federal income taxes; early withdrawals subject to tax penalty. | Withdrawals permitted anytime subject to Federal income taxes; early withdrawals subject to tax penalty. | Withdrawals permitted anytime subject to Federal income taxes; early withdrawals subject to tax penalty. |
| **Vesting** | Contributions are immediately 100% vested. | Contributions are immediately 100% vested. | Employer and employee contributions are immediately vested 100%. |

[1] Maximum compensation on which 2002 contribution can be based is $200,000.

**All forms noted on charts can be downloaded from the IRS Web Site at: www.irs.gov or ordered over the phone at 1-800-TAX-FORM (1-800-829-3676).**

_will do safe harbor anyways – than not immed. vested_

192

| Defined Contribution Plans | | | Defined Benefit |
|---|---|---|---|
| **401(k)** | **Profit-Sharing** | **Money Purchase** | **Defined Benefit** |
| Permits higher level of salary deferrals by employees than other retirement vehicles. | Permits employer to make large contributions for employees. | Permits employer to make large contributions for employees. | Provides a fixed, pre-established benefit for employees. |
| Any employer with one or more employees. | Any employer with one or more employees. | Any employer with one or more employees. | Any employer with one or more employees. |
| No model form to establish this plan. Advice from a financial institution or employee benefit advisor may be necessary. Annual filing of Form 5500 is required. Also may require annual non-discrimination testing to ensure plan does not discriminate in favor of highly compensated employees. | No model form to establish this plan. Advice from a financial institution or employee benefit advisor may be necessary. Annual filing of Form 5500 is required. | No model form to establish this plan. Advice from a financial institution or employee benefit advisor may be necessary. Annual filing of Form 5500 is required. | No model form to establish this plan. Advice from a financial institution or employee benefit advisor would be necessary. Annual filing of Form 5500 is required. An actuary **must** determine annual contributions. |
| Employee salary reduction contributions and/or employer contributions. | Annual employer contribution is discretionary. | Employer contributions are fixed. | Primarily funded by employer. |
| Employee: $11,000 in 2002 with $1,000 annual incremental increases until the limit reaches $15,000 in 2006. Additional contributions can be made by participants age 50 or over. Employer/Employee Combined: Contributions per participant up to the lesser of 100% of compensation[1] or $40,000. Employer can deduct amounts that do not exceed 25% of aggregate compensation for all participants. | Contributions per participant up to the lesser of 100% of compensation[1] or $40,000. Employer can deduct amounts that do not exceed 25% of aggregate compensation for all participants. | Contributions per participant up to the lesser of 100% of compensation[1] or $40,000. Employer can deduct amounts that do not exceed 25% of aggregate compensation for all participants. | Actuarially determined contribution. |
| Employee can elect how much to contribute pursuant to a salary reduction agreement. The employer can make additional contributions, including possible matching contributions, as set by plan terms. | Employer makes contribution as set by plan terms. Employee contributions, if allowed, as set by plan terms. | Employer makes contribution as set by plan terms. Employee contributions, if allowed, as set by plan terms. | Employer generally required to make contribution as set by plan terms. |
| Generally, must be offered to all employees at least 21 years of age who worked at least 1,000 hours in a previous year. | Generally, must be offered to all employees at least 21 years of age who worked at least 1,000 hours in a previous year. | Generally, must be offered to all employees at least 21 years of age who worked at least 1,000 hours in a previous year. | Generally, must be offered to all employees at least 21 years of age who worked at least 1,000 hours in a previous year. |
| Withdrawals permitted after a specified event occurs (e.g., retirement, plan termination, etc.). Plan may permit loans and hardship withdrawals; early withdrawals subject to tax penalty. | Withdrawals permitted after a specified event occurs (e.g., retirement, plan termination, etc.). Plan may permit loans; early withdrawals subject to tax penalty. | Payment of benefits after a specified event occurs (e.g., retirement, plan termination, etc.). Plan may permit loans; early withdrawals subject to tax penalty. | Payment of benefits after a specified event occurs (e.g., retirement, plan termination, etc.). Plan may permit loans; early withdrawals subject to tax penalty. |
| Employee salary deferrals are immediately 100% vested. Employer contributions may vest over time according to plan terms. | Employer contributions may vest over time according to plan terms. Employee contributions, if any, are immediately 100% vested. | Employer contributions may vest over time according to plan terms. Employee contributions, if any, are immediately 100% vested. | Right to benefits may vest over time according to plan terms. |

[2] Maximum compensation on which 2002 employer 2% non-elective contributions can be based is $200,000.

193

## Payroll-Deduction IRAs

Even if an employer does not want to adopt a retirement plan, it can allow its employees to contribute to an IRA through payroll deductions, providing a simple and direct way for eligible employees to save. The decision about whether to contribute, and when and how much to contribute to the IRA (up to $3,000 per year for 2002 through 2004, increasing thereafter) is always made by the employee in this type of arrangement.

Many individuals eligible to contribute to an IRA do not. One reason is that some individuals wait until the end of the year to set aside the money and then find that they do not have sufficient funds to do so. Payroll deductions allow individuals to plan ahead and save smaller amounts each pay period. Payroll deduction contributions are tax-deductible by an individual, to the same extent as other IRA contributions.

## Simplified Employee Pensions (SEPs)

A SEP allows employers to set up a type of IRA for themselves and each of their employees. Employers must contribute a uniform percentage of pay for each employee, although they do not have to make contributions every year. For the year 2002, employer contributions are limited to the lesser of 25 percent of pay or $40,000. (Note: the dollar amount is indexed for inflation and will increase.) Most employers, including those who are self-employed, can establish a SEP.

SEPs have low start-up and operating costs and can be established using a two-page form. And you can decide how much to put into a SEP each year – offering you some flexibility when business conditions vary.

## SIMPLE IRA Plans

This savings option is for employers with 100 or fewer employees and involves a type of IRA.

A SIMPLE IRA plan allows employees to contribute a percentage of their salary each paycheck and requires employer contributions. Under SIMPLE IRA plans, employees can set aside up to $7,000 in 2002 (increasing by $1,000 increments each year thereafter until the limit reaches $10,000 in 2005) by payroll deduction. Employers must either match employee contributions dollar for dollar – up to 3 percent of an employee's compensation – or make a fixed contribution of 2 percent of compensation for all eligible employees.

SIMPLE IRA plans are easy to set up. You fill out a short form to establish a plan and ensure that SIMPLE IRAs (to hold contributions made under the SIMPLE IRA plan) are set up for each employee. A financial institution can do much of the paperwork. Additionally, administrative costs are low.

Employers may either have employees set up their own SIMPLE IRAs at a financial institution of their choice or have all SIMPLE IRAs maintained at one financial institution chosen by the employer.

Employees can decide how and where the money will be invested, and keep their SIMPLE IRAs even when they change jobs.

## 401(k) Plans

401(k) plans have become a widely accepted retirement savings vehicle for small businesses. Today, an estimated 42 million American workers are enrolled in 401(k) plans that have total assets of about $2 trillion.

With a 401(k) plan, employees can choose to defer a portion of their salary. So instead of receiving that amount in their paycheck today, the employee can contribute such amount into a 401(k) plan sponsored by their employer. These deferrals go into a separate account for each employee. Generally, the deferrals (plus earnings) are not taxed by the Federal government or by most state and local governments until distributed.

401(k) plans can vary significantly in their complexity. However, many financial institutions and other organizations offer prototype 401(k) plans, which can greatly lessen the administrative burden on individual employers of establishing and maintaining such plans.

## Profit-Sharing Plans

Employer contributions to a profit-sharing plan are discretionary. Depending on the plan terms, there is often no set amount that an employer needs to contribute each year.

If you do make contributions, you will need to have a set formula for determining how the contributions are allocated among plan participants. The funds go into a separate account for each employee.

As with 401(k) plans, profit-sharing plans can vary greatly in their complexity. Similarly, many financial institutions offer prototype profit-sharing plans that can reduce the administrative burden on individual employers.

## Money Purchase Plans

Money purchase plans are defined contribution plans that require fixed employer contributions (contributions are not discretionary). With a money purchase plan, the plan document specifies the employer contribution that is required each year. For example, let's say that your money purchase plan requires a contribution of 5 percent of each eligible employee's pay. The employer needs to make a contribution of 5 percent of each eligible employee's pay to a separate account within the plan for each employee each year.

Many financial institutions offer prototype money purchase plans that can lessen the administrative burden on individual employers.

## Defined Benefit Plans

Defined benefit plans provide a fixed, pre-established benefit for employees.

Some employers find that defined benefit plans offer business advantages. For instance, employees often value the fixed benefit provided by this type of plan. In addition, employees in DB plans can often receive a greater benefit at retirement than under any other type of retirement plan. On the employer side, businesses can generally contribute (and therefore deduct) more each year than in defined contribution plans. However, defined benefit plans are often more complex and, thus, more costly to establish and maintain than other types of plans.

## To Find Out More...

The following pamphlets and other retirement-related information are available for small businesses:

**From the U.S. Department of Labor:**
- *Simplified Employee Pensions (SEPs) – What Small Businesses Need to Know*
- *Savings Incentive Match Plan for Employee of Small Employers (SIMPLE) – A Small Business Retirement Savings Advantage*

**From the Internal Revenue Service**
- Publication 560, *Retirement Plans for Small Business (SEP, SIMPLE, and Qualified Plans)*
- Publication 590, *Individual Retirement Arrangements*

**U.S. Chamber of Commerce**
Business Information and Development
(202) 463-5381
**www.uschamber.com**

**DOL/U.S.Chamber/SBA Web site**
**www.selectaretirementplan.org**

**U.S. Department of Labor
Pension and Welfare Benefits Administration**
**www.dol.gov/pwba**

**PWBA publication request line:**
1-866-275-7922

**DOL Small Business Advisor**
**www.dol.gov/elaws**

**Internal Revenue Service**
Tax Exempt/Government Entities
(877) 829-5500
**www.irs.gov/ep**

You can order IRS forms and publications 24 hours a day, 7 days a week, by calling:
1-800-TAX-FORM (1-800-829-3676)

**Small Business Administration**
Answer Desk
(800) 827-5722
**www.sba.gov**

Department
of the
Treasury

**Internal
Revenue
Service**

**Publication 560**
Cat. No. 46574N

# Retirement Plans for Small Business

## (SEP, SIMPLE, and Qualified Plans)

For use in preparing

## 2002 Returns

**Get forms and other information
faster and easier by:**

**Computer** • www.irs.gov or **FTP** • ftp.irs.gov

**FAX** • 703-368-9694 (from your FAX machine)

# Contents

# Important Changes for 2002

**Plan amendments to conform to the Economic Growth and Tax Relief Reconciliation Act of 2001 (EGTRRA).** Generally, master and prototype plans are amended by sponsoring organizations. However, you may need to request a determination letter regarding a master or prototype plan you maintain that is a nonstandardized plan if you make changes to adopt some provisions of EGTRRA. Your request should be made on the appropriate form (generally Form 5300 or Form 5307). The request should be filed with Form 8717, *User Fee for Employee Plan Determination Letter Request,* and the applicable user fee. See *User fee,* later.

**Earned income of members of recognized religious sects.** For years beginning after 2001, earned income for retirement plans includes amounts received for services by

196

self-employed members of recognized religious sects opposed to social security benefits who are exempt from self-employment tax.

**Credit for startup costs.** For costs paid or incurred in tax years beginning after December 31, 2001, for retirement plans that first become effective after that date, you may be able to claim a tax credit for part of the ordinary and necessary costs of starting a SEP, SIMPLE, or qualified plan. The credit equals 50% of the cost to set up and administer the plan and educate employees about the plan, up to a maximum of $500 per year for each of the first 3 years of the plan. For plans that become effective after 2002, you can choose to start claiming the credit in the tax year before the tax year in which the plan becomes effective.

You must have had 100 or fewer employees who received at least $5,000 in compensation from you for the preceding year. At least one participant must be a non-highly compensated employee. The employees generally cannot be substantially the same employees for whom contributions were made or benefits accrued under a plan of any of the following employers in the 3-tax-year period immediately before the first year to which the credit applies.

1) You.

2) A member of a controlled group that includes you.

3) A predecessor of (1) or (2).

The credit is part of the general business credit, which can be carried back or forward to other tax years if it cannot be used in the current year. However, the part of the general business credit attributable to the small employer pension plan startup cost credit cannot be carried back to a tax year beginning before January 1, 2002. You cannot deduct the part of the startup costs equal to the credit claimed for a tax year, but you can choose not to claim the allowable credit for a tax year.

To take the credit, get Form 8881, *Credit for Small Employer Pension Plan Startup Costs,* and the instructions.

**Compensation limit.** For years beginning after 2001, the maximum compensation used for figuring contributions and benefits increases to $200,000. This amount is subject to cost-of-living increases after 2002.

**Deduction limits.** After 2001, certain deduction limits change as explained next.

*Elective deferrals.* For years beginning after 2001, elective deferrals are not subject to the deduction limit that applies to SARSEPs and profit-sharing plans (discussed next). Also, elective deferrals are not taken into account when figuring the amount you can deduct for employer contributions that are not elective deferrals.

*SEP and profit-sharing plans.* For years beginning after 2001, your maximum deduction for contributions to a SEP or a profit-sharing plan increases to 25% of the compensation paid or accrued during the year to your eligible employees participating in the plan. Compensation for figuring the deduction for contributions includes elective deferrals.

However, a lower limit may apply to SARSEPs. For more information, see *Limit on Elective Deferrals* in chapter 2.

**Defined benefit plans.** For plan years beginning after 2001, your deduction for contributions to a defined benefit plan can be as much as the plan's unfunded current liability.

**Elective deferrals.** The limit on elective deferrals increases to $11,000 for tax years beginning in 2002 and then increases $1,000 each tax year thereafter until it reaches $15,000 in 2006. These new limits will apply for participants in SARSEPs, 401(k) plans (excluding SIMPLE plans), and deferred compensation plans of state or local governments and tax-exempt organizations. The $15,000 figure is subject to cost-of-living increases after 2006.

*Catch-up contributions.* For tax years beginning after 2001, a plan can permit participants who are age 50 or over at the end of the calendar year to also make catch-up contributions. The catch-up contribution limit for 2002 is $1,000. This limit increases by $1,000 each year thereafter until it reaches $5,000 in 2006. The limit is subject to cost-of-living increases after 2006. The catch-up contribution a participant can make for a year cannot exceed the lesser of the following amounts.

- The catch-up contribution limit.

- The excess of the participant's compensation over the elective deferrals that are not catch-up contributions.

**SIMPLE plan salary reduction contributions.** The limit on salary reduction contributions to a SIMPLE plan increases to $7,000 beginning in 2002 and then increases $1,000 each tax year thereafter until it reaches $10,000 in 2005. The $10,000 figure is subject to adjustment after 2005 for cost-of-living increases.

*Catch-up contributions.* For tax years beginning after 2001, a SIMPLE plan can permit participants who are age 50 or over at the end of the calendar year to make catch-up contributions. The catch-up contribution limit for 2002 is $500. This limit increases by $500 each year thereafter until it reaches $2,500 in 2006. The limit is subject to cost-of-living increases after 2006. The catch-up contributions a participant can make for a year cannot exceed the lesser of the following amounts.

- The catch-up contribution limit.

- The excess of the participant's compensation over the salary reduction contributions that are not catch-up contributions.

**User fee.** The user fee for requesting a determination letter does not apply to certain requests made after 2001, by employers who have 100 or fewer employees, at least one of whom is a non-highly compensated employee participating in the plan. See *User fee* under *Setting Up a Qualified Plan* in chapter 4.

**Limits on contributions and benefits.** For years ending after 2001, the maximum annual benefit for a participant under a defined benefit plan increases to the lesser of the following amounts.

- 100% of the participant's average compensation for his or her highest 3 consecutive calendar years.

- $160,000 (subject to cost-of-living increases after 2002).

For years beginning after 2001, a defined contribution plan's maximum annual contributions and other additions (excluding earnings) to the account of a participant increases to the lesser of the following amounts.

- 100% of the participant's compensation.

- $40,000 (subject to cost-of-living increases after 2002).

For years beginning after 2001, the annual limit on the amount of employer contributions to a SEP increases to the lesser of the following amounts.

- 25% of an eligible employee's compensation.

- $40,000 (subject to cost-of-living adjustments after 2002).

**Excise tax for nondeductible (excess) contributions.** For years beginning after 2001, you can choose to exclude certain nondeductible (excess) contributions when figuring the 10% excise tax. For more information, see *Defined benefit plan exception* under *Excise Tax for Nondeductible (Excess) Contributions* in chapter 4.

**Rollover distributions.** A hardship distribution made after 2001 will not qualify as an eligible rollover distribution.

**Involuntary payment of benefits.** If a participant's employment is terminated, a plan may provide for immediate distribution of the participant's benefit under the plan if the present value of the benefit is not greater than $5,000. For distributions after 2001, benefits attributable to rollover contributions and earnings on the contributions can be ignored in determining the value of these benefits.

For distributions made after the Department of Labor adopts final regulations implementing rules on fiduciary responsibilities relating to this provision, a plan must provide for the automatic rollover of any distribution of more than $1,000 to an IRA under this provision, unless the participant chooses otherwise. The plan administrator must notify the participant in writing that the distribution can be transferred to another IRA.

**Retirement savings contributions credit.** Beginning in 2002, retirement pla (including self-employed individuals) who make contributions to their plan may qualify for the retirement savings contributions credit. The amount of the credit is based on the contributions participants make and their credit rate. The maximum contribution eligible for the credit is $2,000. The credit rate can be as low as 10% or as high as 50%, depending on the participant's adjusted gross income. The credit also depends on the participant's filing status. Form 8880, *Credit for Qualified Retirement Savings Contributions,* and the instructions explain how to claim the credit.

# Important Change for 2003

**Deemed IRA under a qualified plan.** For plan years beginning after 2002, a qualified plan (discussed in chapter 4) can maintain a separate account or annuity under the plan to receive voluntary employee contributions. If the separate account or annuity otherwise meets the requirements of a traditional IRA or Roth IRA, it is deemed a traditional IRA or Roth IRA. A deemed IRA is subject to IRA rules and not to qualified plan rules. Also, the deemed IRA and contributions to it are not taken into account in applying qualified plan rules to any other contributions under the plan. Voluntary employee contributions must be designated as such by employees covered under the plan. They are includible in income.

If you want to provide for a deemed IRA, you will have to amend your plan. For information on amending the plan, see Revenue Procedure 2003–13 in Internal Revenue Bulletin 2003–4.

# Important Reminders

**Plan amendments required by changes in the law.** If you must revise your qualified plan to conform to recent legislation, you may choose to get a determination letter from the IRS approving the revision. Generally, master and prototype plans are amended by sponsoring organizations. However, there are instances when you may need to request a determination letter regarding a master or prototype plan that is a nonstandardized plan you maintain. Your request should be made on the appropriate form (generally Form 5300 or Form 5307). The request should be filed with Form 8717 and the appropriate user fee.

You may have to amend your plan to comply with tax law changes made by the following laws.

- Uniformed Services Employment and Reemployment Rights Act of 1994, Public Law 103–353.
- Uruguay Round Agreements Act, Public Law 103–465.
- Small Business Job Protection Act of 1996, Public Law 104–188.
- Taxpayer Relief Act of 1997, Public Law 105–34.
- Internal Revenue Service Restructuring and Reform Act of 1998, Public Law 105–206.

- Community Renewal Tax Relief Act of 2000, Public Law 106–554.

You generally were required to make these amendments by February 28, 2002. Plans directly affected by the September 11, 2001, terrorist attacks on the United States had until June 30, 2002, to make these amendments. In cases of substantial hardship resulting from the terrorist attacks, the IRS could have granted additional extensions of time up to December 31, 2002, to make the amendments.

For more information about these extensions, see Revenue Procedure 2001–55 in Internal Revenue Bulletin 2001–49.

The time for amending a pre-approved plan (master or prototype or volume submitter plan) is extended to the later of September 30, 2003, or the end of the 12th month beginning after the date on which the IRS issues a GUST opinion or advisory letter for the pre-approved plan. For more information, see Revenue Procedure 2002–73 in Internal Revenue Bulletin 2002–49.

**Photographs of missing children.** The Internal Revenue Service is a proud partner with the National Center for Missing and Exploited Children. Photographs of missing children selected by the Center may appear in this publication on pages that would otherwise be blank. You can help bring these children home by looking at the photographs and calling **1–800–THE–LOST** (1–800–843–5678) if you recognize a child.

# Introduction

This publication discusses retirement plans you can set up and maintain for yourself and your employees. In this publication, "you" refers to the employer. See chapter 1 for the definition of the term employer and the definitions of other terms used in this publication. This publication covers the following types of retirement plans.

- SEP (simplified employee pension) plans.
- SIMPLE (savings incentive match plan for employees) plans.
- Qualified plans (also called H.R. 10 plans or Keogh plans when covering self-employed individuals).

SEP, SIMPLE, and qualified plans offer you and your employees a tax-favored way to save for retirement. You can deduct contributions you make to the plan for your employees. If you are a sole proprietor, you can deduct contributions you make to the plan for yourself. You can also deduct trustees' fees if contributions to the plan

do not cover them. Earnings on the contributions are generally tax free until you or your employees receive distributions from the plan.

Under certain plans, employees can have you contribute limited amounts of their before-tax pay to a plan. These amounts (and earnings on them) are generally tax free until your employees receive distributions from the plan.

**What this publication covers.** This publication contains the information you need to understand the following topics.

- What type of plan to set up.
- How to set up a plan.
- How much you can contribute to a plan.
- How much of your contribution is deductible.
- How to treat certain distributions.
- How to report information about the plan to the IRS and your employees.

**Basic features of retirement plans.** Basic features of SEP, SIMPLE, and qualified plans are discussed below. The key rules for SEP, SIMPLE, and qualified plans are outlined in *Table 1*.

*SEP plans.* SEPs provide a simplified method for you to make contributions to a retirement plan for your employees. Instead of setting up a profit-sharing or money purchase plan with a trust, you can adopt a SEP agreement and make contributions directly to a traditional individual retirement account or a traditional individual retirement annuity (SEP-IRA) set up for each eligible employee.

*SIMPLE plans.* A SIMPLE plan can be set up by an employer who had 100 or fewer employees who received at least $5,000 in compensation from the employer for the preceding calendar year and who meets certain other requirements. Under a SIMPLE plan, employees can choose to make salary reduction contributions rather than receiving these amounts as part of their regular pay. In addition, you will contribute matching or nonelective contributions. The two types of SIMPLE plans are the SIMPLE IRA plan and the SIMPLE 401(k) plan.

*Qualified plans.* The qualified plan rules are more complex than the SEP plan and SIMPLE plan rules. However, there are advantages to qualified plans, such as increased flexibility in designing plans and increased contribution and deduction limits in some cases.

## Table 1. Key Retirement Plan Rules for 2002

| Type of Plan | Last Date for Contribution | Maximum Contribution | Maximum Deduction | When to Set Up Plan |
|---|---|---|---|---|
| SEP | Due date of employer's return (including extensions). | Smaller of $40,000 or 25%[1] of participant's compensation.[2] | 25%[1] of all participants' compensation.[2] | Any time up to due date of employer's return (including extensions). |
| SIMPLE IRA and SIMPLE 401(k) | **Salary reduction contributions:** 30 days after the end of the month for which the contributions are to be made.[3] | **Employee:** Salary reduction contribution, up to $7,000. | Same as maximum contribution. | Any time between 1/1 and 10/1 of the calendar year.<br><br>For a new employer coming into existence after 10/1, as soon as administratively feasible. |
| | **Matching contributions or nonelective contributions:** Due date of employer's return (including extensions). | **Employer contribution:** *Either* dollar-for-dollar matching contributions, up to 3% of employee's compensation,[4] *or* fixed nonelective contributions of 2% of compensation.[2] | Same as maximum contribution. | |
| Qualified | Due date of employer's return (including extensions).<br><br>**Note:** For a defined benefit plan subject to minimum funding requirements, contributions are due in quarterly installments. See *Minimum Funding Requirements* in chapter 4. | Defined Contribution Plans<br><br>**Money Purchase:** Smaller of $40,000 or 100%[1] of participant's compensation.[2]<br><br>**Profit-Sharing:** Smaller of $40,000 or 100%[1] of participant's compensation.[2]<br><br>Defined Benefit Plans<br>Amount needed to provide an annual benefit no larger than the smaller of $160,000 or 100% of the participant's average compensation for his or her highest 3 consecutive calendar years. | Defined Contribution Plans<br><br>**Money Purchase:** 25%[1] of all participants' compensation.[2]<br><br>**Profit-Sharing:** 25%[1] of all participants' compensation.[2]<br><br>Defined Benefit Plans<br>Based on actuarial assumptions and computations. | By the end of the tax year. |

[1]Net earnings from self-employment must take the contribution into account.
[2]Compensation is generally limited to $200,000.
[3]Does not apply to SIMPLE 401(k) plans. The deadline for qualified plans applies instead.
[4]Under a SIMPLE 401(k) plan, compensation is generally limited to $200,000.

**What this publication does not cover.** Although the purpose of this publication is to provide general information about retirement plans you can set up for your employees, it does not contain all the rules and exceptions that apply to these plans. You may also need professional help and guidance.

Also, this publication does not cover all the rules that may be of interest to employees. For example, it does not cover the following topics.

- The comprehensive IRA rules an employee needs to know. These rules are covered in Publication 590, *Individual Retirement Arrangements (IRAs)*.

- The comprehensive rules that apply to distributions from retirement plans. These rules are covered in Publication 575, *Pension and Annuity Income.*

**Comments and suggestions.** We welcome your comments about this publication and your suggestions for future editions.

You can e-mail us while visiting our web site at www.irs.gov.

You can write to us at the following address:

Internal Revenue Service
Tax Forms and Publications
W:CAR:MP:FP
1111 Constitution Ave. NW
Washington, DC 20224

We respond to many letters by telephone. Therefore, it would be helpful if you would include your daytime phone number, including the area code, in your correspondence.

**Help from the Internal Revenue Service (IRS).** See chapter 6 for information about getting publications and forms.

If you own a business and have questions about starting a pension plan, an existing plan, or filing **Form 5500**, call our **Tax Exempt/Government Entities Customer Account Services** at **1–877–829–5500**. Assistance is available Monday through Friday from 8:00 a.m. to 6:30 p.m. EST. **If you have questions about a traditional or Roth IRA or any individual income tax issues, you should call** 1–800–829–1040.

**Note:** All references to "section" in the following discussions are to sections of the Internal Revenue Code (which can be found at most libraries) unless otherwise indicated.

# 1.

# Definitions You Need To Know

Certain terms used in this publication are defined below. The same term used in another publication may have a slightly different meaning.

**Annual additions.** Annual additions are the total of all your contributions in a year, employee contributions (not including rollovers), and forfeitures allocated to a participant's account.

**Annual benefits.** Annual benefits are the benefits to be paid yearly in the form of a straight life annuity (with no extra benefits) under a plan to which employees do not contribute and under which no rollover contributions are made.

**Business.** A business is an activity in which a profit motive is present and economic activity is involved. Service as a newspaper carrier under age 18 is not a business, but service as a newspaper dealer is. Service as a sharecropper under an owner-tenant arrangement is a business. Service as a public official is not.

**Common-law employee.** A common-law employee is any individual who, under common law, would have the status of an employee. A leased employee can also be a common-law employee.

A common-law employee is a person who performs services for an employer who has the right to control and direct the results of the work and the way in which it is done. For example, the employer:

- Provides the employee's tools, materials, and workplace, and
- Can fire the employee.

Common-law employees are not self-employed and cannot set up retirement plans for income from their work, even if that income is self-employment income for social security tax purposes. For example, common-law employees who are ministers, members of religious orders, full-time insurance salespeople, and U.S. citizens employed in the United States by foreign governments cannot set up retirement plans for their earnings from those employments, even though their earnings are treated as self-employment income.

However, an individual may be a common-law employee and a self-employed person as well. For example, an attorney can be a corporate common-law employee during regular working hours and also practice law in the evening as a self-employed person. In another example, a minister employed by a congregation for a salary is a common-law employee even though the salary is treated as self-employment income for social security tax purposes. However, fees reported on Schedule C (Form 1040), *Profit or Loss From Business*, for performing marriages, baptisms, and other personal services are self-employment earnings for qualified plan purposes.

**Compensation.** Compensation for plan allocations is the pay a participant received from you for personal services for a year. You can generally define compensation as including all the following payments.

1) Wages and salaries.

2) Fees for professional services.

3) Other amounts received (cash or noncash) for personal services actually rendered by an employee, including, but not limited to, the following items.

   a) Commissions and tips.

   b) Fringe benefits.

   c) Bonuses.

For a self-employed individual, compensation means the earned income, discussed later, of that individual.

Compensation generally includes amounts deferred in the following employee benefit plans. These amounts are elective deferrals.

- Qualified cash or deferred arrangement (section 401(k) plan).

- Salary reduction agreement to contribute to a tax-sheltered annuity (section 403(b) plan), a SIMPLE IRA plan, or a SARSEP.

- Section 457 nonqualified deferred compensation plan.

- Section 125 cafeteria plan.

However, an employer can choose to exclude elective deferrals under the above plans from the definition of compensation. The limit on elective deferrals is discussed in chapter 2 under *Salary Reduction Simplified Employee Pension (SARSEP)* and in chapter 4.

**Other options.** In figuring the compensation of a participant, you can treat any of the following amounts as the employee's compensation.

- The employee's wages as defined for income tax withholding purposes.

- The employee's wages you report in box 1 of Form W–2, *Wage and Tax Statement*.

- The employee's social security wages (including elective deferrals).

Compensation generally cannot include either of the following items.

- Reimbursements or other expense allowances (unless paid under a nonaccountable plan).

- Deferred compensation (either amounts going in or amounts coming out) other than certain elective deferrals unless you choose not to include those elective deferrals in compensation.

**Contribution.** A contribution is an amount you pay into a plan for all those participating in the plan, including self-employed individuals. Limits apply to how much, under the contribution formula of the plan, can be contributed each year for a participant.

**Deduction.** A deduction is the plan contributions you can subtract from gross income on your federal income tax return. Limits apply to the amount deductible.

**Earned income.** Earned income is net earnings from self-employment, discussed later, from a business in which your services materially helped to produce the income.

You can also have earned income from property your personal efforts helped create, such as royalties from your books or inventions. Earned income includes net earnings from selling or otherwise disposing of the property, but it does not include capital gains. It includes income from licensing the use of property other than goodwill.

Earned income includes amounts received for services by self-employed members of recognized religious sects opposed to social security benefits who are exempt from self-employment tax.

If you have more than one business, but only one has a retirement plan, only the earned income from that business is considered for that plan.

**Employer.** An employer is generally any person for whom an individual performs or did perform any service, of whatever nature, as an employee. A sole proprietor is treated as his or her own employer for retirement plan purposes. However, a partner is not an employer for retirement plan purposes. The partnership is treated as the employer of each partner.

**Highly compensated employee.** A highly compensated employee is an individual who:

- Owned more than 5% of the capital or profits in your business at any time during the year or the preceding year, or

- For the preceding year, received compensation from you of more than $90,000 and, if you so choose, was in the top 20% of employees when ranked by compensation.

**Leased employee.** A leased employee who is not your common-law employee must generally be treated as your employee for retirement plan purposes if he or she does all the following.

- Provides services to you under an agreement between you and a leasing organization.

- Has performed services for you (or for you and related persons) substantially full time for at least 1 year.

- Performs services under your primary direction or control.

**Exception.** A leased employee is not treated as your employee if all the following conditions are met.

1) Leased employees are not more than 20% of your non-highly compensated work force.

2) The employee is covered und
ing organization's qualified pension plan.

3) The leasing organization's plan is a money purchase pension plan that has all the following provisions.

   a) Immediate participation. (This requirement does not apply to any individual whose compensation from the leasing organization in each plan year during the 4-year period ending with the plan year is less than $1,000.)

   b) Full and immediate vesting.

   c) A nonintegrated employer contribution rate of at least 10% of compensation for each participant.

However, if the leased employee is your common-law employee, that employee will be your employee for all purposes, regardless of any pension plan of the leasing organization.

**Net earnings from self-employment.** For SEP and qualified plans, net earnings from self-employment is your gross income from your trade or business (provided your personal services are a material income-producing factor) minus allowable business deductions. Allowable deductions include contributions to SEP and qualified plans for common-law employees and the deduction allowed for one-half of your self-employment tax.

Net earnings from self-employment do not include items excluded from gross income (or their related deductions) other than foreign earned income and foreign housing cost amounts.

For the deduction limits, earned income is net earnings for personal services actually rendered to the business. You take into account the income tax deduction for one-half of self-employment tax and the deduction for contributions to the plan made on your behalf when figuring net earnings.

Net earnings include a partner's distributive share of partnership income or loss (other than separately stated items, such as capital gains and losses). It does not include income passed through to shareholders of S corporations. Guaranteed payments to limited partners are net earnings from self-employment if they are paid for services to or for the partnership. Distributions of other income or loss to limited partners are not net earnings from self-employment.

For SIMPLE plans, net earnings from self-employment is the amount on line 4 of Short Schedule SE (Form 1040), *Self-Employment Tax*, before subtracting any contributions made to the SIMPLE plan for yourself.

**Participant.** A participant is an eligible employee who is covered by your retirement plan. See the discussions of the different types of plans for the definition of an employee eligible to participate in each type of plan.

**Partner.** A partner is an individual who shares ownership of an unincorporated trade or business with one or more persons. For retirement plans, a partner is treated as an employee of the partnership.

**Self-employed individual.** An individual in business for himself or herself is self-employed. Sole proprietors and partners are self-employed. Self-employment can include part-time work.

Not everyone who has net earnings from self-employment for social security tax purposes is self-employed for qualified plan purposes. See *Common-law employee,* earlier. Also see *Net earnings from self-employment.*

In addition, certain fishermen may be considered self-employed for setting up a qualified plan. See Publication 595, *Tax Highlights for Commercial Fishermen,* for the special rules used to determine whether fishermen are self-employed.

**Sole proprietor.** A sole proprietor is an individual who owns an unincorporated business by himself or herself. For retirement plans, a sole proprietor is treated as both an employer and an employee.

# 2.

# Simplified Employee Pension (SEP)

## Topics
This chapter discusses:

- Setting up a SEP
- How much to contribute
- Deducting contributions
- Salary reduction simplified employee pensions (SARSEPs)
- Distributions (withdrawals)
- Additional taxes
- Reporting and disclosure requirements

## Useful Items
You may want to see:

**Publication**

❑ **590** Individual Retirement Arrangements (IRAs)

**Forms (and Instructions)**

❑ **W–2** Wage and Tax Statement

❑ **1040** U.S. Individual Income Tax Return

❑ **5305–SEP** Simplified Employee Pension—Individual Retirement Accounts Contribution Agreement

❑ **5305A–SEP** Salary Reduction Simplified Employee Pension—Individual Retirement Accounts Contribution Agreement

A simplified employee pension (SEP) is a written plan that allows you to make contributions toward your own retirement (if you are self-em-

ployed) and your employees' retirement wi   t getting involved in a more complex qualified plan.

Under a SEP, you make the contributions to a traditional individual retirement arrangement (called a SEP-IRA) set up by or for each eligible employee. A SEP-IRA is owned and controlled by the employee, and you make contributions to the financial institution where the SEP-IRA is maintained.

SEP-IRAs are set up for, at a minimum, each eligible employee (defined later). A SEP-IRA may have to be set up for a leased employee (defined in chapter 1), but does not need to be set up for excludable employees (defined later).

**Eligible employee.** An eligible employee is an individual who meets all the following requirements.

- Has reached age 21.
- Has worked for you in at least 3 of the last 5 years.
- Has received at least $450 in compensation from you for 2002 (subject to cost-of-living adjustments for 2003 and later years).

 *You can use less restrictive participation requirements than those listed, but not more restrictive ones.*

**Excludable employees.** The following employees can be excluded from coverage under a SEP.

- Employees covered by a union agreement and whose retirement benefits were bargained for in good faith by the employees' union and you.
- Nonresident alien employees who have received no U.S. source wages, salaries, or other personal services compensation from you. For more information about nonresident aliens, see Publication 519, *U.S. Tax Guide for Aliens.*

## Setting Up a SEP

There are three basic steps in setting up a SEP.

1) You must execute a formal written agreement to provide benefits to all eligible employees.

2) You must give each eligible employee certain information about the SEP.

3) A SEP-IRA must be set up by or for each eligible employee.

 *Many financial institutions will help you set up a SEP.*

**Formal written agreement.** You must execute a formal written agreement to provide benefits to all eligible employees under a SEP. You can satisfy the written agreemen by adopting an IRS model SEP using *Form 5305–SEP.* However, see *When not to use Form 5305–SEP,* later.

If you adopt an IRS model SEP using Form 5305–SEP, no prior IRS approval or determination letter is required. Keep the original form. Do not file it with the IRS. Also, using Form 5305–SEP will usually relieve you from filing annual retirement plan information returns with the IRS and the Department of Labor. See the Form 5305–SEP instructions for details.

**When not to use Form 5305–SEP.** You cannot use Form 5305–SEP if any of the following apply.

1) You currently maintain any other qualified retirement plan. This does not prevent you from maintaining another SEP.

2) You have any eligible employees for whom IRAs have not been set up.

3) You use the services of leased employees (as described in chapter 1).

4) You are a member of any of the following unless all eligible employees of all the members of these groups, trades, or businesses participate under the SEP.

  a) An affiliated service group described in section 414(m).

  b) A controlled group of corporations described in section 414(b).

  c) Trades or businesses under common control described in section 414(c).

5) You do not pay the cost of the SEP contributions.

**Information you must give to employees.** You must give each eligible employee a copy of Form 5305–SEP, its instructions, and the other information listed in the Form 5305–SEP instructions. An IRS model SEP is not considered adopted until you give each employee this information.

**Setting up the employee's SEP-IRA.** A SEP-IRA must be set up by or for each eligible employee. SEP-IRAs can be set up with banks, insurance companies, or other qualified financial institutions. You send SEP contributions to the financial institution where the SEP-IRA is maintained.

**Deadline for setting up a SEP.** You can set up a SEP for a year as late as the due date (including extensions) of your income tax return for that year.

**Credit for startup costs.** You may be able to claim a tax credit for part of the ordinary and necessary costs of starting a SEP that first became effective in 2002. For more information, see *Credit for startup costs* under *Important Changes for 2002*, earlier.

# How Much Can I Contribute?

The SEP rules permit you to contribute a limited amount of money each year to each employee's SEP-IRA. If you are self-employed, you can contribute to your own SEP-IRA. Contributions must be in the form of money (cash, check, or money order). You cannot contribute property. However, participants may be able to transfer or roll over certain property from one retirement plan to another. See Publication 590 for more information about rollovers.

You do not have to make contributions every year. But if you make contributions, they must be based on a written allocation formula and must not discriminate in favor of highly compensated employees (defined in chapter 1). When you contribute, you must contribute to the SEP-IRAs of all participants who actually performed personal services during the year for which the contributions are made, even employees who die or terminate employment before the contributions are made.

The contributions you make under a SEP are treated as if made to a qualified pension, stock bonus, profit-sharing, or annuity plan. Consequently, contributions are deductible within limits, as discussed later, and generally are not taxable to the plan participants.

A SEP-IRA cannot be designated as a Roth IRA. Employer contributions to a SEP-IRA will not affect the amount an individual can contribute to a Roth IRA.

**Time limit for making contributions.** To deduct contributions for a year, you must make the contributions by the due date (including extensions) of your tax return for the year.

## Contribution Limits

Contributions you make for 2002 to a common-law employee's SEP-IRA cannot exceed the lesser of 25% of the employee's compensation or $40,000 (subject to cost-of-living adjustments for 2003 and later years). Compensation generally does not include your contributions to the SEP.

*Example.* Your employee, Mary Plant, earned $21,000 for 2002. The maximum contribution you can make to her SEP-IRA is $5,250 (25% x $21,000).

**Contributions for yourself.** The annual limits on your contributions to a common-law employee's SEP-IRA also apply to contributions you make to your own SEP-IRA. However, special rules apply when figuring your maximum deductible contribution. See *Deduction Limit for Self-Employed Individuals*, later.

**Annual compensation limit.** You cannot consider the part of an employee's compensation over $200,000 when figuring your contribution limit for that employee. However, $40,000 is the maximum contribution for an eligible employee. (The annual compensation limit of $200,000 is subject to cost-of-living adjustments for 2003 and later years.)

**More than one plan.** If you contribute to a defined contribution plan (defined in chapter 4), annual additions to an account are limited to the lesser of $40,000 or 100% of the participant's compensation. When you figure this limit, you must add your contributions to all defined contribution plans. Because a SEP is considered a defined contribution plan for this limit, your contributions to a SEP must be added to your contributions to other defined contribution plans.

**Tax treatment of excess contributions.** Excess contributions are your contributions to an employee's SEP-IRA (or to your own SEP-IRA) for 2002 that exceed the lesser of the following amounts.

• 25% of the employee's compensation (or, for you, 20% of your net earnings from self-employment).

• $40,000.

Excess contributions are included in the employee's income for the year and are treated as contributions by the employee to his or her SEP-IRA. For more information on employee tax treatment of excess contributions, see chapter 4 in Publication 590.

**Reporting on Form W–2.** Do not include SEP contributions on your employee's Form W–2 unless contributions were made under a salary reduction arrangement (discussed later).

# Deducting Contributions

Generally, you can deduct the contributions you make each year to each employee's SEP-IRA. If you are self-employed, you can deduct the contributions you make each year to your own SEP-IRA.

## Deduction Limit for Contributions for Participants

The most you can deduct for your contributions (other than elective deferrals) for participants is the lesser of the following amounts.

1) Your contributions (including any excess contributions carryover).

2) 25% of the compensation (limited to $200,000 per participant) paid to the participants during 2002 from the business that has the plan, not to exceed $40,000 per participant.

For 2003 and later years, the $200,000 and $40,000 amounts in (2) above are subject to cost-of-living increases.

⚠ CAUTION  *Compensation in (2) above includes elective deferrals (explained, later, under* Salary Reduction Simplified Employee Pension (SARSEP))*. Beginning in 2002, elective deferrals are no longer subject to this deduction limit. However, the combined deduction for a participant's elective deferrals and other SEP contributions cannot exceed $40,000.*

*Your SEP document may limit contributions to lower amounts because of elective deferrals.*

## Deduction Limit for Self-Employed Individuals

If you contribute to your own SEP-IRA, you must make a special computation to figure your maximum deduction for these contributions. When figuring the deduction for contributions made to your own SEP-IRA, compensation is your net earnings from self-employment (defined in chapter 1), which takes into account both the following deductions.

- The deduction for one-half of your self-employment tax.
- The deduction for contributions to your own SEP-IRA.

The deduction for contributions to your own SEP-IRA and your net earnings depend on each other. For this reason, you determine the deduction for contributions to your own SEP-IRA indirectly by reducing the contribution rate called for in your plan. To do this, use the *Rate Table for Self-Employed* or the *Rate Worksheet for Self-Employed,* whichever is appropriate for your plan's contribution rate, in chapter 5. Then figure your maximum deduction by using the *Deduction Worksheet for Self-Employed* in chapter 5.

## Deduction Limits for Multiple Plans

For the deduction limits, treat all your qualified defined contribution plans as a single plan and all your qualified defined benefit plans as a single plan. See *Kinds of Plans* in chapter 4 for the definitions of defined contribution plans and defined benefit plans. If you have both kinds of plans, a SEP is treated as a separate profit-sharing (defined contribution) plan. A qualified plan is a plan that meets the requirements discussed under *Qualification Rules* in chapter 4. For information about the special deduction limits, see *Deduction limit for multiple plans* under *Employer Deduction* in chapter 4.

**SEP and defined contribution plan.** If you also contribute to a qualified defined contribution plan, you must reduce the 25% deduction limit for that plan by the allowable deduction for contributions to the SEP-IRAs of those participating in both the SEP plan and the defined contribution plan.

## Carryover of Excess SEP Contributions

If you made SEP contributions that are more than the deduction limit (nondeductible contributions), you can carry over and deduct the difference in later years. However, the carryover, when combined with the contribution for the later year, is subject to the deduction limit for that year. If you also contributed to a defined benefit plan or defined contribution plan, see *Carryover of Excess Contributions* under *Employer Deduction* in chapter 4 for the carryover limit.

**Excise tax.** If you made nondeductible (excess) contributions to a SEP, you may be subject to a 10% excise tax. For information about the excise tax, see *Excise Tax for Nondeductible (Excess) Contributions* under *Employer Deduction* in chapter 4.

## When To Deduct Contributions

When you can deduct contributions made for a year depends on the tax year on which the SEP is maintained.

- If the SEP is maintained on a calendar year basis, you deduct contributions made for a year on your tax return for the year with or within which the calendar year ends.
- If you file your tax return and maintain the SEP using a fiscal year or short tax year, you deduct contributions made for a year on your tax return for that year.

**Example.** You are a fiscal year taxpayer whose tax year ends June 30. You maintain a SEP on a calendar year basis. You deduct SEP contributions made for calendar year 2002 on your tax return for your tax year ending June 30, 2003.

## Where To Deduct Contributions

Deduct the contributions you make for your common-law employees on your tax return. For example, sole proprietors deduct them on Schedule C (Form 1040), *Profit or Loss From Business,* or Schedule F (Form 1040), *Profit or Loss From Farming,* partnerships deduct them on Form 1065, *U.S. Return of Partnership Income,* and corporations deduct them on Form 1120, *U.S. Corporation Income Tax Return,* Form 1120–A, *U.S. Corporation Short-Form Income Tax Return,* or Form 1120S, *U.S. Income Tax Return for an S Corporation.*

Sole proprietors and partners deduct contributions for themselves on line 31 of Form 1040, *U.S. Individual Income Tax Return.* (If you are a partner, contributions for yourself are shown on the Schedule K-1 (Form 1065), *Partner's Share of Income, Credits, Deductions, etc.,* you get from the partnership.)

---

## Salary Reduction Simplified Employee Pension (SARSEP)

A SARSEP is a SEP set up before 1997 that includes a salary reduction arrangement. (See the *Caution,* next.) Under a SARSEP, your employees can choose to have you contribute part of their pay to their SEP-IRAs rather than receive it in cash. This contribution is called an "elective deferral" because employees choose (elect) to set aside the money, and they defer the tax on the money until it is distributed to them.

⚠ **CAUTION** *You are not allowed to set up a SARSEP after 1996. However, participants (including employees hired after 1996) in a SARSEP set up before 1997 can continue to have you contribute part of their pay to the plan. If you are interested in setting up a retirement plan that includes a salary reduction arrangement, see chapter 3.*

**Who can have a SARSEP?** A SARSEP set up before 1997 is available to you and your eligible employees only if all the following requirements are met.

- At least 50% of your employees eligible to participate choose to make elective deferrals.
- You have 25 or fewer employees who were eligible to participate in the SEP any time during the preceding year.
- The elective deferrals of your highly compensated employees meet the SARSEP ADP test.

**SARSEP ADP test.** Under the SARSEP ADP test, the amount deferred each year by each eligible highly compensated employee as a percentage of pay (the deferral percentage) cannot be more than 125% of the average deferral percentage (ADP) of all non-highly compensated employees eligible to participate. A highly compensated employee is defined in chapter 1.

**Deferral percentage.** The deferral percentage for an employee for a year is figured as follows.

$$\frac{\text{The elective employer contributions}}{\text{(excluding certain catch-up contributions)}}{\text{paid to the SEP for the employee for the year}}$$

$$\text{The employee's compensation}$$
$$\text{(limited to \$200,000)}$$

 *The instructions for Form 5305A–SEP have a worksheet you can use to determine whether the elective deferrals of your highly compensated employees meet the SARSEP ADP test.*

**Employee compensation.** For figuring the deferral percentage, compensation is generally the amount you pay to the employee for the year. Compensation includes the elective deferral and other amounts deferred in certain employee benefit plans. See *Compensation* in chapter 1. Elective deferrals under the SARSEP are included in figuring your employees' deferral percentage even though they are not included in the income of your employees for income tax purposes.

*Compensation of self-employed individuals.* If you are self-employed, compensation is your net earnings from self-employment as defined in chapter 1.

Compensation does not include tax-free items (or deductions related to them) other than foreign earned income and housing cost amounts.

*Choice not to treat deferrals as compensation.* You can choose not to treat elective deferrals (and other amounts deferred in certain employee benefit plans) for a year as compensation under your SARSEP.

**Who cannot have a SARSEP?** A state or local government, any of its political subdivisions, agencies, or instrumentalities, or a tax-exempt organization cannot have a SEP that includes a salary reduction arrangement.

## Limit on Elective Defe

The most a participant can choos      er for calendar year 2002 is the lesser of the following amounts.

1) 25% of the participant's compensation (limited to $200,000 of the participant's compensation).

2) $11,000.

In 2003, the compensation limit in (1) of $200,000 is subject to cost-of-living adjustments. The amount in (2) increases to $12,000.

The $11,000 limit applies to the total elective deferrals the employee makes for the year to a SEP and any of the following.

- Cash or deferred arrangement (section 401(k) plan).
- Salary reduction arrangement under a tax-sheltered annuity plan (section 403(b) plan).
- SIMPLE IRA plan.

**Catch-up contributions.** Beginning in 2002, a SEP can permit participants who are age 50 or over at the end of the calendar year to also make catch-up contributions. The catch-up contribution limit for 2002 is $1,000 ($2,000 for 2003). Elective deferrals are not treated as catch-up contributions for 2002 until they exceed the elective deferral limit (the lesser of 25% of compensation or $11,000), the SARSEP ADP test limit discussed earlier, or the plan limit (if any). However, the catch-up contribution a participant can make for a year cannot exceed the lesser of the following amounts.

- The catch-up contribution limit.
- The excess of the participant's compensation over the elective deferrals that are not catch-up contributions.

Catch-up contributions are not subject to the elective deferral limit (the lesser of 25% of compensation or $11,000).

**Overall limit on SEP contributions.** If you also make nonelective contributions to a SEP-IRA, the total of the nonelective and elective contributions to that SEP-IRA cannot exceed the lesser of 25% of the employee's compensation or $40,000 (subject to cost-of-living adjustments after 2002). The same rule applies to contributions you make to your own SEP-IRA. See *Contribution Limits*, earlier.

**Figuring the elective deferral.** For figuring the 25% limit on elective deferrals, compensation does not include SEP contributions, including elective deferrals or other amounts deferred in certain employee benefit plans.

### Tax Treatment of Deferrals

Beginning in 2002, elective deferrals are no longer subject to the deduction limits discussed earlier under *Deducting Contributions*. However, the combined deduction for a participant's elective deferrals and other SEP contributions cannot exceed $40,000.

Elective deferrals that are not more than the limits discussed under *Limit on Elective Deferrals* are excluded from your employees' wages subject to federal income tax in the year of deferral. However, these deferrals are included in wages for social security, Medicare, and federal unemployment (FUTA) tax.

**Excess deferrals.** For 2002, excess deferrals are the elective deferrals for the year that are more than the $11,000 limit discussed earlier. For a participant who is eligible to make catch-up contributions, excess deferrals are the elective deferrals that are more than $12,000. The treatment of excess deferrals made under a SARSEP is similar to the treatment of excess deferrals made under a qualified plan. See *Treatment of Excess Deferrals* under *Elective Deferrals (401(k) Plans)* in chapter 4.

**Excess SEP contributions.** Excess SEP contributions are elective deferrals of highly compensated employees that are more than the amount permitted under the SARSEP ADP test. You must notify your highly compensated employees within 2½ months after the end of the plan year of their excess SEP contributions. If you do not notify them within this time period, you must pay a 10% tax on the excess. For an explanation of the notification requirements, see Revenue Procedure 91–44 in Cumulative Bulletin 1991–2. If you adopted a SARSEP using Form 5305A–SEP, the notification requirements are explained in the instructions for that form.

**Reporting on Form W–2.** Do not include elective deferrals in the "Wages, tips, other compensation" box of Form W–2. You must, however, include them in the "Social security wages" and "Medicare wages and tips" boxes. You must also include them in box 12. Mark the "Retirement plan" checkbox in box 13. For more information, see the Form W–2 instructions.

## Distributions (Withdrawals)

As an employer, you cannot prohibit distributions from a SEP-IRA. Also, you cannot make your contributions on the condition that any part of them must be kept in the account.

Distributions are subject to IRA rules. For information about IRA rules, including the tax treatment of distributions, rollovers, required distributions, and income tax withholding, see Publication 590.

## Additional Taxes

The tax advantages of using SEP-IRAs for retirement savings can be offset by additional taxes. There are additional taxes for all the following actions.

- Making excess contributions.
- Making early withdrawals.
- Not making required withdrawals.

For information about these taxes, see chapter 1 in Publication 590. Also, a SEP-IRA may be disqualified, or an excise tax may apply, if the account is involved in a prohibited transaction, discussed next.

**Prohibited transaction.** If an employee improperly uses his or her SEP-IRA, such as by borrowing money from it, the employee has engaged in a prohibited transaction. In that case,

the SEP-IRA will no longer qualify as an IRA. For a list of prohibited transactions, see *Prohibited Transactions* in chapter 4.

*Effects on employee.* If a SEP-IRA is disqualified because of a prohibited transaction, the assets in the account will be treated as having been distributed to the employee on the first day of the year in which the transaction occurred. The employee must include in income the fair market value of the assets (on the first day of the year) that is more than any cost basis in the account. Also, the employee may have to pay the additional tax for making early withdrawals.

## Reporting and Disclosure Requirements

If you set up a SEP using Form 5305–SEP, you must give your eligible employees certain information about the SEP when you set it up. See *Setting Up a SEP*, earlier. Also, you must give your eligible employees a statement each year showing any contributions to their SEP-IRAs. You must also give them notice of any excess contributions. For details about other information you must give them, see the instructions for Form 5305–SEP or 5305A–SEP (for a salary reduction SEP).

Even if you did *not* use Form 5305–SEP or Form 5305A–SEP to set up your SEP, you must give your employees information similar to that described above. For more information, see the instructions for either Form 5305–SEP or Form 5305A–SEP.

---

# 3.

# SIMPLE Plans

## Topics
This chapter discusses:

- SIMPLE IRA plan
- SIMPLE 401(k) plan

## Useful Items
You may want to see:

**Forms (and instructions)**

❏ **W–2** Wage and Tax Statement

❏ **5304–SIMPLE** Savings Incentive Match Plan for Employees of Small Employers (SIMPLE)—Not for use with a Designated Financial Institution

❏ **5305–SIMPLE** Savings Incentive Match Plan for Employees of

Employers (SIMPLE)—for Use With a Designated Financial Institution

A savings incentive match plan for employees (SIMPLE plan) is a written arrangement that provides you and your employees with a simplified way to make contributions to provide retirement income. Under a SIMPLE plan, employees can choose to make salary reduction contributions to the plan rather than receiving these amounts as part of their regular pay. In addition, you will contribute matching or nonelective contributions.

SIMPLE plans can only be maintained on a calendar-year basis.

A SIMPLE plan can be set up in either of the following ways.

- Using SIMPLE IRAs (SIMPLE IRA plan).
- As part of a 401(k) plan (SIMPLE 401(k) plan).

 *Many financial institutions will help you set up a SIMPLE plan.*

## SIMPLE IRA Plan

A SIMPLE IRA plan is a retirement plan that uses SIMPLE IRAs for each eligible employee. Under a SIMPLE IRA plan, a SIMPLE IRA must be set up for each eligible employee. For the definition of an eligible employee, see *Who Can Participate in a SIMPLE IRA Plan*, later.

### Who Can Set Up a SIMPLE IRA Plan?

You can set up a SIMPLE IRA plan if you meet both the following requirements.

- You meet the employee limit.
- You do not maintain another qualified plan unless the other plan is for collective bargaining employees.

**Employee limit.** You can set up a SIMPLE IRA plan only if you had 100 or fewer employees who received $5,000 or more in compensation from you for the preceding year. Under this rule, you must take into account *all* employees employed at any time during the calendar year regardless of whether they are eligible to participate. Employees include self-employed individuals who received earned income and leased employees (defined in chapter 1).

Once you set up a SIMPLE IRA plan, you must continue to meet the 100-employee limit each year you maintain the plan.

*Grace period for employers who cease to meet the 100-employee limit.* If you maintain the SIMPLE IRA plan for at least 1 year and you cease to meet the 100-employee limit in a later year, you will be treated as meeting it for the 2 calendar years immediately following the calendar year for which you last met it.

A different rule applies if you do not meet the 100-employee limit because of an acquisition, disposition, or similar transaction. Under this

rule, the SIMPLE IRA plan will be treated as meeting the 100-employee limit for the year of the transaction and the 2 following years if both the following conditions are satisfied.

- Coverage under the plan has not significantly changed during the grace period.
- The SIMPLE IRA plan would have continued to qualify after the transaction if you had remained a separate employer.

⚠ *The grace period for acquisitions, dispositions, and similar transactions also applies if, because of these types of transactions, you do not meet the rules explained under* Other qualified plan *or* Who Can Participate in a SIMPLE IRA Plan, *below.*

**Other qualified plan.** The SIMPLE IRA plan generally must be the only retirement plan to which you make contributions, or to which benefits accrue, for service in any year beginning with the year the SIMPLE IRA plan becomes effective.

*Exception.* If you maintain a qualified plan for collective bargaining employees, you are permitted to maintain a SIMPLE IRA plan for other employees.

### Who Can Participate in a SIMPLE IRA Plan?

**Eligible employee.** Any employee who received at least $5,000 in compensation during any 2 years preceding the current calendar year and is reasonably expected to receive at least $5,000 during the current calendar year is eligible to participate. The term "employee" includes a self-employed individual who received earned income.

You can use less restrictive eligibility requirements (but not more restrictive ones) by eliminating or reducing the prior year compensation requirements, the current year compensation requirements, or both. For example, you can allow participation for employees who received at least $3,000 in compensation during any preceding calendar year. However, you cannot impose any other conditions for participating in a SIMPLE IRA plan.

**Excludable employees.** The following employees do not need to be covered under a SIMPLE IRA plan.

- Employees who are covered by a union agreement and whose retirement benefits were bargained for in good faith by the employees' union and you.
- Nonresident alien employees who have received no U.S. source wages, salaries, or other personal services compensation from you.

**Compensation.** Compensation for employees is the total wages required to be reported on Form W-2. Compensation also includes the salary reduction contributions made under this plan, compensation deferred under a section 457 plan, and the employees' elective deferrals under a section 401(k) plan, a SARSEP, or a section 403(b) annuity contract. If you are self-employed, compensation is your net earn-

ings from self-employment (line 4 of Short Schedule SE (Form 1040)) before subtracting any contributions made to the SIMPLE IRA plan for yourself.

## How To Set Up a SIMPLE IRA Plan

You can use **Form 5304–SIMPLE** or **Form 5305–SIMPLE** to set up a SIMPLE IRA plan. Each form is a model savings incentive match plan for employees (SIMPLE) plan document. Which form you use depends on whether you select a financial institution or your employees select the institution that will receive the contributions.

Use Form 5304–SIMPLE if you allow each plan participant to select the financial institution for receiving his or her SIMPLE IRA plan contributions. Use Form 5305–SIMPLE if you require that all contributions under the SIMPLE IRA plan be deposited initially at a designated financial institution.

The SIMPLE IRA plan is adopted when you have completed all appropriate boxes and blanks on the form and you (and the designated financial institution, if any) have signed it. Keep the original form. Do not file it with the IRS.

**Other uses of the forms.** If you set up a SIMPLE IRA plan using Form 5304–SIMPLE or Form 5305–SIMPLE, you can use the form to satisfy other requirements, including the following.

- Meeting employer notification requirements for the SIMPLE IRA plan. Page 3 of Form 5304–SIMPLE and Page 3 of Form 5305–SIMPLE contain a *Model Notification to Eligible Employees* that provides the necessary information to the employee.

- Maintaining the SIMPLE IRA plan records and proving you set up a SIMPLE IRA plan for employees.

**Deadline for setting up a SIMPLE IRA plan.** You can set up a SIMPLE IRA plan effective on any date between January 1 and October 1 of a year, provided you did not previously maintain a SIMPLE IRA plan. This requirement does not apply if you are a new employer that comes into existence after October 1 of the year the SIMPLE IRA plan is set up and you set up a SIMPLE IRA plan as soon as administratively feasible after you come into existence. If you previously maintained a SIMPLE IRA plan, you can set up a SIMPLE IRA plan effective only on January 1 of a year. A SIMPLE IRA plan cannot have an effective date that is before the date you actually adopt the plan.

**Setting up a SIMPLE IRA.** SIMPLE IRAs are the individual retirement accounts or annuities into which the contributions are deposited. A SIMPLE IRA must be set up for each eligible employee. *Forms 5305–S, SIMPLE Individual Retirement Trust Account,* and *5305–SA, SIMPLE Individual Retirement Custodial Account,* are model trust and custodial account documents the participant and the trustee (or custodian) can use for this purpose.

A SIMPLE IRA cannot be designated as a Roth IRA. Contributions to a SIM    IRA will not affect the amount an individual can contribute to a Roth IRA.

**Deadline for setting up a SIMPLE IRA.** A SIMPLE IRA must be set up for an employee before the first date by which a contribution is required to be deposited into the employee's IRA. See *Time limits for contributing funds*, later, under *Contribution Limits*.

**Credit for startup costs.** You may be able to claim a tax credit for part of the ordinary and necessary costs of starting a SIMPLE IRA plan that first became effective in 2002. For more information, see *Credit for startup costs* under *Important Changes for 2002*, earlier.

## Notification Requirement

If you adopt a SIMPLE IRA plan, you must notify each employee of the following information before the beginning of the election period.

1) The employee's opportunity to make or change a salary reduction choice under a SIMPLE IRA plan.

2) Your choice to make either matching contributions or nonelective contributions (discussed later).

3) A summary description and the location of the plan. The financial institution should provide you with this information.

4) Written notice that his or her balance can be transferred without cost or penalty if you use a designated financial institution.

**Election period.** The election period is generally the 60-day period immediately preceding January 1 of a calendar year (November 2 to December 31 of the preceding calendar year). However, the dates of this period are modified if you set up a SIMPLE IRA plan in mid-year (for example, on July 1) or if the 60-day period falls before the first day an employee becomes eligible to participate in the SIMPLE IRA plan.

A SIMPLE IRA plan can provide longer periods for permitting employees to enter into salary reduction agreements or to modify prior agreements. For example, a SIMPLE IRA plan can provide a 90-day election period instead of the 60-day period. Similarly, in addition to the 60-day election period, a SIMPLE IRA plan can provide quarterly election periods during the 30 days before each calendar quarter, other than the first quarter of each year.

## Contribution Limits

Contributions are made up of salary reduction contributions and employer contributions. You, as the employer, must make either matching contributions or nonelective contributions, defined later. No other contributions can be made to the SIMPLE IRA plan. These contributions, which you can deduct, must be made timely. See *Time limits for contributing funds*, later.

**Salary reduction contributions.** The amount the employee chooses to have you contribute to a SIMPLE IRA on his or her behalf cannot be more than $7,000 for 2002 ($8,000 for 2003). These contributions must be expressed as a percentage of the employee's compensation unless you permit the employee to express them as a specific dollar amount. You cannot place restrictions on the contribution amount (such as limiting the contribution percentage), except to comply with the $7,000 limit.

If an employee is a participant in any other employer plan during the year and has elective salary reductions or deferred compensation under those plans, the salary reduction contributions under a SIMPLE IRA plan also are elective deferrals that count toward the overall annual limit ($11,000 for 2002) on exclusion of salary reductions and other elective deferrals.

**Catch-up contributions.** Beginning in 2002, a SIMPLE IRA plan can permit participants who are age 50 or over at the end of the calendar year to also make catch-up contributions. The catch-up contribution limit for 2002 is $500 ($1,000 for 2003). Salary reduction contributions are not treated as catch-up contributions for 2002 until they exceed $7,000. However, the catch-up contribution a participant can make for a year cannot exceed the lesser of the following amounts.

• The catch-up contribution limit.

• The excess of the participant's compensation over the salary reduction contributions that are not catch-up contributions.

**Employer matching contributions.** You are generally required to match each employee's salary reduction contributions (other than catch-up contributions) on a dollar-for-dollar basis up to 3% of the employee's compensation. This requirement does not apply if you make nonelective contributions as discussed later.

**Example.** In 2002, your employee, John Rose, earned $25,000 and chose to defer 5% of his salary. Your net earnings from self-employment are $40,000, and you choose to contribute 10% of your earnings to your SIMPLE IRA. You make 3% matching contributions. The total contribution you can make for John is $2,000, figured as follows.

Salary reduction contributions
($25,000 × .05) . . . . . . . . . . . . . . $1,250
Employer matching contribution
($25,000 × .03) . . . . . . . . . . . . . . . 750
**Total contributions** . . . . . . . . . . . **$2,000**

The total contribution you can make for yourself is $5,200, figured as follows.

Salary reduction contributions
($40,000 × .10) . . . . . . . . . . . . . . $4,000
Employer matching contribution
($40,000 × .03) . . . . . . . . . . . . . . 1,200
**Total contributions** . . . . . . . . . . . **$5,200**

**Lower percentage.** If you choose a matching contribution less than 3%, the percentage must be at least 1%. You must notify the employees of the lower match within a reasonable period of time before the 60-day election period (discussed earlier) for the calendar year. You cannot choose a percentage less than 3% for more than 2 years during the 5-year period that ends with (and includes) the year for which the choice is effective.

**Nonelective contributions.** Instead of matching contributions, you can choose to make nonelective contributions of 2% of compensation on behalf of each eligible employee who has at least $5,000 (or some lower amount you select) of compensation from you for the year. If you make this choice, you must make nonelective contributions whether or not the employee chooses to make salary reduction contributions. Only $200,000 of the employee's compensation can be taken into account to figure the contribution limit.

If you choose this 2% contribution formula, you must notify the employees within a reasonable period of time before the 60-day election period (discussed earlier) for the calendar year.

**Example 1.** In 2002, your employee, Jane Wood, earned $36,000 and chose to have you contribute 10% of her salary. Your net earnings from self-employment are $50,000, and you choose to contribute 10% of your earnings to your SIMPLE IRA. You make a 2% nonelective contribution. Both of you are under age 50. The total contribution you can make for Jane is $4,320, figured as follows.

Salary reduction contributions
($36,000 × .10) . . . . . . . . . . . . . . $3,600
2% nonelective contributions
($36,000 × .02) . . . . . . . . . . . . . . 720
**Total contributions** . . . . . . . . . . . **$4,320**

The total contribution you can make for yourself is $6,000, figured as follows.

Salary reduction contributions
($50,000 × .10) . . . . . . . . . . . . . . $5,000
Employer matching contribution
($50,000 × .02) . . . . . . . . . . . . . . 1,000
**Total contributions** . . . . . . . . . . . **$6,000**

**Example 2.** Using the same facts as in Example 1, above, the maximum contribution you can make for Jane or for yourself if you each earned $75,000 is $8,500, figured as follows.

Salary reduction contributions
(maximum amount) . . . . . . . . . . . $7,000
2% nonelective contributions
($75,000 × .02) . . . . . . . . . . . . . . 1,500
**Total contributions** . . . . . . . . . . . **$8,500**

**Time limits for contributing funds.** You must make the salary reduction contributions to the SIMPLE IRA within 30 days after the end of the month in which the amounts would otherwise have been payable to the employee in cash. You must make matching contributions or nonelective contributions by the due date (including extensions) for filing your federal income tax return for the year.

## When To Deduct Contributions

You can deduct SIMPLE IRA contributions in the tax year with or within which the calendar year for which contributions were made ends. You can deduct contributions for a particular tax year if they are made for that tax year and are made by the due date (including extensions) of your federal income tax return for that y

**Example 1.** Your tax year is the fiscal year ending June 30. Contributions under a SIMPLE IRA plan for the calendar year 2002 (including contributions made in 2002 before July 1, 2002)

are deductible in the tax year ending June 30, 2003.

**Example 2.** You are a sole proprietor whose tax year is the calendar year. Contributions under a SIMPLE IRA plan for the calendar year 2002 (including contributions made in 2003 by April 15, 2003) are deductible in the 2002 tax year.

## Where To Deduct Contributions

Deduct the contributions you make for your common-law employees on your tax return. For example, sole proprietors deduct them on Schedule C (Form 1040), *Profit or Loss From Business*, or Schedule F (Form 1040), *Profit or Loss From Farming*, partnerships deduct them on Form 1065, *U.S. Return of Partnership Income*, and corporations deduct them on Form 1120, *U.S. Corporation Income Tax Return*, Form 1120–A, *U.S. Corporation Short-Form Income Tax Return*, or Form 1120S, *U.S. Income Tax Return for an S Corporation*.

Sole proprietors and partners deduct contributions for themselves on line 31 of Form 1040, *U.S. Individual Income Tax Return*. (If you are a partner, contributions for yourself are shown on the Schedule K–1 (Form 1065), *Partner's Share of Income, Credits, Deductions, etc.*, you get from the partnership.)

## Tax Treatment of Contributions

You can deduct your contributions and your employees can exclude these contributions from their gross income. SIMPLE IRA contributions are not subject to federal income tax withholding. However, salary reduction contributions are subject to social security, Medicare, and federal unemployment (FUTA) taxes. Matching and nonelective contributions are not subject to these taxes.

**Reporting on Form W–2.** Do not include SIMPLE IRA contributions in the "Wages, tips, other compensation box" of Form W–2. However, salary reduction contributions must be included in the boxes for social security and Medicare wages. Also include the proper code in box 12. For more information, see the instructions for Forms W–2 and W–3.

## Distributions (Withdrawals)

Distributions from a SIMPLE IRA are subject to IRA rules and generally are includible in income for the year received. Tax-free rollovers can be made from one SIMPLE IRA into another SIMPLE IRA. However, a rollover from a SIMPLE IRA to a non-SIMPLE IRA can be made tax free only after a 2-year participation in the SIMPLE IRA plan.

Early withdrawals generally are subject to a 10% additional tax. However, the additional tax is increased to 25% if funds are withdrawn within 2 years of beginning participation.

**More information.** See Publication 590, *Individual Retirement Arrangements*, for information about IRA rules, including those on the tax treatment of distributions, rollovers, and required distributions, and income tax withholding.

## More Information on SIMPLE IRA Plans

If you need more help to set up and maintain SIMPLE IRA plans, see the following IRS notice and revenue procedure.

**Notice 98–4.** This notice contains questions and answers about the implementation and operation of SIMPLE IRA plans, including the election and notice requirements for these plans. Notice 98–4 is in Cumulative Bulletin 1998–1.

**Revenue Procedure 97–29.** This revenue procedure provides guidance to drafters of prototype SIMPLE IRAs on obtaining opinion letters. Revenue Procedure 97–29 is in Cumulative Bulletin 1997–1.

## SIMPLE 401(k) Plan

You can adopt a SIMPLE plan as part of a 401(k) plan if you meet the 100-employee limit as discussed earlier under *SIMPLE IRA Plan*. A SIMPLE 401(k) plan is a qualified retirement plan and generally must satisfy the rules discussed under *Qualification Rules* in chapter 4. However, a SIMPLE 401(k) plan is not subject to the nondiscrimination and top-heavy rules in that discussion if the plan meets the conditions listed below.

1) Under the plan, an employee can choose to have you make salary reduction contributions for the year to a trust in an amount expressed as a percentage of the employee's compensation, but not more than $7,000 for 2002 ($8,000 for 2003). If permitted under the plan, an employee who is age 50 or over can also make a catch-up contribution of up to $500 for 2002 ($1,000 for 2003). See *Catch-up contributions* earlier under *Contribution Limits*.

2) You must make either:

   a) Matching contributions up to 3% of compensation for the year, or

   b) Nonelective contributions of 2% of compensation on behalf of each eligible employee who has at least $5,000 of compensation from you for the year.

3) No other contributions can be made to the trust.

4) No contributions are made, and no benefits accrue, for services during the year under any other qualified retirement plan of the employer on behalf of any employee eligible to participate in the SIMPLE 401(k) plan.

5) The employee's rights to any contributions are nonforfeitable.

No more than $200,000 of the employee's compensation can be taken into account in figuring salary reduction contributions, matching contributions, and nonelective contributions.

**Employee notification.** The notification requirement that applies to SIMPLE IRA plans also applies to SIMPLE 401(k) plans. See *Notification Requirement* in this chapter.

**Credit for startup costs.** You may be able to claim a tax credit for part of the ordinary and necessary costs of starting a SIMPLE 401(k) plan that first became effective in 2002. For more information, see *Credit for startup costs* under *Important Changes for 2002*, earlier.

## More Information on SIMPLE 401(k) Plans

If you need more help to set up and maintain SIMPLE 401(k) plans, see Revenue Procedure 97–9 in Cumulative Bulletin 1997–1. This revenue procedure provides a model amendment you can use to adopt a plan with SIMPLE 401(k) provisions. This model amendment provides guidance to plan sponsors for incorporating 401(k) SIMPLE provisions in plans containing cash or deferred arrangements.

---

# 4.

# Qualified Plans

## Topics
This chapter discusses:

- Kinds of plans
- Setting up a qualified plan
- Minimum funding requirement
- Contributions
- Employer deduction
- Elective deferrals (401(k) plans)
- Distributions
- Prohibited transactions
- Reporting requirements
- Qualification rules

## Useful Items
You may want to see:

**Publication**

❏ **575** Pension and Annuity Income

**Forms (and Instructions)**

❏ **Schedule C (Form 1040)** Profit or Loss From Business

❏ **Schedule F (Form 1040)** Profit or Loss From Farming

❏ **Schedule K-1 (Form 1065)** Partner's Share of Income, Credits, Deductions, etc.

❏ **W–2** Wage and Tax Statement

❏ **1040** U.S. Individual Income Tax Return

❏ **1099–R** Distributions From Pensions, Annuities, Retirement or

Profit-Sharing Plans, IRAs, Insurance Contracts, etc.

❑ **5330** Return of Excise Taxes Related to Employee Benefit Plans

❑ **5500** Annual Return/Report of Employee Benefit Plan

❑ **5500-EZ** Annual Return of One-Participant (Owners and Their Spouses) Retirement Plan

❑ **Schedule A (Form 5500)** Insurance Information

Qualified retirement plans set up by self-employed individuals are sometimes called Keogh or H.R. 10 plans. A sole proprietor or a partnership can set up a qualified plan. A common-law employee or a partner cannot set up a qualified plan. The plans described here can also be set up and maintained by employers that are corporations. All the rules discussed here apply to corporations except where specifically limited to the self-employed.

The plan must be for the exclusive benefit of employees or their beneficiaries. A qualified plan *can include coverage for a self-employed individual.* A self-employed individual is treated as both an employer and an employee.

As an employer, you can usually deduct, subject to limits, contributions you make to a qualified plan, including those made for your own retirement. The contributions (and earnings and gains on them) are generally tax free until distributed by the plan.

## Kinds of Plans

There are two basic kinds of qualified plans—defined contribution plans and defined benefit plans—and different rules apply to each. You can have more than one qualified plan, but your contributions to all the plans must not total more than the overall limits discussed under *Contributions* and *Employer Deduction,* later.

### Defined Contribution Plan

A defined contribution plan provides an individual account for each participant in the plan. It provides benefits to a participant largely based on the amount contributed to that participant's account. Benefits are also affected by any income, expenses, gains, losses, and forfeitures of other accounts that may be allocated to an account. A defined contribution plan can be either a profit-sharing plan or a money purchase pension plan.

**Profit-sharing plan.** A profit-sharing plan is a plan for sharing your business profits with your employees. However, you do not have to make contributions out of net profits to have a profit-sharing plan.

The plan does not need to provide a definite formula for figuring the profits to be shared. But, if there is no formula, there must be systematic and substantial contributions.

The plan must provide a definite formula for allocating the contribution among the participants and for distributing the accumulated funds to the employees after they reach a certain age,

after a fixed number of years, or upon certain other occurrences.

In general, you can be more flexible in making contributions to a profit-sharing plan than to a money purchase pension plan (discussed next) or a defined benefit plan (discussed later).

Forfeitures under a profit-sharing plan can be allocated to the accounts of remaining participants in a nondiscriminatory way or they can be used to reduce your contributions.

**Money purchase pension plan.** Contributions to a money purchase pension plan are fixed and are not based on your business profits. For example, if the plan requires that contributions be 10% of the participants' compensation without regard to whether you have profits (or the self-employed person has earned income), the plan is a money purchase pension plan. This applies even though the compensation of a self-employed individual as a participant is based on earned income derived from business profits.

### Defined Benefit Plan

A defined benefit plan is any plan that is not a defined contribution plan. Contributions to a defined benefit plan are based on what is needed to provide definitely determinable benefits to plan participants. Actuarial assumptions and computations are required to figure these contributions. Generally, you will need continuing professional help to have a defined benefit plan.

Forfeitures under a defined benefit plan cannot be used to increase the benefits any employee would otherwise receive under the plan. Forfeitures must be used instead to reduce employer contributions.

## Setting Up a Qualified Plan

There are two basic steps in setting up a qualified plan. First you adopt a written plan. Then you invest the plan assets.

You, the employer, are responsible for setting up and maintaining the plan.

 *If you are self-employed, it is not necessary to have employees besides yourself to sponsor and set up a qualified plan. If you have employees, see* Participation, *under* Qualification Rules, *later.*

**Set-up deadline.** To take a deduction for contributions for a tax year, your plan must be set up (adopted) by the last day of that year (December 31 for calendar year employers).

**Credit for startup costs.** You may be able to claim a tax credit for part of the ordinary and necessary costs of starting a qualified plan that first became effective in 2002. For more information, see *Credit for startup costs* under *Important Changes for 2002,* earlier.

### Adopting a Written Plan

You must adopt a written plan. The plan can be an IRS-approved master or prototype plan offered by a sponsoring organization. Or it can be an individually designed plan.

**Written plan requirement.** To qualify, the plan you set up must be in writing and must be communicated to your employees. The plan's provisions must be stated in the plan. It is not sufficient for the plan to merely refer to a requirement of the Internal Revenue Code.

**Master or prototype plans.** Most qualified plans follow a standard form of plan (a master or prototype plan) approved by the IRS. Master and prototype plans are plans made available by plan providers for adoption by employers (including self-employed individuals). Under a master plan, a single trust or custodial account is established, as part of the plan, for the joint use of all adopting employers. Under a prototype plan, a separate trust or custodial account is established for each employer.

**Plan providers.** The following organizations generally can provide IRS-approved master or prototype plans.

- Banks (including some savings and loan associations and federally insured credit unions).

- Trade or professional organizations.

- Insurance companies.

- Mutual funds.

**Individually designed plan.** If you prefer, you can set up an individually designed plan to meet specific needs. Although advance IRS approval is not required, you can apply for approval by paying a fee and requesting a determination letter. You may need professional help for this. Revenue Procedure 2003–6 in Internal Revenue Bulletin 2003–1 may help you decide whether to apply for approval.

Internal Revenue Bulletins are available on the IRS web site at **www.irs.gov.** They are also available at most IRS offices and at certain libraries.

**User fee.** The fee mentioned earlier for requesting a determination letter does not apply to certain requests made in 2002 and later years, by employers who have 100 or fewer employees who received at least $5,000 of compensation from the employer for the preceding year. At least one of them must be a non-highly compensated employee participating in the plan. The fee does not apply to requests made by the later of the following dates.

- The end of the 5th plan year the plan is in effect.

- The end of any remedial amendment period for the plan that begins within the first 5 plan years.

The request cannot be made by the sponsor of a prototype or similar plan the sponsor intends to market to participating employers.

For more information about whether the user fee applies, see Notice 2002–1 in Internal Revenue Bulletin 2002–2.

### Investing Plan Assets

In setting up a qualified plan, you arrange how the plan's funds will be used to build its assets.

- You can establish a trust or custodial account to invest the funds.

- You, the trust, or the custodial account can buy an annuity contract from an insurance company. Life insurance can be included only if it is incidental to the retirement benefits.

- You, the trust, or the custodial account can buy face-amount certificates from an insurance company. These certificates are treated like annuity contracts.

You set up a trust by a legal instrument (written document). You may need professional help to do this.

You can set up a custodial account with a bank, savings and loan association, credit union, or other person who can act as the plan trustee.

You do not need a trust or custodial account, although you can have one, to invest the plan's funds in annuity contracts or face-amount certificates. If anyone other than a trustee holds them, however, the contracts or certificates must state they are not transferable.

**Other plan requirements.** For information on other important plan requirements, see *Qualification Rules*, later.

# Minimum Funding Requirement

In general, if your plan is a money purchase pension plan or a defined benefit plan, you must actually pay enough into the plan to satisfy the minimum funding standard for each year. Determining the amount needed to satisfy the minimum funding standard for a defined benefit plan is complicated. The amount is based on what should be contributed under the plan formula using actuarial assumptions and formulas. For information on this funding requirement, see section 412 and its regulations.

**Quarterly installments of required contributions.** If your plan is a defined benefit plan subject to the minimum funding requirements, you must make quarterly installment payments of the required contributions. If you do not pay the full installments timely, you may have to pay interest on any underpayment for the period of the underpayment.

**Due dates.** The due dates for the installments are 15 days after the end of each quarter. For a calendar-year plan, the installments are due April 15, July 15, October 15, and January 15 (of the following year).

**Installment percentage.** Each quarterly installment must be 25% of the required annual payment.

**Extended period for making contributions.** Additional contributions required to satisfy the minimum funding requirement for a plan year will be considered timely if made by 8½ months after the end of that year.

# Contributions

A qualified plan is generally funded by your contributions. However, employees participating in the plan may be permitted to make contributions.

**Contributions deadline.** You can make deductible contributions for a tax year up to the due date of your return (plus extensions) for that year.

**Self-employed individual.** You can make contributions on behalf of yourself only if you have net earnings (compensation) from self-employment in the trade or business for which the plan was set up. Your net earnings must be from your personal services, not from your investments. If you have a net loss from self-employment, you cannot make contributions for yourself for the year, even if you can contribute for common-law employees based on their compensation.

## When Contributions Are Considered Made

You generally apply your plan contributions to the year in which you make them. But you can apply them to the previous year if all the following requirements are met.

1) You make them by the due date of your tax return for the previous year (plus extensions).

2) The plan was established by the end of the previous year.

3) The plan treats the contributions as though it had received them on the last day of the previous year.

4) You do either of the following.

   a) You specify in writing to the plan administrator or trustee that the contributions apply to the previous year.

   b) You deduct the contributions on your tax return for the previous year. (A partnership shows contributions for partners on Schedule K (Form 1065), *Partner's Share of Income, Credits, Deductions, etc.*)

**Employer's promissory note.** Your promissory note made out to the plan is not a payment that qualifies for the deduction. Also, issuing this note is a prohibited transaction subject to tax. See *Prohibited Transactions*, later.

## Employer Contributions

There are certain limits on the contributions and other annual additions you can make each year for plan participants. There are also limits on the amount you can deduct. See *Deduction Limits*, later.

## Limits on Contributions and Benefits

Your plan must provide that contributions or benefits cannot exceed certain limits. The limits differ depending on whether your plan is a defined contribution plan or a defined benefit plan.

**Defined benefit plan.** For 2002, the annual benefit for a participant under a defined benefit plan cannot exceed the lesser of the following amounts.

1) 100% of the participant's average compensation for his or her highest 3 consecutive calendar years.

2) $160,000.

For 2003 and later years, the amount in (2) is subject to cost-of-living adjustments.

**Defined contribution plan.** For 2002, a defined contribution plan's annual contributions and other additions (excluding earnings) to the account of a participant cannot exceed the lesser of the following amounts.

1) 100% of the participant's compensation.

2) $40,000.

Catch-up contributions (discussed later under *Limit on Elective Deferrals*) are not subject to the above limit.

For 2003, and later years, the amount in (2) is subject to cost-of-living adjustments.

**Excess annual additions.** Excess annual additions are the amounts contributed to a defined contribution plan that are more than the limits discussed previously. A plan can correct excess annual additions caused by any of the following actions.

- A reasonable error in estimating a participant's compensation.

- A reasonable error in determining the elective deferrals permitted (discussed later).

- Forfeitures allocated to participants' accounts.

**Correcting excess annual additions.** A plan can provide for the correction of excess annual additions in the following ways.

1) Allocate and reallocate the excess to other participants in the plan to the extent of their unused limits for the year.

2) If these limits are exceeded, do one of the following.

   a) Hold the excess in a separate account and allocate (and reallocate) it to participants' accounts in the following year (or years) before making any contributions for that year (see also *Carryover of Excess Contributions*, later).

   b) Return employee after-tax contributions or elective deferrals (see *Employee Contributions* and *Elective Deferrals (401(k) Plans)*, later).

**Tax treatment of returned contributions or distributed elective deferrals.** The return of employee after-tax contributions or the distribution of elective deferrals to correct excess annual additions is considered a corrective payment rather than a distribution of accrued benefits. The penalties for early distributions and excess distributions do not apply.

These disbursements are not wages reportable on Form W–2. You must report them on a separate Form 1099–R as follows.

- Report the total distribution, including employee contributions, in box 1. If the distribution includes any gain from the contribution, report the gain in box 2a. Report the return of employee contributions in box 5. Enter Code E in box 7.

- Report a distribution of an elective deferral in boxes 1 and 2a. Include any gain from the contribution. Leave box 5 blank and enter Code E in box 7.

Participants must report these amounts on the line for *Pensions and annuities* on Form 1040 or Form 1040A, *U.S. Individual Income Tax Return.*

## Employee Contributions

Participants may be permitted to make nondeductible contributions to a plan in addition to your contributions. Even though these employee contributions are not deductible, the earnings on them are tax free until distributed in later years. Also, these contributions must satisfy the nondiscrimination test of section 401(m). See Notice 98–1 for further guidance and transition relief relating to recent statutory amendments to the nondiscrimination rules under sections 401(k) and 401(m). Notice 98–1 is in Cumulative Bulletin 1998–1.

## Employer Deduction

You can usually deduct, subject to limits, contributions you make to a qualified plan, including those made for your own retirement. The contributions (and earnings and gains on them) are generally tax free until distributed by the plan.

### Deduction Limits

The deduction limit for your contributions to a qualified plan depends on the kind of plan you have.

**Defined contribution plans.** The deduction for contributions to a defined contribution plan (profit-sharing plan or money purchase pension plan) cannot be more than 25% of the compensation paid (or accrued) during the year to your eligible employees participating in the plan. If

you are self-employed, you must reduce this limit in figuring the deduction for contributions you make for your own account. See *Deduction Limit for Self-Employed Individuals*, later..

When figuring the deduction limit, the following rules apply.

- Elective deferrals (discussed later) are not subject to the limit.

- Compensation includes elective deferrals.

- The maximum compensation that can be taken into account for each employee is $200,000.

**Defined benefit plans.** The deduction for contributions to a defined benefit plan is based on actuarial assumptions and computations. Consequently, an actuary must figure your deduction limit.

⚠ **CAUTION** *In figuring the deduction for contributions, you cannot take into account any contributions or benefits that are more than the limits discussed earlier under* Limits on Contributions and Benefits. *However, for plan years beginning in 2002 and later years, your deduction for contributions to a defined benefit plan can be as much as the plan's unfunded current liability.*

**Deduction limit for multiple plans.** If you contribute to both a defined contribution plan and a defined benefit plan and at least one employee is covered by both plans, your deduction for those contributions is limited. Your deduction cannot be more than the greater of the following amounts.

- 25% of the compensation paid (or accrued) during the year to your eligible employees participating in the plan. If you are self-employed, you must reduce this 25% limit in figuring the deduction for contributions you make for your own account.

- Your contributions to the defined benefit plans, but not more than the amount needed to meet the year's minimum funding standard for any of these plans.

This limit does not apply if contributions to the defined contribution plan consist only of elective deferrals.

⚠ **CAUTION** *For this rule, a SEP is treated as a separate profit-sharing (defined contribution) plan.*

## Deduction Limit for Self-Employed Individuals

If you make contributions for yourself, you need to make a special computation to figure your maximum deduction for these contributions. Compensation is your net earnings from self-employment, defined in chapter 1. This nition takes into account both the following items.

- The deduction for one-half of your self-employment tax.

- The deduction for contributions on your behalf to the plan.

The deduction for your own contributions and your net earnings depend on each other. For this reason, you determine the deduction for your own contributions indirectly by reducing the contribution rate called for in your plan. To do this, use either the *Rate Table for Self-Employed* or the *Rate Worksheet for Self-Employed* in chapter 5. Then figure your maximum deduction by using the *Deduction Worksheet for Self-Employed* in chapter 5.

**Multiple plans.** The deduction limit for multiple plans (discussed earlier) also applies to contributions you make as an employer on your own behalf.

## Where To Deduct Contributions

Deduct the contributions you make for your common-law employees on your tax return. For example, sole proprietors deduct them on Schedule C (Form 1040), *Profit or Loss From Business,* or Schedule F (Form 1040), *Profit or Loss From Farming,* partnerships deduct them on Form 1065, *U.S. Return of Partnership Income,* and corporations deduct them on Form 1120, *U.S. Corporation Income Tax Return,* Form 1120–A, *U.S. Corporation Short-Form Income Tax Return,* or Form 1120S, *U.S. Income Tax Return for an S Corporation.*

Sole proprietors and partners deduct contributions for themselves on line 31 of Form 1040, *U.S. Individual Income Tax Return.* (If you are a partner, contributions for yourself are shown on the Schedule K-1 (Form 1065), *Partner's Share of Income, Credits, Deductions, etc.,* you get from the partnership.)

Table 4–1. **Carryover of Excess Contributions Illustrated—Profit-Sharing Plan (000's omitted)**

| Year | Participants' Compensation | Participants' share of required contribution (10% of annual profit) | Deductible limit for current year (15% of compensation)[1] | Contribution | Excess contribution carryover used[2] | Total deduction including carryovers | Excess contribution carryover available at end of year |
|---|---|---|---|---|---|---|---|
| 1999 . . . . . . . | $1,000 | $100 | $150 | $100 | $ 0 | $100 | $ 0 |
| 2000 . . . . . . . | 400 | 125 | 60 | 125 | 0 | 60 | 65 |
| 2001 . . . . . . . | 500 | 50 | 75 | 50 | 25 | 75 | 40 |
| 2002 . . . . . . . | 600 | 100 | 150 | 100 | 40 | 140 | 0 |

[1]25% for 2002 and later years.
[2]There were no carryovers from years before 1999.

## Carryover of Excess Contributions

If you contribute more to the plans than you can deduct for the year, you can carry over and deduct the difference in later years, combined with your contributions for those years. Your combined deduction in a later year is limited to 25% of the participating employees' compensation for that year. For purposes of this limit, a SEP is treated as a profit-sharing (defined contribution) plan. However, this percentage limit must be reduced to figure your maximum deduction for contributions you make for yourself. See *Deduction Limit for Self-Employed Individuals*, earlier. The amount you carry over and deduct may be subject to the excise tax discussed next.

*Table 4–1* illustrates the carryover of excess contributions to a profit-sharing plan.

## Excise Tax for Nondeductible (Excess) Contributions

If you contribute more than your deduction limit to a retirement plan, you have made nondeductible contributions and you may be liable for an excise tax. In general, a 10% excise tax applies to nondeductible contributions made to qualified pension and profit-sharing plans and to SEPs.

**Special rule for self-employed individuals.** The 10% excise tax does not apply to any contribution made to meet the minimum funding requirements in a money purchase pension plan or a defined benefit plan. Even if that contribution is more than your earned income from the trade or business for which the plan is set up, the difference is not subject to this excise tax. See *Minimum Funding Requirement*, earlier.

**Exceptions.** The following exceptions may enable you to choose not to take certain nondeductible contributions into account when figuring the 10% excise tax.

*Contributions to one or more defined contribution plans.* If contributions to one or more defined contribution plans are not deductible only because they are more than the combined plan deduction limit, the 10% excise tax does not apply to the extent the difference is not more than the greater of the following amounts.

- 6% of the participants' compensation (including elective deferrals) for the year.

- The sum of employer matching contributions and the elective deferrals to a 401(k) plan.

*Defined benefit plan exception.* For years beginning after 2001, in figuring the 10% excise tax, you can choose not to take into account as nondeductible contributions for any year contributions to a defined benefit plan that are not more than the full funding limit figured without considering the current liability limit. Apply the overall limits on deductible contributions first to contributions to defined contribution plans and then to contributions to defined benefit plans. If you use this new exception, you cannot also use the exception discussed above under *Contributions to one or more defined contribution plans.*

**Reporting the tax.** You must report the tax on your nondeductible contributions on *Form 5330*.

Form 5330 includes a computation of the tax. See the separate instructions for completing the form.

## Elective Deferrals (401(k) Plans)

Your qualified plan can include a cash or deferred arrangement under which participants can choose to have you contribute part of their before-tax compensation to the plan rather than receive the compensation in cash. A plan with this type of arrangement is popularly known as a "401(k) plan." (As a self-employed individual participating in the plan, you can contribute part of your before-tax net earnings from the business.) This contribution is called an "elective deferral" because participants choose (elect) to set aside the money, and they defer the tax on the money until it is distributed to them.

In general, a qualified plan can include a cash or deferred arrangement only if the qualified plan is one of the following plans.

- A profit-sharing plan.

- A money purchase pension plan in existence on June 27, 1974, that included a salary reduction arrangement on that date.

**Automatic enrollment in a 401(k) plan.** Your 401(k) plan can have an automatic enrollment feature. Under this feature, you can automatically reduce an employee's pay by a fixed percentage and contribute that amount to the 401(k) plan on his or her behalf unless the employee affirmatively chooses not to have his or her pay reduced or chooses to have it reduced by a different percentage. These contributions qualify as elective deferrals. For more information about 401(k) plans with an automatic enrollment feature, see Revenue Ruling 2000–8 in Cumulative Bulletin 2000–1.

**Partnership.** A partnership can have a 401(k) plan.

**Restriction on conditions of participation.** The plan cannot require, as a condition of participation, that an employee complete more than 1 year of service.

**Matching contributions.** If your plan permits, you can make matching contributions for an employee who makes an elective deferral to your 401(k) plan. For example, the plan might provide that you will contribute 50 cents for each dollar your participating employees choose to defer under your 401(k) plan.

**Nonelective contributions.** You can, under a qualified 401(k) plan, also make contributions (other than matching contributions) for your participating employees without giving them the choice to take cash instead.

**Employee compensation limit.** No more than $200,000 of the employee's compensation can be taken into account when figuring contributions. (чок?)

**SIMPLE 401(k) plan.** If you had 100 or fewer employees who earned $5,000 or more in compensation during the preceding year, you may be able to set up a SIMPLE 401(k) plan. A

SIMPLE 401(k) plan is not subject to the nondiscrimination and top-heavy plan requirements discussed later under *Qualification Rules*. For details about SIMPLE 401(k) plans, see *SIMPLE 401(k) Plan* in chapter 3.

## Limit on Elective Deferrals

There is a limit on the amount an employee can defer each year under these plans. This limit applies without regard to community property laws. Your plan must provide that your employees cannot defer more than the limit that applies for a particular year. For 2002, the basic limit on elective deferrals is $11,000. (For 2003, this limit increases to $12,000.) If, in conjunction with other plans, the deferral limit is exceeded, the difference is included in the employee's gross income.

**Catch-up contributions.** Beginning in 2002, a 401(k) plan can permit participants who are age 50 or over at the end of the calendar year to also make catch-up contributions. The catch-up contribution limit for 2002 is $1,000 ($2,000 for 2003). Elective deferrals are not treated as catch-up contributions for 2002 until they exceed the $11,000 limit, the ADP test limit of Internal Revenue Code section 401(k)(3), or the plan limit (if any). However, the catch-up contribution a participant can make for a year cannot exceed the lesser of the following amounts.

- The catch-up contribution limit.

- The excess of the participant's compensation over the elective deferrals that are not catch-up contributions.

**Self-employed individual's matching contributions.** Matching contributions to a 401(k) plan on behalf of a self-employed individual are not subject to the limit on elective deferrals. These matching contributions receive the same treatment as the matching contributions for other employees.

**Treatment of contributions.** Your contributions to a 401(k) plan are generally deductible by you and tax free to participating employees until distributed from the plan. Participating employees have a nonforfeitable right to the accrued benefit resulting from these contributions. Deferrals are included in wages for social security, Medicare, and federal unemployment (FUTA) tax.

**Reporting on Form W–2.** You must report the total amount deferred in boxes 3, 5, and 12 of your employee's Form W–2. See the Form W–2 instructions.

## Treatment of Excess Deferrals

If the total of an employee's deferrals is more than the limit for 2002, the employee can have the difference (called an excess deferral) paid out of any of the plans that permit these distributions. He or she must notify the plan by April 15, 2003 (or an earlier date specified in the plan), of the amount to be paid from each plan. The plan must then pay the employee that amount by April 15, 2003.

**Excess withdrawn by April 15.** If the employee takes out the excess deferral by April 15,

2003, it is not reported again by including it in the employee's gross income for 2003. However, any income earned on the excess deferral taken out is taxable in the tax year in which it is taken out. The distribution is not subject to the additional 10% tax on early distributions.

If the employee takes out part of the excess deferral and the income on it, the distribution is treated as made proportionately from the excess deferral and the income.

Even if the employee takes out the excess deferral by April 15, the amount is considered contributed for satisfying (or not satisfying) the nondiscrimination requirements of the plan, unless the distributed amount is for a non-highly compensated employee who participates in only one employer's 401(k) plan or plans. See *Contributions or benefits must not discriminate*, later, under *Qualification Rules*.

**Excess not withdrawn by April 15.** If the employee does not take out the excess deferral by April 15, 2003, the excess, though taxable in 2002, is not included in the employee's cost basis in figuring the taxable amount of any eventual benefits or distributions under the plan. In effect, an excess deferral left in the plan is taxed twice, once when contributed and again when distributed. Also, if the entire deferral is allowed to stay in the plan, the plan may not be a qualified plan.

**Reporting corrective distributions on Form 1099–R.** Report corrective distributions of excess deferrals (including any earnings) on Form 1099–R. For specific information about reporting corrective distributions, see the *Instructions for Forms 1099, 1098, 5498, and W–2G.*

**Tax on excess contributions of highly compensated employees.** The law provides tests to detect discrimination in a plan. If tests, such as the actual deferral percentage test (ADP test) (see section 401(k)(3)) and the actual contribution percentage test (ACP test) (see section 401(m)(2)), show that contributions for highly compensated employees are more than the test limits for these contributions, the employer may have to pay a 10% excise tax. Report the tax on *Form 5330.*

The tax for the year is 10% of the excess contributions for the plan year ending in your tax year. Excess contributions are elective deferrals, employee contributions, or employer matching or nonelective contributions that are more than the amount permitted under the ADP test or the ACP test.

See Notice 98–1 for further guidance and transition relief relating to recent statutory amendments to the nondiscrimination rules under sections 401(k) and 401(m). Notice 98–1 is in Cumulative Bulletin 1998–1.

# Distributions

Amounts paid to plan participants from a qualified plan are called distributions. Distributions may be nonperiodic, such as lump-sum distributions, or periodic, such as annuity payments. Also, certain loans may be treated as distributions. See *Loans Treated as Distributions* in Publication 575.

# Required Distributions

A qualified plan must provide that each participant will either:

- Receive his or her entire interest (benefits) in the plan by the required beginning date (defined later), or
- Begin receiving regular periodic distributions by the required beginning date in annual amounts calculated to distribute the participant's entire interest (benefits) over his or her life expectancy or over the joint life expectancy of the participant and the designated beneficiary (or over a shorter period).

These distribution rules apply individually to each qualified plan. You cannot satisfy the requirement for one plan by taking a distribution from another. The plan must provide that these rules override any inconsistent distribution options previously offered.

**Minimum distribution.** If the account balance of a qualified plan participant is to be distributed (other than as an annuity), the plan administrator must figure the minimum amount required to be distributed each distribution calendar year. This minimum is figured by dividing the account balance by the applicable life expectancy. For details on figuring the minimum distribution, see *Tax on Excess Accumulation* in Publication 575.

*Minimum distribution incidental benefit requirement.* Minimum distributions must also meet the minimum distribution incidental benefit requirement. This requirement ensures the plan is used primarily to provide retirement benefits to the employee. After the employee's death, only "incidental" benefits are expected to remain for distribution to the employee's beneficiary (or beneficiaries). For more information about other distribution requirements, see Publication 575.

**Required beginning date.** Generally, each participant must receive his or her entire benefits in the plan or begin to receive periodic distributions of benefits from the plan by the required beginning date.

A participant must begin to receive distributions from his or her qualified retirement plan by April 1 of the first year after the later of the following years.

1) Calendar year in which he or she reaches age 70½.

2) Calendar year in which he or she retires.

However, the plan may require the participant to begin receiving distributions by April 1 of the year after the participant reaches age 70½ even if the participant has not retired.

If the participant is a 5% owner of the employer maintaining the plan or if the distribution is from a traditional or SIMPLE IRA, the participant must begin receiving distributions by April 1 of the first year after the calendar year in which the participant reached age 70½. For more information, see *Tax on Excess Accumulation* in Publication 575.

*Distributions after the starting year.* The distribution required to be made by April 1 is treated as a distribution for the starting year. (The starting year is the year in which the participant meets (1) or (2) above, whichever applies.)

After the starting year, the partici[pant must] receive the required distribution for [each year by] December 31 of that year. If no [distribution is] made in the starting year, require[d distributions] for 2 years must be made in the n[ext year, one] by April 1 and one by December 3[1.]

*Distributions after participant's death.* See Publication 575 for the special rules covering distributions made after the death of a participant.

# Distributions From 401(k) Plans

Generally, distributions cannot be made until one of the following occurs.

- The employee retires, dies, becomes disabled, or otherwise severs employment.
- The plan ends and no other defined contribution plan is established or continued.
- In the case of a 401(k) plan that is part of a profit-sharing plan, the employee reaches age 59½ or suffers financial hardship. For the rules on hardship distributions, including the limits on them, see section 1.401(k)–1(d)(2) of the regulations.

 *Certain distributions listed above may be subject to the tax on early distributions discussed later.*

**Qualified domestic relations order (QDRO).** These distribution restrictions do not apply if the distribution is to an alternate payee under the terms of a QDRO, which is defined in Publication 575.

# Tax Treatment of Distributions

Distributions from a qualified plan minus a pro-rated part of any cost basis are subject to income tax in the year they are distributed. Since most recipients have no cost basis, a distribution is generally fully taxable. An exception is a distribution that is properly rolled over as discussed next under *Rollover.*

The tax treatment of distributions depends on whether they are made periodically over several years or life (periodic distributions) or are nonperiodic distributions. See *Taxation of Periodic Payments* and *Taxation of Nonperiodic Payments* in Publication 575 for a detailed description of how distributions are taxed, including the 10-year tax option or capital gain treatment of a lump-sum distribution.

**Rollover.** The recipient of an eligible rollover distribution from a qualified plan can defer the tax on it by rolling it over into a traditional IRA or another eligible retirement plan. However, it may be subject to withholding as discussed under *Withholding requirement,* later.

*Eligible rollover distribution.* This is a distribution of all or any part of an employee's balance in a qualified retirement plan that is not any of the following.

1) A required minimum distribution. See *Required Distributions,* earlier.

2) Any of a series of substantially equal payments made at least once a year over any of the following periods.

   a) The employee's life or life expectancy.

   b) The joint lives or life expectancies of the employee and beneficiary.

   c) A period of 10 years or longer.

3) A hardship distribution.

4) The portion of a distribution that represents the return of an employee's nondeductible contributions to the plan. See *Employee Contributions*, earlier. Also, see the *Tip* below.

5) A corrective distribution of excess contributions or deferrals under a 401(k) plan and any income allocable to the excess, or of excess annual additions and any allocable gains. See *Correcting excess annual additions*, earlier, under *Limits on Contributions and Benefits*.

6) Loans treated as distributions.

7) Dividends on employer securities.

8) The cost of life insurance coverage.

**TIP** *A distribution of the employee's nondeductible contributions may qualify as a rollover distribution. The transfer must be made either (1) through a direct rollover to a defined contribution plan that separately accounts for the taxable and nontaxable parts of the rollover or (2) through a rollover to a traditional IRA.*

**More information.** For more information about rollovers, see *Rollovers* in Publications 575 and 590.

**Withholding requirement.** If, during a year, a qualified plan pays to a participant one or more eligible rollover distributions (defined earlier) that are reasonably expected to total $200 or more, the payor must withhold 20% of each distribution for federal income tax.

**Exceptions.** If, instead of having the distribution paid to him or her, the participant chooses to have the plan pay it directly to an IRA or another eligible retirement plan (a *direct rollover*), no withholding is required.

If the distribution is not an eligible rollover distribution, defined earlier, the 20% withholding requirement does not apply. Other withholding rules apply to distributions such as long-term periodic distributions and required distributions (periodic or nonperiodic). However, the participant can still choose not to have tax withheld from these distributions. If the participant does not make this choice, the following withholding rules apply.

- For periodic distributions, withholding is based on their treatment as wages.

- For nonperiodic distributions, 10% of the taxable part is withheld.

**Estimated tax payments.** If no income tax is withheld or not enough tax is withheld, the recipient of a distribution may have to make estimated tax payments. For more information,

see *Withholding Tax and Estimated Tax* in Publication 575.

## Tax on Early Distributions

If a distribution is made to an employee under the plan before he or she reaches age 59½, the employee may have to pay a 10% additional tax on the distribution. This tax applies to the amount received that the employee must include in income.

**Exceptions.** The 10% tax will not apply if distributions before age 59½ are made in any of the following circumstances.

- Made to a beneficiary (or to the estate of the employee) on or after the death of the employee.

- Made due to the employee having a qualifying disability.

- Made as part of a series of substantially equal periodic payments beginning after separation from service and made at least annually for the life or life expectancy of the employee or the joint lives or life expectancies of the employee and his or her designated beneficiary. (The payments under this exception, except in the case of death or disability, must continue for at least 5 years or until the employee reaches age 59½, whichever is the longer period.)

- Made to an employee after separation from service if the separation occurred during or after the calendar year in which the employee reached age 55.

- Made to an alternate payee under a qualified domestic relations order (QDRO).

- Made to an employee for medical care up to the amount allowable as a medical expense deduction (determined without regard to whether the employee itemizes deductions).

- Timely made to reduce excess contributions under a 401(k) plan.

- Timely made to reduce excess employee or matching employer contributions (excess aggregate contributions).

- Timely made to reduce excess elective deferrals.

- Made because of an IRS levy on the plan.

**Reporting the tax.** To report the tax on early distributions, file *Form 5329, Additional Taxes on Qualified Plans (Including IRAs) and Other Tax-Favored Accounts*. See the form instructions for additional information about this tax.

## Tax on Excess Benefits

If you are or have been a 5% owner of the business maintaining the plan, amounts you receive at any age that are more than the benefits provided for you under the plan formula are subject to an additional tax. This tax also applies to amounts received by your successor. The tax is 10% of the excess benefit includible in income.

**5% owner.** You are a 5% owner if you meet either of the following conditions at any during the 5 plan years immediately before the plan year that ends within the tax year you receive the distribution.

- You own more than 5% of the capital or profits interest in the employer.

- You own or are considered to own more than 5% of the outstanding stock (or more than 5% of the total voting power of all stock) of the employer.

**Reporting the tax.** Include on Form 1040, line 61, any tax you owe for an excess benefit. On the dotted line next to the total, write "Sec. 72(m)(5)" and write in the amount.

**Lump-sum distribution.** The amount subject to the additional tax is not eligible for the optional methods of figuring income tax on a lump-sum distribution. The optional methods are discussed under *Lump-Sum Distributions* in Publication 575.

## Excise Tax on Reversion of Plan Assets

A 20% or 50% excise tax is generally imposed on the cash and fair market value of other property an employer receives directly or indirectly from a qualified plan. If you owe this tax, report it in Part XIII of *Form 5330*. See the form instructions for more information.

## Notification of Significant Benefit Accrual Reduction

For plan amendments taking effect after June 6, 2001, the employer or the plan will have to pay an excise tax if both the following occur.

- A defined benefit plan or money purchase pension plan is amended to provide for a significant reduction in the rate of future benefit accrual.

- The plan administrator fails to notify the affected individuals and the employee organizations representing them of the reduction in writing. Affected individuals are the participants and alternate payees whose rate of benefit accrual under the plan may reasonably be expected to be significantly reduced by the amendment.

A plan amendment that eliminates or reduces any early retirement benefit or retirement-type subsidy reduces the rate of future benefit accrual.

The notice must be written in a manner calculated to be understood by the average plan participant and must provide enough information to allow each individual to understand the effect of the plan amendment. It must be provided within a reasonable time before the amendment takes effect or September 7, 2001, whichever is later.

The tax is $100 per participant or alternate payee for each day the notice is late. It is imposed on the employer, or, in the case of a multi-employer plan, on the plan.

There are certain exceptions ¹ tions on, the tax. The tax does not ₂ the following situations.

- The amendment takes effect after June 6, 2001, and notice was provided before April 25, 2001, to participants and beneficiaries adversely affected by the amendment (or their representatives) to notify them of the nature and effective date of the amendment.

- The person liable for the tax was unaware of the failure and exercised reasonable diligence to meet the notice requirements.

- The person liable for the tax exercised reasonable diligence to meet the notice requirements and provided the notice within 30 days starting on the first date the person knew or should have known that the failure to provide notice existed.

If the person liable for the tax exercised reasonable diligence to meet the notice requirement, the tax cannot be more than $500,000 during the tax year. The tax can also be waived to the extent it would be excessive or unfair if the failure is due to reasonable cause and not to willful neglect.

# Prohibited Transactions

Prohibited transactions are transactions between the plan and a *disqualified person* that are prohibited by law. (However, see *Exemption*, later.) If you are a disqualified person who takes part in a prohibited transaction, you must pay a tax (discussed later).

Prohibited transactions generally include the following transactions.

1) A transfer of plan income or assets to, or use of them by or for the benefit of, a disqualified person.

2) Any act of a fiduciary by which he or she deals with plan income or assets in his or her own interest.

3) The receipt of consideration by a fiduciary for his or her own account from any party dealing with the plan in a transaction that involves plan income or assets.

4) Any of the following acts between the plan and a disqualified person.

   a) Selling, exchanging, or leasing property.

   b) Lending money or extending credit.

   c) Furnishing goods, services, or facilities.

**Exemption.** Certain transactions are exempt from being treated as prohibited transactions. For example, a prohibited transaction does not take place if you are a disqualified person and receive any benefit to which you are entitled as a plan participant or beneficiary. However, the benefit must be figured and paid under the same terms as for all other participants and beneficiaries. For other transactions that are exempt, see section 4975 and the related regulations.

**Disqualified person.** You are a disqualified person if you are any of the following.

1) A fiduciary of the plan.

2) A person providing services to the plan.

3) An employer, any of whose employees are covered by the plan.

4) An employee organization, any of whose members are covered by the plan.

5) Any direct or indirect owner of 50% or more of any of the following.

   a) The combined voting power of all classes of stock entitled to vote, or the total value of shares of all classes of stock of a corporation that is an employer or employee organization described in (3) or (4).

   b) The capital interest or profits interest of a partnership that is an employer or employee organization described in (3) or (4).

   c) The beneficial interest of a trust or unincorporated enterprise that is an employer or an employee organization described in (3) or (4).

6) A member of the family of any individual described in (1), (2), (3), or (5). (A member of a family is the spouse, ancestor, lineal descendant, or any spouse of a lineal descendant.)

7) A corporation, partnership, trust, or estate of which (or in which) any direct or indirect owner described in (1) through (5) holds 50% or more of any of the following.

   a) The combined voting power of all classes of stock entitled to vote or the total value of shares of all classes of stock of a corporation.

   b) The capital interest or profits interest of a partnership.

   c) The beneficial interest of a trust or estate.

8) An officer, director (or an individual having powers or responsibilities similar to those of officers or directors), a 10% or more shareholder, or highly compensated employee (earning 10% or more of the yearly wages of an employer) of a person described in (3), (4), (5), or (7).

9) A 10% or more (in capital or profits) partner or joint venturer of a person described in (3), (4), (5), or (7).

10) Any disqualified person, as described in (1) through (9) above, who is a disqualified person with respect to any plan to which a section 501(c)(22) trust is permitted to make payments under section 4223 of ERISA.

## Tax on Prohibited Transactions

The initial tax on a prohibited transaction is 15% of the amount involved for each year (or part of a year) in the taxable period. If the transaction is not corrected within the taxable period, an additional tax of 100% of the amount involved is imposed. For information on correcting the transaction, see *Correcting a prohibited transaction*, later.

Both taxes are payable by any disqualified person who participated in the transaction (other than a fiduciary acting only as such). If more than one person takes part in the transaction, each person can be jointly and severally liable for the entire tax.

**Amount involved.** The amount involved in a prohibited transaction is the greater of the following amounts.

- The money and fair market value of any property given.

- The money and fair market value of any property received.

If services are performed, the amount involved is any excess compensation given or received.

**Taxable period.** The taxable period starts on the transaction date and ends on the earliest of the following days.

- The day the IRS mails a notice of deficiency for the tax.

- The day the IRS assesses the tax.

- The day the correction of the transaction is completed.

**Payment of the 15% tax.** Pay the 15% tax with *Form 5330.*

**Correcting a prohibited transaction.** If you are a disqualified person who participated in a prohibited transaction, you can avoid the 100% tax by correcting the transaction as soon as possible. Correcting the transaction means undoing it as much as you can without putting the plan in a worse financial position than if you had acted under the highest fiduciary standards.

*Correction period.* If the prohibited transaction is not corrected during the taxable period, you usually have an additional 90 days after the day the IRS mails a notice of deficiency for the 100% tax to correct the transaction. This correction period (the taxable period plus the 90 days) can be extended if either of the following occurs.

- The IRS grants reasonable time needed to correct the transaction.

- You petition the Tax Court.

If you correct the transaction within this period, the IRS will abate, credit, or refund the 100% tax.

# Reporting Requirements

You may have to file an annual return/report form by the last day of the 7th month after the plan year ends. See the following list of forms to choose the right form for your plan.

**Form 5500-EZ.** You can use Form 5500-EZ if the plan meets all the following conditions.

- The plan is a one-participant plan, defined below.

- The plan meets the minimum coverage requirements of section 410(b) without being combined with any other plan you may have that covers other employees of your business.

- The plan only provides benefits for you, you and your spouse, or one or more partners and their spouses.

- The plan does not cover a business that is a member of an affiliated service group, a controlled group of corporations, or a group of businesses under common control.

- The plan does not cover a business that leases employees.

**One-participant plan.** Your plan is a one-participant plan if either of the following is true.

- The plan covers only you (or you and your spouse) and you (or you and your spouse) own the entire business (whether incorporated or unincorporated).

- The plan covers only one or more partners (or partner(s) and spouse(s)) in a business partnership.

**Form 5500–EZ not required.** You do not have to file Form 5500–EZ (or Form 5500) if you meet the conditions mentioned above and either of the following conditions.

- You have a one-participant plan that had total plan assets of $100,000 or less at the end of every plan year beginning after December 31, 1993.

- You have two or more one-participant plans that together had total plan assets of $100,000 or less at the end of every plan year beginning after December 31, 1993.

**Example.** You are a sole proprietor and your plan meets all the conditions for filing Form 5500–EZ. The total plan assets are more than $100,000. You should file Form 5500–EZ.

 All one-participant plans must file Form 5500–EZ for their final plan year, even if the total plan assets have always been less than $100,000. The final plan year is the year in which distribution of all plan assets is completed.

**Form 5500.** If you do not meet the requirements for filing Form 5500–EZ, you must file Form 5500.

**Schedule A (Form 5500).** If any plan benefits are provided by an insurance company, insurance service, or similar organization, complete and attach Schedule A (Form 5500) to Form 5500. Schedule A is not needed for a plan that covers only one of the following.

1) An individual or an individual and spouse who wholly own the trade or business, whether incorporated or unincorporated.

2) Partners in a partnership or the partners and their spouses.

 Do not file a Schedule A (Form 5500) with a Form 5500–EZ.

**Schedule B (Form 5500).** For most defined benefit plans, complete and attach Schedule B (Form 5500), *Actuarial Information*, to Form 5500 or Form 5500–EZ.

**Schedule P (Form 5500).** This schedule is used by a fiduciary (trustee or custodian) of a trust described in section 401(a) or a custodial account described in section 401(f) to protect it under the statute of limitations provided in section 6501(a). The filing of a completed Schedule P (Form 5500), *Annual Return of Fiduciary of Employee Benefit Trust*, by the fiduciary satisfies the annual filing requirement under section 6033(a) for the trust or custodial account created as part of a qualified plan. This filing starts the running of the 3-year limitation period that applies to the trust or custodial account. For this protection, the trust or custodial account must qualify under section 401(a) and be exempt from tax under section 501(a). The fiduciary should file, under section 6033(a), a Schedule P as an attachment to Form 5500 or Form 5500–EZ for the plan year in which the trust year ends. The fiduciary cannot file Schedule P separately. See the *Instructions for Form 5500* for more information.

**Form 5310.** If you terminate your plan and are the plan sponsor or plan administrator, you can file **Form 5310,** *Application for Determination for Terminating Plan.* Your application must be accompanied by the appropriate user fee and **Form 8717,** *User Fee for Employee Plan Determination Letter Request.*

**More information.** For more information about reporting requirements, see the forms and their instructions.

# Qualification Rules

To qualify for the tax benefits available to qualified plans, a plan must meet certain requirements (qualification rules) of the tax law. Generally, unless you write your own plan, the financial institution that provided your plan will take the continuing responsibility for meeting qualification rules that are later changed. The following is a brief overview of important qualification rules that generally have not yet been discussed. It is not intended to be all-inclusive. See *Setting Up a Qualified Plan,* earlier.

 Generally, the following qualification rules also apply to a SIMPLE 401(k) retirement plan. A SIMPLE 401(k) plan is, however, not subject to the top-heavy plan rules and nondiscrimination rules if the plan satisfies the provisions discussed in chapter 3 under SIMPLE 401(k) Plan.

**Plan assets must not be diverted.** Your plan must make it impossible for its assets to be used for, or diverted to, purposes other than the benefit of employees and their beneficiaries. As a general rule, the assets cannot be diverted to the employer.

**Minimum coverage requirement must be met.** To be a qualified plan, a defined benefit plan must benefit at least the lesser of the following.

1) 50 employees.

2) The greater of:

   a) 40% of all employees, or

   b) Two employees.

If there is only one employee, the plan must benefit that employee.

**Contributions or benefits must not discriminate.** Under the plan, contributions or benefits to be provided must not discriminate in favor of highly compensated employees.

**Contributions and benefits must not be more than certain limits.** Your plan must not provide for contributions or benefits that are more than certain limits. The limits apply to the annual contributions and other additions to the account of a participant in a defined contribution plan and to the annual benefit payable to a participant in a defined benefit plan. These limits were discussed earlier under *Contributions.*

**Minimum vesting standard must be met.** Your plan must satisfy certain requirements regarding when benefits vest. A benefit is vested (you have a fixed right to it) when it becomes nonforfeitable. A benefit is nonforfeitable if it cannot be lost upon the happening, or failure to happen, of any event.

**Participation.** In general, an employee must be allowed to participate in your plan if he or she meets both the following requirements.

- Has reached age 21.

- Has at least 1 year of service (2 years if the plan is not a 401(k) plan and provides that after not more than 2 years of service the employee has a nonforfeitable right to all his or her accrued benefit).

 A plan cannot exclude an employee because he or she has reached a specified age.

**Leased employee.** A leased employee, defined in chapter 1, who performs services for you (recipient of the services) is treated as your employee for certain plan qualification rules. These rules include those in all the following areas.

- Nondiscrimination in coverage, contributions, and benefits.

- Minimum age and service requirements.

- Vesting.

- Limits on contributions and benefits.

- Top-heavy plan requirements.

Contributions or benefits provided by the leasing organization for services performed for you are treated as provided by you.

**Benefit payment must begin when required.** Your plan must provide that, unless the participant chooses otherwise, the payment of benefits to the participant must begin within 60 days after the close of the latest of the following periods.

215

- The plan year in which the participant reaches the earlier of age 65 or the normal retirement age specified in the plan.

- The plan year in which the 10th anniversary of the year in which the participant began participating in the plan occurs.

- The plan year in which the participant separates from service.

***Early retirement.*** Your plan can provide for payment of retirement benefits before the normal retirement age. If your plan offers an early retirement benefit, a participant who separates from service before satisfying the early retirement age requirement is entitled to that benefit if he or she meets both the following requirements.

- Satisfies the service requirement for the early retirement benefit.

- Separates from service with a nonforfeitable right to an accrued benefit. The benefit, which may be actuarially reduced, is payable when the early retirement age requirement is met.

**Survivor benefits.** Defined benefit and certain money purchase pension plans must provide automatic survivor benefits in both the following forms.

- A qualified joint and survivor annuity for a vested participant who does not die before the annuity starting date.

- A qualified pre-retirement survivor annuity for a vested participant who dies before the annuity starting date and who has a surviving spouse.

The automatic survivor benefit also applies to any participant under a profit-sharing plan unless all the following conditions are met.

- The participant does not choose benefits in the form of a life annuity.

- The plan pays the full vested account balance to the participant's surviving spouse (or other beneficiary if the surviving spouse consents or if there is no surviving spouse) if the participant dies.

- The plan is not a direct or indirect transferee of a plan that must provide automatic survivor benefits.

***Loan secured by benefits.*** If survivor benefits are required for a spouse under a plan, he or she must consent to a loan that uses as security the accrued benefits in the plan.

***Waiver of survivor benefits.*** Each plan participant may be permitted to waive the joint and survivor annuity or the pre-retirement survivor annuity (or both), but only if the participant has the written consent of the spouse. The plan also must allow the participant to withdraw the waiver. The spouse's consent must be witnessed by a plan representative or notary public.

***Waiver of 30-day waiting period before annuity starting date.*** A plan may permit a participant to waive (with spousal consent) the 30-day minimum waiting period after a written

explanation of the terms and conditions of a joint and survivor annuity is provided to each participant.

The waiver is allowed only if the distribution begins more than 7 days after the written explanation is provided.

***Involuntary cash-out of benefits not more than dollar limit.*** A plan may provide for the immediate distribution of the participant's benefit under the plan if the present value of the benefit is not greater than $5,000.

However, the distribution cannot be made after the annuity starting date unless the participant and the spouse (or surviving spouse of a participant who died) consent in writing to the distribution. If the present value is greater than $5,000, the plan must have the written consent of the participant and the spouse (or surviving spouse) for any immediate distribution of the benefit.

For distributions in 2002 and later years, benefits attributable to rollover contributions and earnings on them can be ignored in determining the present value of these benefits.

For distributions made after the Department of Labor adopts final regulations implementing rules on fiduciary responsibilities relating to this provision, a plan must provide for the automatic rollover of any distribution of more than $1,000 to an IRA under this provision, unless the participant chooses otherwise. The plan administrator must notify the participant in writing that the distribution can be transferred to another IRA.

**Consolidation, merger, or transfer of assets or liabilities.** Your plan must provide that, in the case of any merger or consolidation with, or transfer of assets or liabilities to, any other plan, each participant would (if the plan then terminated) receive a benefit equal to or more than the benefit he or she would have been entitled to just before the merger, etc. (if the plan had then terminated).

**Benefits must not be assigned or alienated.** Your plan must provide that its benefits cannot be assigned or alienated.

***Exception for certain loans.*** A loan from the plan (not from a third party) to a participant or beneficiary is not treated as an assignment or alienation if the loan is secured by the participant's accrued nonforfeitable benefit and is exempt from the tax on prohibited transactions under section 4975(d)(1) or would be exempt if the participant were a disqualified person. A disqualified person is defined earlier under *Prohibited Transactions*.

***Exception for qualified domestic relations order (QDRO).*** Compliance with a QDRO does not result in a prohibited assignment or alienation of benefits. QDRO is defined in Publication 575.

Payments to an alternate payee under a QDRO before the participant attains age 59½ are not subject to the 10% additional tax that would otherwise apply under certain circumstances. The interest of the alternate payee is not taken into account in determining whether a distribution to the participant is a lump-sum distribution. Benefits distributed to an alternate payee under a QDRO can be rolled over tax free to an individual retirement account or to an individual retirement annuity.

**No benefit reduction for social security increases.** Your plan must not permit a benefit reduction for a post-separation increase in the social security benefit level or wage base for any participant or beneficiary who is receiving benefits under your plan, or who is separated from service and has nonforfeitable rights to benefits. This rule also applies to plans supplementing the benefits provided by other federal or state laws.

**Elective deferrals must be limited.** If your plan provides for elective deferrals, it must limit those deferrals to the amount in effect for that particular year. See *Limit on Elective Deferrals*, earlier.

**Top-heavy plan requirements.** A top-heavy plan is one that mainly favors partners, sole proprietors, and other key employees.

A plan is top heavy for any plan year for which the total value of accrued benefits or account balances of key employees is more than 60% of the total value of accrued benefits or account balances of all employees. Additional requirements apply to a top-heavy plan primarily to provide minimum benefits or contributions for non-key employees covered by the plan.

Most qualified plans, whether or not top heavy, must contain provisions that meet the top-heavy requirements and will take effect in plan years in which the plans are top heavy. These qualification requirements for top-heavy plans are explained in section 416 and its regulations.

***SIMPLE 401(k) plan exception.*** The top-heavy plan requirements do not apply to SIMPLE 401(k) plans.

# 5.

# Table and Worksheets for the Self-Employed

As discussed in chapters 2 and 4, if you are self-employed, you must use the following rate table or rate worksheet and deduction worksheet to figure your deduction for contributions you made for yourself to a SEP-IRA or qualified plan.

First, use either the rate table or rate worksheet to find your reduced contribution rate. Then complete the deduction worksheet to figure your deduction for contributions.

⚠️ **CAUTION** *The table and the worksheets that follow apply only to self-employed individuals who have only one defined contribution plan, such as a profit-sharing plan. A SEP plan is treated as a profit-sharing plan. However, do not use this worksheet for SAR-SEPs.*

## Deduction Worksheet for Self-Employed

**Step 1**

Enter your net profit from line 31, Schedule C (Form 1040); line 3, Schedule C-EZ (Form 1040); line 36, Schedule F (Form 1040); or line 15a*, Schedule K-1 (Form 1065) . . . . . . . . . . . . . . . . . . . . . . . . . . . . . . . . . . . . . . . . _____

*General partners should reduce this amount by the same additional expenses subtracted from line 15a to determine the amount on line 1 or 2 of Schedule SE

**Step 2**

Enter your deduction for self-employment tax from line 29, Form 1040 . . . . . . _____

**Step 3**

Net earnings from self-employment. Subtract step 2 from step 1 . . . . . . . . . . . _____

**Step 4**

Enter your rate from the *Rate Table for Self-Employed* or *Rate Worksheet for Self-Employed* . . . . . . . . . . . . . . . . . . . . . . . . . . . . . . . . . . . . . . . . . . . . _____

**Step 5**

Multiply step 3 by step 4 . . . . . . . . . . . . . . . . . . . . . . . . . . . . . . _____

**Step 6**

Multiply $200,000 by your plan contribution rate (not the reduced rate) . . . . . . . _____

**Step 7**

Enter the **smaller** of step 5 or step 6 . . . . . . . . . . . . . . . . . . . . . . _____

**Step 8**

Contribution dollar limit . . . . . . . . . . . . . . . . . . . . . . . . . . . . . . . . . . . . $40,000

• **If you made any elective deferrals, go to step 9.**

• **Otherwise, skip steps 9 through 18 and enter the smaller of step 7 or step 8 on step 19.**

**Step 9**

Enter your allowable elective deferrals made during 2002. Do not enter more than $11,000 . . . . . . . . . . . . . . . . . . . . . . . . . . . . . . . . . . . . . . . . . . _____

**Step 10**

Subtract step 9 from step 8 . . . . . . . . . . . . . . . . . . . . . . . . . . . . . . _____

**Step 11**

Subtract step 9 from step 3 . . . . . . . . . . . . . . . . . . . . . . . _____

**Step 12**

Enter one-half of step 11 . . . . . . . . . . . . . . . . . . . . . . . . . . . . . . . _____

**Step 13**

Enter the **smallest** of step 7, 10, or 12 . . . . . . . . . . . . . . . . . . . . . _____

**Step 14**

Subtract step 13 from step 3 . . . . . . . . . . . . . . . . . . . . . . . . . . . . . _____

**Step 15**

Enter the **smaller** of step 9 or step 14 . . . . . . . . . . . . . . . . . . . . . _____

• **If you made catch-up contributions, go to step 16.**

• **Otherwise, skip steps 16 through 18 and go to step 19.**

**Step 16**

Subtract step 15 from step 14 . . . . . . . . . . . . . . . . . . . . . . . . . . . . _____

**Step 17**

Enter your catch-up contributions, if any. Do not enter more than $1,000 . . . . . . _____

**Step 18**

Enter the **smaller** of step 16 or step 17 . . . . . . . . . . . . . . . . . . . . . . . . _____

**Step 19**

Add steps 13, 15, and 18. This is your ***maximum deductible contribution*** . . . . _____

**Next:** Enter your deduction on line 31, Form 1040.

**Rate table for self-employed.** If your plan's contribution rate is a whole percentage (for example, 12% rather than 12½%), you can use the following table to find your reduced contribution rate. Otherwise, use the rate worksheet provided later.

First, find your plan contribution rate (the contribution rate stated in your plan) in *Column A* of the table. Then read across to the rate under *Column B*. Enter the rate from *Column B* in step 4 of the *Deduction Worksheet for Self-Employed*.

### Rate Table for Self-Employed

| Column A<br>If the plan contri-<br>bution rate is:<br>(shown as %) | Column B<br>Your<br>rate is:<br>(shown as decimal) |
|---|---|
| 1 . . . . . . . . . . . . . . | .009901 |
| 2 . . . . . . . . . . . . . . | .019608 |
| 3 . . . . . . . . . . . . . . | .029126 |
| 4 . . . . . . . . . . . . . . | .038462 |
| 5 . . . . . . . . . . . . . . | .047619 |
| 6 . . . . . . . . . . . . . . | .056604 |
| 7 . . . . . . . . . . . . . . | .065421 |
| 8 . . . . . . . . . . . . . . | .074074 |
| 9 . . . . . . . . . . . . . . | .082569 |
| 10 . . . . . . . . . . . . . . | .090909 |
| 11 . . . . . . . . . . . . . . | .099099 |
| 12 . . . . . . . . . . . . . . | .107143 |
| 13 . . . . . . . . . . . . . . | .115044 |
| 14 . . . . . . . . . . . . . . | .122807 |
| 15 . . . . . . . . . . . . . . | .130435 |
| 16 . . . . . . . . . . . . . . | .137931 |
| 17 . . . . . . . . . . . . . . | .145299 |
| 18 . . . . . . . . . . . . . . | .152542 |
| 19 . . . . . . . . . . . . . . | .159664 |
| 20 . . . . . . . . . . . . . . | .166667 |
| 21 . . . . . . . . . . . . . . | .173554 |
| 22 . . . . . . . . . . . . . . | .180328 |
| 23 . . . . . . . . . . . . . . | .186992 |
| 24 . . . . . . . . . . . . . . | .193548 |
| 25* . . . . . . . . . . . . . . | .200000* |

*The deduction for annual employer contributions (other than elective deferrals) to a SEP plan, a profit-sharing plan, or a money purchase plan, cannot be more than 20% of your net earnings (figured without deducting contributions for yourself) from the business that has the plan.

***Example.*** You are a sole proprietor with no employees. If your plan's contribution rate is 10% of a participant's compensation, your rate is 0.090909. Enter this rate in step 4 of the *Deduction Worksheet for Self-Employed*.

## Deduction Worksheet for Self-Employed

**Step 1**

Enter your net profit from line 31, Schedule C (Form 1040); line 3, Schedule C-EZ (Form 1040); line 36, Schedule F (Form 1040); or line 15a*, Schedule K-1 (Form 1065) . . . . . . . . . . . . . . . . . . . . . . . . . . . . . . . . . . . . . . . . . .  $200,000

*General partners should reduce this amount by the same additional expenses subtracted from line 15a to determine the amount on line 1 or 2 of Schedule SE

**Step 2**

Enter your deduction for self-employment tax from line 29, Form 1040 . . . . . .  7,942

**Step 3**

Net earnings from self-employment. Subtract step 2 from step 1 . . . . . . . . . . .  192,058

**Step 4**

Enter your rate from the *Rate Table for Self-Employed* or *Rate Worksheet for Self-Employed* . . . . . . . . . . . . . . . . . . . . . . . . . . . . . . . . . . . . . . . . . . .  0.078

**Step 5**

Multiply step 3 by step 4 . . . . . . . . . . . . . . . . . . . . . . . . . . . . . . . . . . . . .  14,981

**Step 6**

Multiply $200,000 by your plan contribution rate (not the reduced rate) . . . . . . .  17,000

**Step 7**

Enter the **smaller** of step 5 or step 6 . . . . . . . . . . . . . . . . . . . . . . . . . . . .  14,981

**Step 8**

Contribution dollar limit . . . . . . . . . . . . . . . . . . . . . . . . . . . . . . . . . . . . . . .  $40,000

- **If you made any elective deferrals, go to step 9.**
- **Otherwise, skip steps 9 through 18 and enter the smaller of step 7 or step 8 on step 19.**

**Step 9**

Enter your allowable elective deferrals made during 2002. Do not enter more than $11,000 . . . . . . . . . . . . . . . . . . . . . . . . . . . . . . . . . . . . . . . . . . . . . .  _____

**Step 10**

Subtract step 9 from step 8 . . . . . . . . . . . . . . . . . . . . . . . . . . . . . . . . . . . .  _____

**Step 11**

Subtract step 9 from step 3 . . . . . . . . . . . . . . . . . . . . . . . . . . . . . . . . . . . .  _____

**Step 12**

Enter one-half of step 11 . . . . . . . . . . . . . . . . . . . . . . . . . . . . . . . . . . . . . .  _____

**Step 13**

Enter the **smallest** of step 7, 10, or 12 . . . . . . . . . . . . . . . . . . . . . . . . . . .  _____

**Step 14**

Subtract step 13 from step 3 . . . . . . . . . . . . . . . . . . . . . . . . . . . . . . . . . . .  _____

**Step 15**

Enter the **smaller** of step 9 or step 14 . . . . . . . . . . . . . . . . . . . . . . . . . . . .  _____

- **If you made catch-up contributions, go to step 16.**
- **Otherwise, skip steps 16 through 18 and go to step 19.**

**Step 16**

Subtract step 15 from step 14 . . . . . . . . . . . . . . . . . . . . . . . . . . . . . . . . . .  _____

**Step 17**

Enter your catch-up contributions, if any. Do not enter more than $1,000 . . . . . .  _____

**Step 18**

Enter the **smaller** of step 16 or step 17 . . . . . . . . . . . . . . . . . . . . . . . . . . .  _____

**Step 19**

Add steps 13, 15, and 18. This is your ***maximum deductible contribution*** . . . .  $14,981

**Next:** Enter your deduction on line 31, Form 1040.

---

**Rate worksheet for self-employed.** If your plan's contribution rate is not a whole percentage (for example, 10½%), you cannot use the *Rate Table for Self-Employed.* Use the following worksheet instead.

### Rate Worksheet for Self-Employed

1) Plan contribution rate as a decimal (for example, 10½% = 0.105) . . . .  _____
2) Rate in line 1 plus 1 (for example, 0.105 + 1 = 1.105) . . . . . . . . . . .  _____
3) Self-employed rate as a decimal rounded to at least 3 decimal places (line 1 ÷ line 2) . . . . . . . . . . . . .  ══════

**Figuring your deduction.** Now that you have your self-employed rate from either the rate table or rate worksheet, you can figure your maximum deduction for contributions for yourself by completing the *Deduction Worksheet for Self-Employed.*

***Community property laws.*** If you reside in a community property state and you are married and filing a separate return, disregard community property laws for step 1 of the *Deduction Worksheet for Self-Employed.* Enter on step 1 the total net profit you actually earned.

***Example.*** You are a sole proprietor with no employees. The terms of your plan provide that you contribute 8½% (.085) of your compensation to your plan. Your net profit from line 31, Schedule C (Form 1040) is $200,000. You have no elective deferrals or catch-up contributions. Your self-employment tax deduction on line 29 of Form 1040 is $7,942. See the filled-in portions of both Schedule SE (Form 1040), *Self-Employment Income,* and Form 1040, later.

You figure your self-employed rate and maximum deduction for employer contributions you made for yourself as follows.

### Rate Worksheet for Self-Employed

1) Plan contribution rate as a decimal (for example, 10½% = 0.105) . . . .  0.085
2) Rate in line 1 plus 1 (for example, 0.105 + 1 = 1.105) . . . . . . . . . . .  1.085
3) Self-employed rate as a decimal rounded to at least 3 decimal places (line 1 ÷ line 2) . . . . . . . . . . . . .  0.078

## Portion of Schedule SE (Form 1040)

**Section A—Short Schedule SE. Caution.** Read above to see if you can use Short Schedule SE.

| | | | |
|---|---|---|---|
| 1 | Net farm profit or (loss) from Schedule F, line 36, and farm partnerships, Schedule K-1 (Form 1065), line 15a . . . . . . . . . . . . . . . . . . . . . . | **1** | |
| 2 | Net profit or (loss) from Schedule C, line 31; Schedule C-EZ, line 3; Schedule K-1 (Form 1065), line 15a (other than farming); and Schedule K-1 (Form 1065-B), box 9. Ministers and members of religious orders, see page SE-1 for amounts to report on this line. See page SE-2 for other income to report . . . . . . . . . . . . . . . . . . . . . . . | **2** | 200,000 |
| 3 | Combine lines 1 and 2 . . . . . . . . . . . . . . . . . . . . . . | **3** | 200,000 |
| 4 | **Net earnings from self-employment.** Multiply line 3 by 92.35% (.9235). If less than $400, **do not** file this schedule; you do not owe self-employment tax . . . . . . . . . ▶ | **4** | 184,700 |
| 5 | **Self-employment tax.** If the amount on line 4 is:<br><br>• $84,900 or less, multiply line 4 by 15.3% (.153). Enter the result here and on **Form 1040, line 56.**<br>• More than $84,900, multiply line 4 by 2.9% (.029). Then, add $10,527.60 to the result. Enter the total here and on **Form 1040, line 56.** | **5** | 15,884 |
| 6 | **Deduction for one-half of self-employment tax.** Multiply line 5 by 50% (.5). Enter the result here and on **Form 1040, line 29** . . . . . | **6** | 7,942 |

For Paperwork Reduction Act Notice, see Form 1040 instructions.   Cat. No. 11358Z   Schedule SE (Form 1040) 2002

## Portion of Form 1040

| | | | | |
|---|---|---|---|---|
| **Adjusted Gross Income** | 23 | Educator expenses (see page 29) . . . . . . . | **23** | |
| | 24 | IRA deduction (see page 29) . . . . . . . . . | **24** | |
| | 25 | Student loan interest deduction (see page 31) . . . | **25** | |
| | 26 | Tuition and fees deduction (see page 32) . . . . | **26** | |
| | 27 | Archer MSA deduction. Attach Form 8853 . . . . | **27** | |
| | 28 | Moving expenses. Attach Form 3903 . . . . . . | **28** | |
| | 29 | One-half of self-employment tax. Attach Schedule SE . . | **29** | 7,942 |
| | 30 | Self-employed health insurance deduction (see page 33) | **30** | |
| | 31 | Self-employed SEP, SIMPLE, and qualified plans . . . | **31** | 14,981 |
| | 32 | Penalty on early withdrawal of savings . . . . . | **32** | |
| | 33a | Alimony paid   b Recipient's SSN ▶ | **33a** | |
| | 34 | Add lines 23 through 33a . . . . . . . . . . . | **34** | 22,923 |
| | 35 | Subtract line 34 from line 22. This is your **adjusted gross income** . . . . . . ▶ | **35** | |

For Disclosure, Privacy Act, and Paperwork Reduction Act Notice, see page 76.   Cat. No. 11320B   Form **1040** (2002)

# 6.

# How To Get Tax Help

You can get help with unresolved tax issues, order free publications and forms, ask tax questions, and get more information from the IRS in several ways. By selecting the method that is best for you, you will have quick and easy access to tax help.

**Contacting your Taxpayer Advocate.** If you have attempted to deal with an IRS problem unsuccessfully, you should contact your Taxpayer Advocate.

The Taxpayer Advocate represents your interests and concerns within the IRS by protecting your rights and resolving problems that have not been fixed through normal channels. While Taxpayer Advocates cannot change the tax law or make a technical tax decision, they can clear up problems that resulted from previous con-

tacts and ensure that your case is given a complete and impartial review.

To contact your Taxpayer Advocate:

- Call the Taxpayer Advocate at **1–877–777–4778.**
- Call, write, or fax the Taxpayer Advocate office in your area.
- Call **1–800–829–4059** if you are a TTY/TDD user.

For more information, see Publication 1546, *The Taxpayer Advocate Service of the IRS.*

**Free tax services.** To find out what services are available, get Publication 910, *Guide to Free Tax Services.* It contains a list of free tax publications and an index of tax topics. It also describes other free tax information services, including tax education and assistance programs and a list of TeleTax topics.

**Personal computer.** With your personal computer and modem, you can access the IRS on the Internet at **www.irs.gov.** While visiting our web site, you can:

- See answers to frequently asked tax questions or request help by e-mail.

- Download forms and publications or search for forms and publications by topic or keyword.
- Order IRS products on-line.
- View forms that may be filled in electronically, print the completed form, and then save the form for recordkeeping.
- View Internal Revenue Bulletins published in the last few years.
- Search regulations and the Internal Revenue Code.
- Receive our electronic newsletters on hot tax issues and news.
- Learn about the benefits of filing electronically (IRS e-file).
- Get information on starting and operating a small business.

You can also reach us with your computer using File Transfer Protocol at **ftp.irs.gov.**

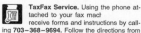

**TaxFax Service.** Using the phone attached to your fax mach receive forms and instructions by calling **703–368–9694.** Follow the directions from the prompts. When you order forms, enter the catalog number for the form you need. The items you request will be faxed to you.

For help with transmission problems, call the FedWorld Help Desk at **703–487–4608.**

 **Phone.** Many services are available by phone.

- *Ordering forms, instructions, and publications.* Call **1–800–829–3676** to order current and prior year forms, instructions, and publications.
- *Asking tax questions.* Call the IRS with your tax questions at **1–800–829–4933.**
- *Retirement plan assistance.* If you own a business and have questions about starting a pension plan, an existing plan, or filing **Form 5500,** call our **Tax Exempt/ Government Entities Customer Account Services** at **1–877–829–5500.** Assistance is available Monday through Friday from 8:00 a.m. to 6:30 p.m. EST. **If you have questions about a traditional or Roth IRA or any individual income tax issues, you should call 1–800–829–1040.**
- *Solving problems.* Take advantage of Everyday Tax Solutions service by calling your local IRS office to set up an in-person appointment at your convenience. Check your local directory assistance or **www.irs.gov** for the numbers.
- *TTY/TDD equipment.* If you have access to TTY/TDD equipment, call **1–800–829–4059** to ask tax questions or to order forms and publications.
- *TeleTax topics.* Call **1–800–829–4477** to listen to pre-recorded messages covering various tax topics.

***Evaluating the quality of our telephone services.*** To ensure that IRS representatives give accurate, courteous, and professional answers, we use several methods to evaluate the quality

of our telephone services. One method is for a second IRS representative to sometimes listen in on or record telephone calls. Another is to ask some callers to complete a short survey at the end of the call.

 **Walk-in.** Many products and services are available on a walk-in basis.

- *Products.* You can walk in to many post offices, libraries, and IRS offices to pick up certain forms, instructions, and publications. Some IRS offices, libraries, grocery stores, copy centers, city and county governments, credit unions, and office supply stores have an extensive collection of products available to print from a CD-ROM or photocopy from reproducible proofs. Also, some IRS offices and libraries have the Internal Revenue Code, regulations, Internal Revenue Bulletins, and Cumulative Bulletins available for research purposes.
- *Services.* You can walk in to your local IRS office to ask tax questions or get help with a tax problem. Now you can set up an appointment by calling your local IRS office number and, at the prompt, leaving a message requesting Everyday Tax Solutions help. A representative will call you back within 2 business days to schedule an in-person appointment at your convenience.

 **Mail.** You can send your order for forms, instructions, and publications to the Distribution Center nearest to you and receive a response within 10 workdays after your request is received. Find the address that applies to your part of the country.

- **Western part of U.S.:**
  Western Area Distribution Center
  Rancho Cordova, CA 95743–0001
- **Central part of U.S.:**
  Central Area Distribution Center

P.O. Box 8903
Bloomington, IL 61702–8903
- **Eastern part of U.S. and foreign addresses:**
  Eastern Area Distribution Center
  P.O. Box 85074
  Richmond, VA 23261–5074

**CD-ROM for tax products.** You can order IRS Publication 1796, *Federal Tax Products on CD-ROM,* and obtain:

- Current tax forms, instructions, and publications.
- Prior-year tax forms and instructions.
- Popular tax forms that may be filled in electronically, printed out for submission, and saved for recordkeeping.
- Internal Revenue Bulletins.

The CD-ROM can be purchased from National Technical Information Service (NTIS) by calling **1–877–233–6767** or on the Internet at **http://www.irs.gov/cdorders.** The first release is available in early January and the final release is available in late February.

**CD-ROM for small businesses.** IRS Publication 3207, *Small Business Resource Guide,* is a must for every small business owner or any taxpayer about to start a business. This handy, interactive CD contains all the business tax forms, instructions and publications needed to successfully manage a business. In addition, the CD provides an abundance of other helpful information, such as how to prepare a business plan, finding financing for your business, and much more. The design of the CD makes finding information easy and quick and incorporates file formats and browsers that can be run on virtually any desktop or laptop computer.

It is available in March. You can get a free copy by calling **1-800-829-3676** or by visiting the website at **www.irs.gov/smallbiz.**

220

**Index**

To help us develop a more useful index, please let us know if you have ideas for index entries. See "Comments and Suggestions" in the "Introduction" for the ways you can reach us.

221

## Tax Publications for Business Taxpayers

See *How To Get Tax Help* for a variety of ways to get publications, including by computer, phone, and mail.

### General Guides

| | |
|---|---|
| 1 | Your Rights as a Taxpayer |
| 17 | Your Federal Income Tax (For Individuals) |
| 334 | Tax Guide for Small Business (For Individuals Who Use Schedule C or C-EZ) |
| 509 | Tax Calendars for 2003 |
| 553 | Highlights of 2002 Tax Changes |
| 910 | Guide to Free Tax Services |

### Employer's Guides

| | |
|---|---|
| 15 | Circular E, Employer's Tax Guide |
| 15-A | Employer's Supplemental Tax Guide |
| 15-B | Employer's Tax Guide to Fringe Benefits |
| 51 | Circular A, Agricultural Employer's Tax Guide |
| 80 | Circular SS, Federal Tax Guide For Employers in the U.S. Virgin Islands, Guam, American Samoa, and the Commonwealth of the Northern Mariana Islands |
| 179 | Circular PR Guía Contributiva Federal Para Patronos Puertorriqueños |
| 926 | Household Employer's Tax Guide |

### Specialized Publications

| | |
|---|---|
| 225 | Farmer's Tax Guide |
| 378 | Fuel Tax Credits and Refunds |
| 463 | Travel, Entertainment, Gift, and Car Expenses |

| | |
|---|---|
| 505 | Tax Withholding and Estimated Tax |
| 510 | Excise Taxes for 2003 |
| 515 | Withholding of Tax on Nonresident Aliens and Foreign Entities |
| 517 | Social Security and Other Information for Members of the Clergy and Religious Workers |
| 527 | Residential Rental Property |
| 533 | Self-Employment Tax |
| 534 | Depreciating Property Placed in Service Before 1987 |
| 535 | Business Expenses |
| 536 | Net Operating Losses (NOLs) for Individuals, Estates, and Trusts |
| 537 | Installment Sales |
| 538 | Accounting Periods and Methods |
| 541 | Partnerships |
| 542 | Corporations |
| 544 | Sales and Other Dispositions of Assets |
| 551 | Basis of Assets |
| 556 | Examination of Returns, Appeal Rights, and Claims for Refund |
| 560 | Retirement Plans for Small Business (SEP, SIMPLE, and Qualified Plans) |
| 561 | Determining the Value of Donated Property |
| 583 | Starting a Business and Keeping Records |
| 587 | Business Use of Your Home (Including Use by Day-Care Providers) |
| 594 | The IRS Collection Process |
| 595 | Tax Highlights for Commercial Fishermen |

| | |
|---|---|
| 597 | Information on the United States-Canada Income Tax Treaty |
| 598 | Tax on Unrelated Business Income of Exempt Organizations |
| 686 | Certification for Reduced Tax Rates in Tax Treaty Countries |
| 901 | U.S. Tax Treaties |
| 908 | Bankruptcy Tax Guide |
| 911 | Direct Sellers |
| 925 | Passive Activity and At-Risk Rules |
| 946 | How To Depreciate Property |
| 947 | Practice Before the IRS and Power of Attorney |
| 954 | Tax Incentives for Empowerment Zones and Other Distressed Communities |
| 1544 | Reporting Cash Payments of Over $10,000 |
| 1546 | The Taxpayer Advocate Service of the IRS |

### Spanish Language Publications

| | |
|---|---|
| 1SP | Derechos del Contribuyente |
| 579SP | Cómo Preparar la Declaración de Impuesto Federal |
| 594SP | Comprendiendo el Proceso de Cobro |
| 850 | English-Spanish Glossary of Words and Phrases Used in Publications Issued by the Internal Revenue Service |
| 1544SP | Informe de Pagos en Efectivo en Exceso de $10,000 (Recibidos en una Ocupación o Negocio) |

## Commonly Used Tax Forms

See *How To Get Tax Help* for a variety of ways to get forms, including by computer, fax, phone, and mail. Items with an asterisk are available by fax. For these orders only, use the catalog number when ordering.

| Form Number and Title | | Catalog Number |
|---|---|---|
| W-2 | Wage and Tax Statement | 10134 |
| W-4 | Employee's Withholding Allowance Certificate* | 10220 |
| 940 | Employer's Annual Federal Unemployment (FUTA) Tax Return* | 11234 |
| 940-EZ | Employer's Annual Federal Unemployment (FUTA) Tax Return* | 10983 |
| 941 | Employer's Quarterly Federal Tax Return | 17001 |
| 1040 | U.S. Individual Income Tax Return* | 11320 |
| Sch A & B | Itemized Deductions & Interest and Ordinary Dividends* | 11330 |
| Sch C | Profit or Loss From Business* | 11334 |
| Sch C-EZ | Net Profit From Business* | 14374 |
| Sch D | Capital Gains and Losses* | 11338 |
| Sch D-1 | Continuation Sheet for Schedule D | 10424 |
| Sch E | Supplemental Income and Loss* | 11344 |
| Sch F | Profit or Loss From Farming* | 11346 |
| Sch H | Household Employment Taxes* | 12187 |
| Sch J | Farm Income Averaging* | 25513 |
| Sch R | Credit for the Elderly or the Disabled* | 11359 |
| Sch SE | Self-Employment Tax* | 11358 |
| 1040-ES | Estimated Tax for Individuals* | 11340 |
| 1040X | Amended U.S. Individual Income Tax Return* | 11360 |
| 1065 | U.S. Return of Partnership Income | 11390 |
| Sch D | Capital Gains and Losses | 11393 |
| Sch K-1 | Partner's Share of Income, Credits, Deductions, etc. | 11394 |
| 1120 | U.S. Corporation Income Tax Return | 11450 |
| 1120-A | U.S. Corporation Short-Form Income Tax Return | 11456 |

| Form Number and Title | | Catalog Number |
|---|---|---|
| 1120S | U.S. Income Tax Return for an S Corporation | 11510 |
| Sch D | Capital Gains and Losses and Built-In Gains | 11516 |
| Sch K-1 | Shareholder's Share of Income, Credits, Deductions, etc. | 11520 |
| 2106 | Employee Business Expenses* | 11700 |
| 2106-EZ | Unreimbursed Employee Business Expenses* | 20604 |
| 2210 | Underpayment of Estimated Tax by Individuals, Estates, and Trusts* | 11744 |
| 2441 | Child and Dependent Care Expenses* | 11862 |
| 2848 | Power of Attorney and Declaration of Representative* | 11980 |
| 3800 | General Business Credit | 12392 |
| 3903 | Moving Expenses* | 12490 |
| 4562 | Depreciation and Amortization* | 12906 |
| 4797 | Sales of Business Property* | 13086 |
| 4868 | Application for Automatic Extension of Time To File U.S. Individual Income Tax Return* | 13141 |
| 5329 | Additional Taxes on Qualified Plans (Including IRAs) and Other Tax-Favored Accounts | 13329 |
| 6252 | Installment Sale Income* | 13601 |
| 8283 | Noncash Charitable Contributions* | 62299 |
| 8300 | Report of Cash Payments Over $10,000 Received in a Trade or Business* | 62133 |
| 8582 | Passive Activity Loss Limitations* | 63704 |
| 8606 | Nondeductible IRAs* | 63966 |
| 8822 | Change of Address* | 12081 |
| 8829 | Expenses for Business Use of Your Home* | 13232 |

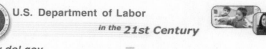

## U.S. Department of Labor
### *in the* 21st Century

**www.dol.gov**                                                          Search / A-Z Index

**May 21, 2003**    DOL Home > Find It! By Topic > Health Plans > ERISA

# Find It! By Topic

## Health Plans & Benefits

### Employee Retirement Income Security Act — ERISA

- DOL Web Pages on This Topic

The Employee Retirement Income Security Act of 1974 (ERISA) is a federal law that sets minimum standards for most voluntarily established pension and health plans in private industry to provide protection for individuals in these plans.

ERISA requires plans to provide participants with plan information including important information about plan features and funding; provides fiduciary responsibilities for those who manage and control plan assets; requires plans to establish a grievance and appeals process for participants to get benefits from their plans; and gives participants the right to sue for benefits and breaches of fiduciary duty.

There have been a number of amendments to ERISA, expanding the protections available to health benefit plan participants and beneficiaries. One important amendment, the Consolidated Omnibus Budget Reconciliation Act (COBRA), provides some workers and their families with the right to continue their health coverage for a limited time after certain events, such as the loss of a job. Another amendment to ERISA is the Health Insurance Portability and Accountability Act (HIPAA) which provides important new protections for working Americans and their families who have preexisting medical conditions or might otherwise suffer discrimination in health coverage based on factors that relate to an individual's health. Other important amendments include the Newborns' and Mothers' Health Protection Act, the Mental Health Parity Act, and the Women's Health and Cancer Rights Act.

In general, ERISA does not cover group health plans established or maintained by governmental entities, churches for their employees, or plans which are maintained solely to comply with applicable workers compensation, unemployment, or disability laws. ERISA also does not cover plans maintained outside the United States primarily for the benefit of nonresident aliens or unfunded excess benefit plans.

**DOL Web Pages on This Topic:**

Compliance Assistance

### Subtopics

- Compliance Assistance
- Consumer Information on Health Plans
- Continuation of Health Coverage (COBRA)
- Employee Retirement Income Security Act (ERISA)
- Fiduciary Responsibilities
- Health Benefits Education
- Mental Health Benefits
- Newborns' & Mothers' Protections (Newborns' Act)
- Participant Rights
- Plan Information
- Portability of Health Coverage (HIPAA)
- Womens' Health & Cancer Rights Protections

Compliance Assistance

21st Century Workforce Initiative

Secretary's Speeches & Testimonies

News Releases

Doing Business With DOL

Research Library

State Labor Offices

About DOL

DOL Agencies

Provides publications and other materials to assist employers and employee benefit plan practitioners in understanding and complying with the requirements of ERISA as it applies to the administration of employee pension and welfare benefit plans.

Consumer Information on Health Plans
Provides fact sheets, booklets, and other health plan information from the Department's Employee Benefits Security Administration (EBSA).

▲ Back to Top                                                    www.dol.gov

Frequently Asked Questions I Freedom of Information Act I Customer Survey
Privacy & Security Statement I Disclaimers I E-mail to a Friend

U.S. Department of Labor                        1-866-4-USA-DOL
Frances Perkins Building                      TTY:  1-877-889-5627
200 Constitution Avenue, NW                          Contact Us
Washington, DC 20210

# U.S. Department of Labor
### Employee Benefits
### Security Administration

## www.dol.gov/ebsa

Go    Search / A-Z Index

## Simple Retirement Solutions for Small Business

This pamphlet constitutes a small entity compliance guide for purposes of the Small Business Regulatory Enforcement Fairness Act of 1996. This brochure does not constitute legal, accounting or other professional service. It is a joint project of the U.S. Department of Labor, the U.S. Small Business Administration and private-sector partners. Its publication does not imply endorsement of any co-sponsor's or participant's opinions, products or services.

**Question:** I'm a small employer, and I'm considering a retirement plan for my workers. But I don't want to do anything too complicated. Are there simple options for employers like me?

### On This Page

Printer Friendly Version

A Few Pension Facts

SIMPLE - Savings Incentive Match Plans for Employees of Small Employers

SEPs - Simplified Employee Pensions

401(k) and Profit-Sharing Plans

Payroll Deduction IRAs

Find Out More

**About EBSA**
EBSA Offices
ERISA Advisory Council
Meet the Assistant Secretary
Organization Chart

**Compliance Assistance**
Unified Agenda
Class Exemptions
Individual Exemptions
EXPRO Exemptions
Advisory Opinions
Information Letters
Technical Releases
Field Assistance Bulletins
Proposed Rules
Final Rules
Notices
Meetings
Public Comments

**Newsroom**
Fact Sheets
Press Releases
Speeches
Testimony

**Consumer Health Plan Information**

**Consumer Pension Plan Information**

**Forms and Document Requests**
Form 5500
ERISA Public Disclosure System

**Laws and Regulations**
Statute Title 29, Cha. 18
Executive Orders
Code of Fed Regulations

**Programs/Initiatives**
ERISA Enforcement
Delinquent Filer Voluntary Compliance Program
Voluntary Fiduciary Correction Program

**Publications/Reports**
Health Publications
Pension Publications
Health Reports
Pension Reports
EBSA Annual Reports
Advisory Council Reports

**Related Resources**

**Frequently Asked Questions**

**Contact Us**

Starting a small business retirement savings plan can be easier than most business people think. There are a number of retirement options that provide tax advantages to both employers and employees.

### Why save?

By starting a retirement savings plan, you will be helping your employees save for the future. Retirement plans may also help you attract and retain a qualified pool of employees and offer your business tax savings.

You will help secure your own retirement as well. What's more, you will be joining more than one million small businesses with 100 or fewer employees that offer workplace retirement savings plans.

Experts estimate that Americans will need 60 to 80 percent of their pre-retirement income - lower-income earners may need up to 90 percent to maintain their current standard of living when they stop working. So, now is the time to look into retirement plan options. As an employer, you have an important role to play in helping America's workers save.

⭐ *Back To Top*

### A Few Pension Facts

Most private-sector retirement plans are either **defined benefit plans** or **defined contribution plans**. Defined benefit plans promise a specified benefit at retirement, for example, $100 a month at retirement. The amount of the benefit is often based on a set percentage of pay multiplied by the number of years the employee worked for the employer offering the plan. Employer contributions must be sufficient to fund the promised benefit.

Defined contribution plans, on the other hand, do not promise a specific amount of benefit at retirement. In these plans, employees or their employer (or both) contribute to employees' individual accounts under the plan, sometimes at a set rate (such as 5 percent of salary annually).

Small businesses may choose to offer a defined benefit plan or a defined contribution plan. Many financial institutions and pension practitioners make available both defined benefit and defined contribution "prototype" plans that have been pre-approved by the IRS.

This brochure focuses on a few of the defined contribution options - SIMPLE plans, SEPs, 401(k) plans, and payroll deduction IRAs. Other types of defined contribution plans include employee stock ownership plans and money purchase plans.

All retirement plans have important tax, business and other implications for employers and employees. Therefore, you may want to discuss any retirement savings plan with a tax or financial advisor.

Here's a brief look at some plans that can help you and your employees save.

*Back To Top*

## SIMPLE - Savings Incentive Match Plans for Employees of Small Employers

This savings option for employers of 100 or fewer employees involves a type of individual retirement account (IRA) and is the result of the Small Business Job Protection Act of 1996.

A SIMPLE plan allows employees to contribute a percentage of their salary each pay check and to have their employer contribute also. Under SIMPLE plans, employees can set aside up to $6,000 each year by payroll deduction. Employers either match employee contributions dollar for dollar - up to 3 percent of an employee's wage - or make a fixed contribution of 2 percent of pay for all eligible employees.

SIMPLE plans are easy to set up - you fill out a short form to establish a plan and ensure that IRA accounts are set up for each employee. Much of the paperwork is done by the financial institution that handles SIMPLE plan accounts, however, and administrative costs are low.

Employers may choose either to permit employees to select the IRA to which their contributions will be sent, or to send contributions for all employees to one financial institution (which will forward contributions of employees who elect a different IRA).

Employees are 100% vested in contributions, decide how and where the money will be invested, and keep their IRA accounts even when they change jobs.

*Back To Top*

## SEPs - Simplified Employee Pensions

A SEP allows employers to set up a type of individual retirement account - known as a SEP-IRA - for themselves and their employees. Employers must contribute a uniform percentage of pay for each employee, although they do not have to make contributions every year. Employer contributions are limited to the lesser of 15 percent of an employee's annual salary or $24,000. (Note: this amount is indexed for inflation and will vary). SEPs can be started by most employers, including those who are self-employed.

SEPs have low start-up and operating costs and can be established using a single quarter-page form. And you decide how much to put into a SEP each year - offering you some flexibility when business conditions vary.

*Back To Top*

## 401(k) and Profit-Sharing Plans

401(k) plans have become a widely-accepted retirement savings vehicle for small businesses. Today, an estimated 25 million American workers are enrolled in 401(k) plans that hold total assets of about $1 trillion.

Employees contribute a percentage of their pay to the 401(k) plan on a tax-deferred basis through payroll deductions. The maximum amount an employee can deposit is $10,000. (Note: This amount is adjusted for inflation and will vary.) Employers also may contribute to an employee's 401(k) account by making employee contributions usually up to a percentage of an employee's pay/

While more complex, 401(k) plans offer higher contribution limits than SIMPLE plans and IRAs, allowing employees to potentially accumulate greater savings.

Employers also may make profit-sharing contributions to a plan that are unrelated to any amounts an employee chooses to contribute. The amount of these contributions is often set as a percentage of employees' pay; however, the employer can change the percentage or amount from year to year. A plan may combine these profit-sharing contributions with 401(k) contributions (and matching contributions).

───────────────── *Back To Top* ─────────────────

## Payroll Deduction IRAs

Even if an employer does not want to adopt a retirement plan, it can allow its employees to save through payroll deduction, providing a simple and direct way for eligible employees to contribute to an IRA through payroll deductions, providing a simple and direct way for eligible employees to save.  The decision about whether to contribute, and when and how much to contribute to the IRA (up to $2,000) is always made by the employee in this type of arrangement.

Many individuals eligible to contribute to an IRA do not. One reason is that some individuals wait until the end of the year to set aside the money and then find that they do not have sufficient funds to do so. Payroll deductions allow individuals to plan ahead and save smaller amounts each pay period. Payroll deduction contributions are tax-deductible by an individual to the same extent as other IRA contributions.

───────────────── *Back To Top* ─────────────────

## Find Out More

The following two pamphlets and other pension-related publications are available on the Employee Benefits Security Administration web site:

- Simplified Employee Pensions (SEPs) - What Small Businesses Need to Know

- Savings Incentive Match Plans for Employees of Small Employers (SIMPLE) - A Small Business Retirement Savings Advantage

These and other pension-related publications are also available by calling EBSA's Toll-Free Employee & Employer Hotline at: 1.866.444.EBSA (3272).

For more information contact:

- U.S. Chamber of Commerce
  Business Information and Development
  Tel  202.463.5381

- Small Business Administration
  Answer Desk
  Tel  1.800.827.5722

▲ Back to Top 　　　　　　　www.dol.gov/ebsa 　　　　　　　　　　www.dol.gov

─────────────────────────────────────────────────
**Frequently Asked Questions | Freedom of Information Act | Customer Survey
Privacy & Security Statement | Disclaimers | E-mail to a Friend**

**U.S. Department of Labor**　　　　　　　　　　　　　　　　**1.866.444.3272**
Frances Perkins Building　　　　　　　　　　　　　TTY: **1.877.889.5627**
200 Constitution Avenue, NW　　　　　　　　　　　　　　　**Contact Us**
Washington, DC 20210

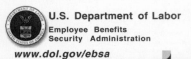

**U.S. Department of Labor**
Employee Benefits
Security Administration

*www.dol.gov/ebsa*

[Go]  Search / A-Z Index

May 21, 2003    <u>DOL</u> > <u>EBSA</u> >  >

## A Look at 401(k) Plan Fees for Employers

A participant-directed retirement savings plan, such as a 401(k) plan, is an important tool to help your employees achieve a secure retirement. As part of offering this type of program, you or someone you choose must select the investment options from which your employees will choose, select the service providers for the plan, and monitor the performance of the investments and the provision of services. All of these duties require you to consider the costs to the plan. This brochure can help you ask the right questions to better understand and evaluate the fees and expenses related to your plan.

You or the person you select to carry out these responsibilities must comply with the standards provided under the Employee Retirement Income Security Act of 1974 (ERISA). This federal law protects private-sector pension plans. The law's standards include ensuring that you act prudently and solely in the interest of the plan's participants and beneficiaries.

Understanding fees and expenses is important in providing for the services necessary for your plan's operation. This responsibility is ongoing. After careful evaluation during the initial selection, the plan's fees and expenses should be monitored to determine whether they continue to be reasonable. While ERISA does not set a specific level of fees, it does require that fees charged to a plan be "reasonable."

Of course, the process of selecting a service provider and investment options should address many factors, including those related to fees and expenses. You must consider the plan's performance over time for each investment option. This selection process and continual monitoring will make it possible for your employees to make sound investment decisions. As part of your evaluation process, here are 10 questions to help focus your consideration of fees and expenses:

- Have you given each of your prospective service providers complete and identical information with regard to your plan?

- Do you know what features you want to provide (e.g., loans, number of investment options, types of investments, Internet trading)?

- Have you decided which fees and expenses you, as plan sponsor, will pay, which your employees will pay, and/or which you will share?

- Do you know which fees and expenses are charged directly to the plan and which are deducted from investment returns?

- Do you know what services are covered under the base fee and what services incur an extra charge? Do you know what the fees are for extra or customized services?

- Do you understand that some investment options have higher fees than others because of the nature of the investment?

- Does the prospective service arrangement have any restrictions, such as charges for early termination of your relationship with the provider?

- Does the prospective arrangement assist your employees in making informed investment decisions for their individual accounts (e.g., providing investment education, information on fees, and the like) and how are you charged for this service?

- Have you considered asking potential providers to present uniform fee information that includes all fees charged?

- What information will you receive on a regular basis from the prospective provider so that you can monitor the provision of services and the investments that you select and make changes, if necessary?

## Remember...

Provide all prospective service providers with complete and identical information about the plan and what you are looking for so you can make a meaningful comparison. This information includes the number of plan participants and plan assets as of a specified date.

Consider the specific services you would like provided. For example, the types and frequency of reports to employer, communications to participants, educational materials and meetings for participants and the availability and frequency of participant investment transfers, the level of responsibility you want the prospective service provider to assume, what services must be included and what are possible extras or customized services, and optional features such as loans, Internet trading and telephone transfers.

- Make informed decisions in selecting and monitoring your plan service providers and investments.

- Fees are just one of several factors you need to consider in your decision making.

- All services have costs. Compare all services to be provided with the total cost for each prospective provider.

- Consider obtaining estimates from more than one service provider before making your decision.

- Cheaper is not necessarily better.

- Ask each prospective provider to be specific about which services are covered for the estimated fees and which are not. To help in gathering this information and in making equivalent comparisons, you may want to use the same format for each prospective provider. See EBSA's Web site for an example of a uniform fee disclosure format to assist in your selection and monitoring process.

- Fees and expenses can have a significant impact on your employees' retirement savings.

This brochure highlights the importance of a process for selecting and monitoring your 401(k) plan's service providers and investment options. Continue to ask questions - as an informed plan sponsor, you can make better decisions for your plan and your employees.

A copy of this brochure and the following resources are available on EBSA's Web site:

- American Bankers Association/American Council of Life Insurance/Investment Company Institute - 401(k) Plan Fee Disclosure Form

- What You Should Know about Your Pension Rights

- A Look at 401(k) Plan Fees for Employees

This material will be made available to sensory impaired individuals upon request:
Voice phone: 202.219.8921
TDD: 1.800.326.2577

(▲) Back to Top                   www.dol.gov/ebsa                              www.dol.gov

Frequently Asked Questions I Freedom of Information Act I Customer Survey
Privacy & Security Statement I Disclaimers I E-mail to a Friend

U.S. Department of Labor                                         1.866.444.3272
Frances Perkins Building                                    TTY: 1.877.889.5627
200 Constitution Avenue, NW                                        Contact Us
Washington, DC 20210

## ABC PLAN
## 401(k) PLAN FEE DISCLOSURE FORM
### For Services Provided by XYZ Company[1]

### Overview

The Employee Retirement Income Security Act of 1974, as amended (ERISA) requires employee benefit plan fiduciaries to act solely in the interests of, and for the exclusive benefit of, plan participants and beneficiaries. As part of that obligation, plan fiduciaries should consider cost, among other things, when choosing investment options for the plan and selecting plan service providers.

This 401(k) plan fee disclosure form may assist you in making informed cost-benefit decisions with respect to your plan. The purpose of this form is to help you determine the total cost of the plan. It is also intended to provide you with a means to compare investment product fees and plan administration expenses charged by competing service providers, regardless of how a particular service provider structures its fees.

The 401(k) plan fees included in this disclosure form represent the following: _____ actual 401(k) plan expenses for the period X/XX/XX through X/XX/XX or _____ estimated 401(k) plan expenses[2] for the period X/XX/XX through X/XX/XX. Additional investment product information regarding fees may be obtained from the product prospectus, annuity contract or other similar documents. Additional information relating to plan administration services and expenses is contained in documentation provided by the service provider, including the contract for plan services. Other plan expenses may include legal fees for initial plan design and ongoing amendments resulting from changes in pension law or plan design and the cost of a mandatory annual audit. You need to contact your legal advisor or accountant to determine these charges.

Selecting a service provider requires that you evaluate and differentiate services offered by competing companies. Cost is one of the criteria, but not the only criterion, for making this evaluation. Other factors of equal or greater importance to consider include the quality and type of services provided, the anticipated performance of competing providers and their investment products and other factors specific to your plan's needs. *The service provider offering the lowest cost services is not necessarily the best choice for your plan.*

### Calculation of Fees

#### In general, fees are calculated in four ways:

Asset-based: expenses are based on the amount of assets in the plan and generally are expressed as percentages or basis points.
Per-person: expenses are based upon the number of eligible employees or actual participants in the plan.
Transaction-based: expenses are based on the execution of a particular plan service or transaction.
Flat rate: fixed charge that does not vary, regardless of plan size.

Fees may be calculated using one or any combination of these methods. Plan administration-related expenses can also be charged as one-time fees or ongoing expenses. One-time fees are typically related to start-ups, conversions (moving from one provider to another) and terminations of service. Ongoing fees are recurring expenses relating to continuing plan operation.

---

[1] There may be plan expenses incurred by other providers, other than the company completing this form. For a complete list of expenses charged to your plan, please contact all plan service providers with whom you contract or may contract and request fee information with respect to their services.

[2] If you are considering a conversion from an existing plan service provider to a new service provider, you will need to provide the service provider(s) with certain information about the plan, including the number of plan participants, the number of eligible participants and the amount of plan assets in order for the service provider(s) to be able to complete this form. Similarly, if you are considering starting a plan, you will need to provide the service provider(s) with estimates of plan participants and plan assets. When providing potential service providers with information regarding your plan, it is critical that you provide identical information to all of the competing companies in order to ensure equivalent comparisons.

**ABC PLAN**
**401(k) PLAN FEE DISCLOSURE FORM**
**For Services Provided by XYZ Company**
**Total Plan Expenses**

Contact Name: _____

Institution: _____

Phone: _____

| | Amount/<br>Estimate[3] |
|---|---|
| **I.   Investment Product Fees (See Schedule A)** | |
| A.  Collective Investment Fund(s) | $_____ |
| B.  Insurance/Annuity Product(s) | $_____ |
| C.  Mutual Fund(s) | $_____ |
| D.  Individually Managed Account(s) | $_____ |
| E.  Brokerage Window | $_____ |
| F.  Other Product(s) (Specify) | $_____ |
| Total Investment Product Fees | $_____ |
| **II.   Plan Administration Expenses (See Schedule B)** | |
| Total Plan Administration Expenses | $_____ |
| **III.   Plan Start-Up or Conversion Related Charges (See Schedule C)** | |
| One Time Start-Up/Conversion expenses | $_____ |
| **IV.   Service Provider Termination Related Charges (See Schedule D)** | |
| Service Provider Termination expenses | $_____ |
| **Total Plan Expenses** | $_____ |

**For definitions of terms used throughout this disclosure form, see Schedule E.**

---

[3] Amounts are calculated based on rates charged, which are identified in attached schedules as applied to relevant information (for example amount of assets or number of participants). Certain calculations may be estimates based on information provided by you, the plan sponsor, and may vary as circumstances change.

## Investment Product Fees/Estimates

| Collective Investment Fund | Assets (X/X/XX) | Management Fee | Other (Specify) | Total Cost |
|---|---|---|---|---|
| Fund 1 | | | | |
| Fund 2 | | | | |
| Fund 3 | | | | |
| Fund 4 | | | | |
| TOTAL | | | | |

| Insurance /Annuity Product | Assets (X/X/XX) | Management Fee | Mortality Risk and Administrative Expense (M&E Fee) | Other (Specify) | Total Cost |
|---|---|---|---|---|---|
| Fund 1 | | | | | |
| Fund 2 | | | | | |
| Separate Account 1 | | | | | |
| Separate Account 2 | | | | | |
| TOTAL | | | | | |

| Mutual Fund | Assets (X/X/XX) | Expense Ratio[4] | Front-end Load | Other (Specify) | Total Cost |
|---|---|---|---|---|---|
| Fund 1 | | | | | |
| Fund 2 | | | | | |
| Fund 3 | | | | | |
| Fund 4 | | | | | |
| TOTAL | | | | | |

| Individually-Managed Account | Assets (X/X/XX) | Management Fee | Other (Specify) | Total Cost |
|---|---|---|---|---|
| Product 1 | | | | |
| Product 2 | | | | |
| Product 3 | | | | |
| Product 4 | | | | |
| TOTAL | | | | |

---

Fees represent product-related charges paid by the plan. Fees associated with participants' transfer of account balances between investment options, including investment transfer expenses and any contingent back-end loads, redemption fees and surrender charges should be included in "other" expenses. In addition, any wrap fees or pricing charges for non-publicly traded assets should be included in the "other" expenses column. For investment product termination fees associated with plan termination or conversion, see Schedule D. Insurance companies incur marketing and distribution costs, which are recouped through charges assessed against the plan.

[4] Includes 12b-1 fee and management fee. (See the fee table in the fund prospectus.)

## ABC PLAN
## 401(k) PLAN FEE DISCLOSURE FORM
## For Services Provided by XYZ Company
## Schedule A, continued

### Investment Product Fees/Estimates

| Brokerage Window[5] | Assets (X/X/XX) | Commission (Range) | Transaction Fee (Range) | Other (Specify) | Total Cost |
|---|---|---|---|---|---|
| Total Transactions | | | | | |

| Other Product[6] | Assets (X/X/XX) | Management Fee | Other (Specify) | Total Cost |
|---|---|---|---|---|
| Product 1 | | | | |
| Product 2 | | | | |
| Product 3 | | | | |
| Product 4 | | | | |

Total Investment Product Fees $_____

---

[5] When providing potential service providers with information/assumptions regarding the brokerage window plan feature, it is critical that you provide identical information to all of the competing companies in order to ensure equivalent comparisons.

Fees associated with participants' transfer of account balances between investment options, including investment transfer expenses and any contingent back-end loads, redemption fees and surrender charges should be included in "other" expenses. In addition, any wrap fees or pricing charges for non-publicly traded assets should be included in the "other" expenses column. For investment product termination fees associated with plan termination or conversion, see Schedule D. Insurance companies incur marketing and distribution costs, which are recouped through charges assessed against the plan.

[6] Other products could include investment vehicles such as REITs and limited partnerships.

### ABC PLAN DISCLOSURE FORM
### For Services Provided by XYZ Company
### Schedule B

## PLAN ADMINISTRATION EXPENSES

| **Expense Type** | **Rate/ Estimate**[*] | **Bundled Service Arrangement ( )[7]** | **Total Cost**[**] | |
|---|---|---|---|---|
| Administration/Recordkeeping Fees: | | | | |
| Daily valuation | $_____ | ☐ | $_____ | |
| Payroll processing | $_____ | ☐ | $_____ | |
| Balance inquiry | $_____ | ☐ | $_____ | |
| Investment transfer | $_____ | ☐ | $_____ | |
| Contract administration charge | $_____ | ☐ | $_____ | |
| Distribution processing | $_____ | ☐ | $_____ | |
| QDRO processing | $_____ | ☐ | $_____ | |
| Participant statements | $_____ | ☐ | $_____ | |
| Plan sponsor reports | $_____ | ☐ | $_____ | |
| VRU/Internet services | $_____ | ☐ | $_____ | |
| Other (specify) | $_____ | ☐ | $_____ | |
| **Subtotal** | | | | $_____ |
| | | | | |
| Participant Education/Advice: | | | | |
| Participant education materials/distribution | $_____ | ☐ | $_____ | |
| Education meetings (frequency__ ) | $_____ | ☐ | $_____ | |
| Investment advice programs | $_____ | ☐ | $_____ | |
| Other (specify) | $_____ | ☐ | $_____ | |
| **Subtotal** | | | | $_____ |
| | | | | |
| Trustee/Custodial Services: | | | | |
| Certified annual trust statement | $_____ | ☐ | $_____ | |
| Safekeeping of plan assets | $_____ | ☐ | $_____ | |
| Other (specify) | $_____ | ☐ | $_____ | |
| **Subtotal** | | | | $_____ |

---

[*] Amounts represent the method by which the fee is calculated, for example as a percentage of plan assets under management, based upon number of participants or based upon number of transactions. For start-up or take-over situations, fees are based upon estimates and/or certain assumptions, i.e., regarding assets under management and number of participants. When providing potential service providers with information/assumptions regarding your plan, it is critical that you provide identical information to all of the competing companies in order to ensure equivalent comparisons. Without a standardized set of assumptions, service providers will certainly use differing assumptions, defeating the intended purpose of clarifying fee comparisons among service providers.

[7] Services provided under a bundled services arrangement are indicated by a check mark next to the specific service.

[**] Amounts represent flat dollar amount charges or total charges based upon the particular method of calculation. In some instances, these amounts represent estimates based on assumptions provided by you, the plan sponsor.

# ABC PLAN DISCLOSURE FORM
## For Services Provided by XYZ Company
### Schedule B, continued

| Expense Type | Rate/<br>Estimate[*] | Bundled Service<br>Arrangement<br>( ) | Total Cost[**] |
|---|---|---|---|
| Compliance Services: | | | |
|   Nondiscrimination testing | $_____ | ☐ | $_____ |
|   Signature ready form 5500 | $_____ | ☐ | $_____ |
|   Annual audit | $_____ | ☐ | $_____ |
|   Other (specify) | $_____ | ☐ | $_____ |
| **Subtotal** | | | $_____ |
| | | | |
| Plan Amendment Fee: | | | |
|   Plan amendment fee | $_____ | ☐ | $_____ |
|   Plan document/determination | | | |
|   letter fee | $_____ | ☐ | $_____ |
|   Other (specify) | $_____ | ☐ | $_____ |
| **Subtotal** | | | $_____ |
| | | | |
| Loan Administration: | | | |
|   Loan origination fee | $_____ | ☐ | $_____ |
|   Loan processing fee | $_____ | ☐ | $_____ |
|   Loan maintenance and repayment | | | |
|   tracking fee | $_____ | ☐ | $_____ |
|   Other (specify) | $_____ | ☐ | $_____ |
| **Subtotal** | | | $_____ |
| | | | |
|   Total separate charges | | | $_____ |
|   Total bundled services | | | $_____ |
|   (Less offsets/credits paid to plan) | | | $(_____) |
| | | | |
| **Total Plan Administration Expenses** | | | $_____ |

---

\* Amounts represent the method by which the fee is calculated, for example as a percentage of plan assets under management, based upon number of participants or based upon number of transactions. For start-up or take-over situations, fees are based upon estimates and/or certain assumptions, i.e., regarding assets under management and number of participants. When providing potential service providers with information/assumptions regarding your plan, it is critical that you provide identical information to all of the competing companies in order to ensure equivalent comparisons. Without a standardized set of assumptions, service providers will certainly use differing assumptions, defeating the intended purpose of clarifying fee comparisons among service providers.

\*\* Amounts represent flat dollar amount charges or total charges based upon the particular method of calculation. In some instances, these amounts represent estimates based on assumptions provided by you, the plan sponsor.

## ONE TIME START-UP/CONVERSION EXPENSES

| Expense Type | Rate/ Estimate[*] | Total Cost[**] |
|---|---|---|
| Start-up/conversion education program | $ _____ | $_____ |
| Start-up/conversion enrollment expense | $ _____ | $_____ |
| Installation fee | $ _____ | $_____ |
| Start-up/conversion plan document fee/filing fee | $ _____ | $_____ |
| Other (specify) | $ _____ | $_____ |
| **Total Start-up/Conversion expenses** | | $_____ |

---

\* Amounts represent the method by which the fee is calculated, for example as a percentage of plan assets under management, based upon number of participants or based upon number of transactions. For start-up or take-over situations, fees are based upon estimates and/or certain assumptions, i.e., regarding assets under management and number of participants. When providing potential service providers with information/assumptions regarding your plan, it is critical that you provide identical information to all of the competing companies in order to ensure equivalent comparisons. Without a standardized set of assumptions, service providers will certainly use differing assumptions, defeating the intended purpose of clarifying fee comparisons among service providers.

\*\* Amounts represent flat dollar amount charges or total charges based upon the particular method of calculation. In some instances, these amounts represent estimates based on assumptions provided by you, the plan sponsor.

**ABC PLAN**
**401(k) PLAN DISCLOSURE FORM**
**For Services Provided by XYZ Company**
**Schedule D**

## SERVICE PROVIDER TERMINATION EXPENSES

| Expense Type | Rate/ Estimate[*] | Total Cost[**] |
|---|---|---|
| Investment Product Expenses | | |
| Contract termination charges | $ _____ | $ _____ |
| Back-end load | $ _____ | $ _____ |
| Product termination fee | $ _____ | $ _____ |
| Other (specify) | $ _____ | $ _____ |
| **Total** | | $ _____ |
| Plan Administration Expenses | | |
| Service provider termination charge | $ _____ | $ _____ |
| Service contract termination charge | $ _____ | $ _____ |
| Other (specify) | $ _____ | $ _____ |
| **Total Termination Expenses** | | $ _____ |

---

[*] Amounts represent the method by which the fee is calculated, for example as a percentage of plan assets under management, based upon number of participants or based upon number of transactions. For start-up or take-over situations, fees are based upon estimates and/or certain assumptions, i.e., regarding assets under management and number of participants. When providing potential service providers with information/assumptions regarding your plan, it is critical that you provide identical information to all of the competing companies in order to ensure equivalent comparisons. Without a standardized set of assumptions, service providers will certainly use differing assumptions, defeating the intended purpose of clarifying fee comparisons among service providers.

[**] Amounts represent flat dollar amount charges or total charges based upon the particular method of calculation. In some instances, these amounts represent estimates based on assumptions provided by you, the plan sponsor.

## DEFINITION OF TERMS

**Administration/Recordkeeping Fee:** Fee for providing recordkeeping and other plan participant administrative type services. For start-up or takeover plans, these fees typically include charges for contacting and processing information from the prior service provider and "matching up" or mapping participant information. Use of this term is not meant to identify any ERISA Section 3(16)(A) obligations.

**Annual Audit:** Federal law requires that all ERISA-covered plans with more than 100 participants be audited by an independent auditor. It is also common to refer to a DOL or IRS examination of a plan as a plan audit. Any charge imposed by a service provider in connection with this audit is reflected on Schedule B.

**Back-End Load:** Sales charges due upon the sale or transfer of mutual funds, insurance/annuity products or other investments, which may be reduced and/or eliminated over time.

**Balance Inquiry:** Fee that may be charged each time a participant inquires about his or her balance.

**Brokerage Commission:** A fee paid to a broker or other intermediary for executing a trade.

**Brokerage Window:** A plan investment option allowing a participant to establish a self-directed brokerage account.

**Bundled Services:** Arrangements whereby plan service providers offer 401(k) plan establishment, investment services and administration for an all-inclusive fee. Bundled services by their nature are priced as a package and cannot be priced on a per service basis.

**Collective Investment Fund:** A tax-exempt pooled fund operated by a bank or trust company that commingles the assets of trust accounts for which the bank provides fiduciary services.

**Contract Administration Charge:** An omnibus charge for costs of administering the insurance/annuity contract, including costs associated with the maintenance of participant accounts and all investment-related transactions initiated by participants.

**Contract Termination Charge:** A charge to the plan for "surrendering" or "terminating" its insurance/annuity contract prior to the end of a stated time period. The charge typically decreases over time.

**Conversion:** The process of changing from one service provider to another.

**Distribution Expense:** The costs typically associated with processing paperwork and issuing a check for a distribution of plan assets to a participant. May include the generation of IRS Form 1099R. This fee may apply to hardship and other in-service withdrawals as well as to separation-from-service or retirement distributions.

**Eligible Employee:** Any employee who is eligible to participate in and receive benefits from a plan.

**Expense Ratio:** The cost of investing and administering assets, including management fees, in a mutual fund or other collective fund expressed as a percentage of total assets.

**Front-End Load:** Sales charges incurred when an investment in a mutual fund is made.

**Individually Managed Account:** An investment account managed for a single plan.

**Installation Fee:** One-time fee for initiating a new plan or initiating new services.

**Investment Transfer Expense:** Fee associated with a participant changing his or her investment allocation, or making transfers among funding accounts under the plan.

**Loan Maintenance and Repayment Tracking Fee:** Fee charged to monitor outstanding loans and repayment schedule.

**Loan Origination Fee:** Fee charged when a plan loan is originally taken.

**Loan Processing Fee:** Fee charged to process a plan loan application.

**Management Fee:** Fee charged for the management of pooled investments such as collective investment funds, insurance/annuity products, mutual funds and individually managed accounts.

**Mortality Risk and Administrative Expense (M&E Fee):** Fee charged by an insurance company to cover the cost of the insurance features of an annuity contract, including the guarantee of a lifetime income payment, interest and expense guarantees, and any death benefit provided during the accumulation period.

**Nondiscrimination Testing Expense:** Tax qualified retirement plans must be administered in compliance with several regulations requiring numerical measurements. The fee charged for the process of determining whether the plan is in compliance is collectively called nondiscrimination testing expense.

**Participant:** Person who has an account in the plan.

**Participant Education Materials/Distribution Expenses:** All costs (including travel expenses) associated with providing print, video, software and/or live instruction to educate employees about how the plan works, the plan investment funds, and asset allocation strategies. There may be a one-time cost associated with implementing a new plan, as well as ongoing costs for an existing program.

**Plan Document/Determination Letter Fee (Filing Fee):** Fee charged for a written plan document. Fee can also include the costs associated with preparing and filing IRS required documentation, including the request for a determination letter (document issued by the IRS stating whether the plan meets the qualifications for tax-advantaged treatment).

**Plan Loan:** The law allows participants to borrow from their accounts up to prescribed limits. This is an optional plan feature.

**Product Termination Fee:** Investment-product charges associated with terminating one or all of a service provider's investment products.

**QDRO (Qualified Domestic Relations Order):** A judgment, decree or order that creates or recognizes an alternate payee's (such as former spouse, child, etc.) right to receive all or a portion of a participant's retirement plan benefits.

**Separate Account:** An asset account established by a life insurance company, separate from other funds of the life insurance company, offering investment funding options for pension plans.

**Service Provider Termination Charge:** Plan administrative costs associated with terminating a relationship with a service provider, with the permanent termination of a plan, or with the termination of specific plan services. These may be termed "surrender" or "transfer" charges.

**Signature Ready Form 5500:** Fee to prepare Form 5500, a form which all qualified retirement plans (excluding SEPs and SIMPLE IRAs) must file annually with the IRS.

**Start-up/Enrollment Expense:** Costs associated with providing materials to educate employees about the plan, and enrolling employees in the plan. This may be part of, or included in, the education programs. There may be a one-time cost associated with implementing a new plan, as well as ongoing enrollment costs.

**Trustee Services:** Fees charged by the individual, bank or trust company with fiduciary responsibility for holding plan assets.

**VRU:** Voice Response Unit.

**Wrap Fee:** An inclusive fee generally based on the percentage of assets in an investment program, which typically provides asset allocation, execution of transactions and other administrative services.

**12b-1 Fee:** A charge to shareholders to cover a mutual fund's shareholder servicing, distribution and marketing costs.

*Special Edition*

A Newsletter Supplement
Summer 2001

Provisions
impacting
plan members
are notated with
this symbol . . .

# Economic Growth and Tax Relief Reconciliation Act of 2001

We're delighted to share some exciting news with you about the Economic Growth and Tax Relief Reconciliation Act of 2001 (EGTRRA). President Bush signed this expansive new piece of pension legislation into law on June 7, 2001.

A few of the changes that EGTRRA encompasses include:
* Increased annual limit on 401(k) and 403(b) deferrals
* Increased annual compensation limit for contribution/ benefit purposes from $170,000 to $200,000
* Increased dollar limit for individual contributions/ benefits purposes
* Simplified and modified top-heavy rules
* Allowance of rollovers between different types of plans
* "Catch-up" contributions for participants age 50 and older

These are just a few highlights. This special edition will outline additional details. It is also organized in a way that we think you will find useful as a reference tool. Provisions are categorized into changes that apply to:
* Defined contribution (DC) plans only (including 401(k))
* Defined benefit (DB) plans only
* All types of plans (including DC and DB)

We'll continue communicating significant developments and further guidance on EGTRRA in the months ahead. Your Pension Service Associate or Plan Consultant are here for your convenience. As with past legislation, we're ready to discuss the general implications of EGTRRA with you.

TRUSTAR
RETIREMENT SERVICES

## Provisions That Apply to Defined Contribution (DC) Plans (including 401(k))

| Subject | Current Law | EGTRRA |
|---------|-------------|--------|
| Elective Deferral Limits | • Elective deferral limit is $7,000 (indexed to $10,500 in 2001) <br> • Elective deferrals in a SIMPLE plan are limited to $6,000 | • Increases the elective deferral limit in 401(k) and 403(b) plans to: <br><br> **Year**   **Limit** <br> 2002   $11,000 <br> 2003   12,000 <br> 2004   13,000 <br> 2005   14,000 <br> 2006   15,000   (indexed in $500 increments) <br><br> • Increases elective deferral limit in a SIMPLE plan to: <br><br> **Year**   **Limit** <br> 2002   $7,000 <br> 2003   8,000 <br> 2004   9,000 <br> 2005   10,000   (indexed in $500 increments) |
| Catch-Up Contributions | No provision. | Members who are age 50 and older may make additional elective deferral contributions to a 401(k) or 403(b) plan equal to: <br><br> **Year**   **Amount** <br> 2002   $1,000 <br> 2003   2,000 <br> 2004   3,000 <br> 2005   4,000 <br> 2006   5,000   (indexed) <br><br> SIMPLE plan: <br> **Year**   **Amount** <br> 2002   $ 500 <br> 2003   1,000 <br> 2004   1,500 <br> 2005   2,000 <br> 2006   2,500   (indexed) <br><br> • Catch-up contributions are not subject to the §415 limit for individual employees, the employer's deduction limit, or non-discrimination testing as long as the provision is available to all plan members. <br> • Applies to employees for whom no other elective deferrals can be made because they've hit allowable limits. |

242

## Provisions That Apply to Defined Contribution (DC) Plans (including 401(k))

| Subject | Current Law | EGTRRA |
|---|---|---|
| Contribution Limits Under §415 | • In a DC plan, the maximum contribution a member can receive in any year is the lesser of 25% of pay or $35,000.<br>• In a 403(b) plan, contributions are limited to the maximum exclusion allowance. | • Increases the DC plan maximum to the lesser of 100% of pay or $40,000 (indexed in $1,000 increments).<br>• Repeals the maximum exclusion allowance under 403(b) plans. |
| Deduction Limit | • Employer contributions (including elective deferrals) to a profit sharing plan are limited to 15% of all covered employees' total pay.<br>• "Total pay" means pay excluding elective deferrals. | • Increases an employer's deduction limit for contributions to a profit sharing or stock bonus plan to 25% of covered employees' total pay.<br>• "Total pay" means pay including deferrals under a 401(k), 403(b), or 457 plan.<br>• Elective deferral contributions are not included in the 25% of pay deduction limit. They are separately deductible. |
| 401(k)/(m) Multiple Use Test | • Under the actual deferral percentage (ADP) test, 401(k) contributions must satisfy either the "125% rule" or the "2 percentage points/200% rule."<br>• Under the actual contribution percentage (ACP) test, 401(m) contributions must satisfy one of the same two rules.<br>• The multiple use test prohibits a plan from using the "2 percentage point/200% rule" in both the ADP and ACP test. | Eliminates the multiple use test. |
| Employer Matching Contributions | Employer matching contributions are subject to the general vesting requirements that apply to qualified plans. Contributions must vest at least as fast as either:<br>• 100% after completing five years of service, or<br>• 20% after three years of service plus 20% each subsequent year (100% after seven years of service). | Speeds up the vesting for employer matching contributions. Matching contributions must vest at least as fast as either:<br>• 100% after completing three years of service<br>or<br>• 20% after two years of service plus 20% each subsequent year (100% after six years of service). |
| Contribution/ Benefit Cutback Under § 411(d)(6) | The cutback rules prohibit an employer from reducing or eliminating many plan features. | • Facilitates the transfer of benefits from one DC plan to another primarily due to mergers and acquisitions.<br>• Allows plan features to not be protected if the member consents and:<br>  – The transfer is a direct transfer,<br>  – The transfer is allowed by both plans,<br>  – The member received proper notice and elected the transfer, and<br>  – The member could have elected a lump sum.<br>• Directs the IRS to issue regulations allowing the elimination of optional forms of benefits under defined benefit plans. |

## Provisions That Apply to Defined Contribution (DC) Plans (including 401(k)

| Subject | Current Law | EGTRRA |
|---|---|---|
| Coverage Testing Groups with Taxable and Non-taxable Entities | Prior to the Small Business Job Protection Act, tax-exempt entities couldn't sponsor a 401(k) plan. Employees of tax-exempt entities could be excluded when testing a 401(k) plan sponsored by a taxable entity if at least 95% of the taxable entity employees were eligible for the 401(k) plan. This special rule was eliminated beginning with the 1997 plan year. | Retroactively to 1997, employees of a tax-exempt entity who are eligible to make deferrals under a 403(b) plan may be excluded when testing the 401(k) plan for coverage if:<br>• No employee of the tax-exempt entity is eligible to participate in the 401(k) plan, *and*<br>• 95% of the non-excludible employees who aren't tax-exempt employees are eligible to participate in the 401(k)/(m) plan. |
| Same Desk Rule | Under the same desk rule, a distribution to a terminated employee is not allowed if the employee continues performing the same function for a successor employer. This applies to 401(k), 403(b) and 457 plans. | Eliminates the same desk rule. Allows the distribution of 401(k), 403(b) and 457 deferrals when an employee performs the same function for a successor employer. |
| 401(k) Hardship Withdrawals | Plans using the safe harbor hardship provision must require employees to stop making elective deferrals for 12 months after they take a hardship withdrawal from their 401(k) plan. | Reduces the suspension period to six months. Also, hardship withdrawal is not eligible for rollover. |
| Plans for Domestic Workers | Employers of household workers may establish a retirement plan for their employees. However, contributions aren't deductible, thus are subject to the 10% excise tax on nondeductible contributions. | Contributions to a SIMPLE 401(k) or a SIMPLE IRA which are non-deductible because the contributions are not a trade or business expense under Code §162 are not subject to the 10% excise tax on non-deductible contributions. |
| Roth 401(k) and 403(b) plans | Earnings on after-tax contributions to a defined contribution plan are subject to income tax when they're distributed. | Taxable years beginning after 12-31-2005:<br>• Plan members can elect a tax treatment for their deferrals similar to Roth IRA contributions.<br>• Contributions are tested along with pre-tax deferrals in the ADP test.<br>• Earnings are tax-free if they are left in the plan at least five years.<br>• Total employee contribution cannot exceed the maximum deferral amount.<br>• Regular distribution rules apply.<br>• Must be accounted for separately from other contributions.<br>• Can be rolled over to another Roth account or a Roth IRA. |
| Deemed IRAs | No provision | Beginning in 2003, plan members can make voluntary contributions to a separate account under the plan that meets the IRA or Roth IRA requirements. The account is deemed an IRA. It is subject to the IRA rules, not the qualified plan rules. |
| Plan Loans for Self-Employed | Prohibitive transaction rules prevent some owner-employees of an S corporation, partners of a partnership, and sole proprietors from taking a plan loan. | Allows plans to make loans to owner-employees of S corporations, partners of a partnership, and sole proprietorships. Loans in IRAs are still prohibited. |

## Provisions That Apply to Defined Benefit (DB) Plans

| Subject | Current Law | EGTRRA |
|---------|-------------|--------|
| Benefit Limits Under §415 | • The maximum annual accrued benefit for any employee is the lesser of 100% of a three-year average pay or $90,000 (indexed to $140,000 in 2001).<br>• The dollar limit is reduced when benefits begin prior to Social Security retirement age.<br>• The dollar limit is increased when benefits begin after Social Security retirement age. | • Increases the plan maximum to the lesser of 100% of pay or $160,000 (indexed in $5,000 increments).<br>• Reduces the dollar limit when benefits begin prior to age 62.<br>• Increases the dollar limit when benefits begin after age 65. |
| Excise Tax on Non-Deductible Contributions | A 10% excise tax is imposed on employers who make contributions to qualified plans that are not deductible. | Eliminates the 10% excise tax on non-deductible contributions made to a plan up to the full funding limit. |
| Plan Valuations | The valuation date must generally be a date within the applicable plan year. This means that a plan's minimum funding requirements, deduction limits and full funding limitation for a year are not known until after the beginning of the year or, in some cases, after the year is over. | Permits use of a valuation date that is up to one year prior to the beginning of the plan year. This applies at the election of the employer and is not available to underfunded plans. |
| Full Funding Limit | Contributions that exceed 150% of current liability are not tax deductible. This limit will be phased to 170% in 2005. | • Phases out the current liability limit:<br><br>**Year** — **Full Funding Limit**<br>2002 — 165% of current liability<br>2003 — 170% of current liability<br>2004 — No current liability limit<br><br>• Allows funding up to the unfunded termination liability (rather than the unfunded current liability) for a plan that terminates within the plan year. This applies to all plans covered by the PBGC. |
| Multi-Employer Plans | Under section 415(b), maximum annual benefits are the lesser of $130,000 or 100% of the highest three-year average compensation. For early retirees, that limit must be actuarially reduced. | Multi-employer plans will be exempt from the section 415(b) percentage of compensation limit (the dollar limit will still apply). In addition, multi-employer plans will not be aggregated with single employer plans or other multi-employer plans for the purpose of applying the percentage of compensation limitation. |
| Service Credit for Governmental Plans | Employees of state and local governments can purchase service credits in their state DB plan to make up for time spent in another state or district. Money saved in 403(b) plans can't be used to purchase these service credits. | Allows state and local government employees to use funds from their 403(b) or 457 plan to purchase credits. |

245

## Provisions That Apply to Defined Benefit (DB) Plans

| Subject | Current Law | EGTRRA |
|---------|-------------|--------|
| ERISA 204(h) Notice | • Written notice must be given to participants if a DB, money purchase, or target plan is amended to significantly reduce the rate of future benefit accruals.<br>• Notice must be given after the amendment is signed and at least 15 days before it's effective.<br>• Notice doesn't have to explain how participants' benefits may be affected. | • Requires DB or MP plans with more than 100 members to give a written notice of a plan amendment that significantly reduces future rates of accrual to all plan participants and alternate payees affected by the amendment.<br>• Includes amendments that eliminate or significantly reduce any early retirement benefits or retirement type subsidies.<br>• Treasury may require a simplified notice, or exempt a plan from the notice if the plan:<br>  – has less than 100 participants, or<br>  – offers participants a choice between the old and the new benefit formulas.<br>• Does not apply to governmental or non-electing church plans.<br>• Treasury may allow use of new technology to provide notice.<br>• Requires that the notice be given within a reasonable time period before the amendment effective date.<br>• Requires that the notice set forth the plan amendment and its effective date and provide sufficient information to allow the participant to understand the effect of the amendment.<br>• Requires the employer to pay an excise tax of $100 per day per omitted participant. Maximum penalty is $500,000 if failure is not willful neglect. |

## Provisions That Apply to All Plans

| Subject | Current Law | EGTRRA |
|---------|-------------|--------|
| Compensation Limit | Annual compensation limit to determine contributions and benefits is $150,000 (indexed to $170,000 in 2001). | Increases the compensation limit to $200,000 (indexed in $5,000 increments). |
| Rollovers | • Prohibits 401(a) qualified plans from accepting rollovers from 403(b) and 457 plans and visa versa.<br>• Prohibits 401(a) qualified plans from accepting rollovers from IRAs (other than conduit IRAs).<br>• Surviving spouse may roll benefits to an IRA, but not to a qualified plan.<br>• Rollovers must be made within 60 days of distribution, or they are treated as taxable. | • Permits rollovers from a 401(a), 403(b), or 457 plan, or an IRA to a DC plan of a subsequent employer, regardless of plan type.<br>• Permits the rollover of after-tax contributions to another qualified plan or IRA.<br>• Surviving spouse may roll benefits to an IRA or to his/her qualified plan.<br>• Grants the IRS authority to waive the 60-day period when failure to comply is due to casualty, disaster, or other events beyond the reasonable control of the individual. |

| Provisions That Apply to All Plans | | |
|---|---|---|
| **Subject** | **Current Law** | **EGTRRA** |
| Rollover of After-Tax Contributions | After-tax employee contributions can't be rolled over to another qualified plan. | • Permits the rollover of after-tax employee contributions to another qualified plan or IRA.<br>• A rollover from one qualified plan to another must be a direct rollover and the receiving plan must provide separate accounting for the contribution. |
| Minimum Distributions | A plan member must receive a minimum distribution starting at the later of age 70 1/2 or retirement (deferral until retirement does not apply to 5% owners and IRAs). | The IRS is directed to update the life expectancy tables that are used to calculate the minimum distribution. |
| Small Amount Payouts | Employers may distribute, without the member's consent, benefit amounts of less than $5,000. Rollover contributions are taken into account when determining if the member's account is more than $5,000. | Allows rollovers to be disregarded when determining whether a member's vested benefit exceeds $5,000. |
| Self-Employed Individuals | For self-employed, "pay" means net earnings subject to self-employment tax. Participants of certain religious faiths elect to be exempt from self-employment tax on religious grounds, thus have no pay for making contributions. | Amends the definition of pay for all qualified plans and IRAs to include an individual's net earnings that would be subject to self-employment tax if the employee was not exempt from the tax on religious grounds. |
| Small Business Credit for Start-Up Expenses | No provision. | • Provides a three-year tax credit for small businesses that adopt a qualified DB or DC plan.<br>• Credit covers 50% of the first $1,000 in administrative and retirement education expenses in each of the first three years.<br>• Limited to businesses with 100 or fewer employees.<br>• Plan must have at least one non-highly compensated employee. |
| Employer-Provided Investment Education | Employer provided retirement advice is not income to employees. | Clarifies that employer provided individual retirement and financial planning services are treated as a non-taxable fringe benefit if the services are available to all eligible employees on the same terms. |
| Sunset Provision | | All provisions of the bill do not apply to taxable, plan, or limitation years beginning after December 31, 2010. |

## Trustar Retirement Services Mission Statement

At Trustar, our mission is to provide recordkeeping, trustee, and trading services for retirement plans. Our customers are individuals, employee groups, employers, and distributor/investor partners. The four core values are the soul of our company. They define how we conduct ourselves, shape our business approach and form our unique perspective on the world. These basic values are necessary for our success.

### Strength

- Attracting a diverse group of quality employees.
- Balancing continued growth with profitability.
- Seeking above average, long range rates of return from our investments.
- Empowering each business, while leveraging competencies to enhance overall company effectiveness.

### Customer Service

- Providing excellent service, as defined by the market.
- Being market-driven.
- Maintaining and improving our financial soundness.
- Offering the lowest possible cost for high quality service.

### Quality

- Continuously improving our operations.
- Determining our customer's needs and designing products to fill them.
- Increasing name recognition.
- Enhancing our quality reputation.

### Integrity

- Operating in an ethical and legal manner.
- Supporting the communities in which we operate.

---

**Trustar<sup>SM</sup> Retirement Services**
P.O. Box 8963
Wilmington, DE 19899-8963

248

# APPENDIX

# COMMON DEFINITIONS

Here are simple definitions of some retirement planning lingo:

**accrued benefit**   The benefit you have earned based on the number of years you have worked while enrolled in a defined benefit pension plan. There may be a vesting schedule against this accrued benefit depending on the number of years you have worked for the company.

**catch-up provision**   A provision in some plans that permits employees over age 50 to put additional money into their plan to achieve greater retirement benefits.

**eligibility**   The criteria used to determine whether an employee may participate in a plan. On all qualified plans (except Simple 401(k)s, Simple IRAs, and SEP-IRAs), eligibility is based on the employee's age, number of years employed, and the number of hours worked per year.

**entry date**   The date that an employee enters the plan. Most often, it is the first date of the plan year, which usually

249

coincides with the first date of the fiscal year. Some plans have monthly or other entry dates.

**integration**    A rule that allows companies to make a higher percentage contribution for higher paid employees and a lower percentage contribution for lower paid employees. There is a five percent maximum on the differential under current law. Also synonymous with "permitted disparity."

**nonqualified plan**    An agreement to pay a special benefit to a key employee.

**permitted disparity**    See Integration.

**qualified plan**    A deductible retirement plan under section 401A of the Internal Revenue Code.

**retirement date**    Usually age 65, but under current law, there is no penalty for an age 62 retirement date.

**retirement plan census**    A listing of all employees, their dates of birth, dates of employment, and their approximate or exact annual earnings. You also need to note those employees who have worked less than 1,000 hours.

**top-heavy plan**    When 60 percent or more of the plan's benefits is allocated to the highly compensated. A top-heavy plan may require a minimum contribution to the lower paid employees and/or the vesting schedule may be accelerated for everyone.

**vesting**    A schedule that delineates the rules on when employees will have rights to their retirement benefits. All employees in a plan must have the same vesting schedule. Three basic vesting schedules are allowed for small companies:

1. 100 percent immediately.

2. Graduated vesting:

|      | 0% | 20% | 40% | 60% | 80% | 100% |
|------|----|-----|-----|-----|-----|------|
| Year | 1  | 2   | 3   | 4   | 5   | 6    |

3. Cliff vesting:

|      | 0% | 0% | 0% | 100% |
|------|----|----|----|------|
| Year | 1  | 2  | 3  | 4    |

# INDEX

— Simples, Roth + Trad w/ other Qualified plans?
(401k etc. or
Simple w/ Roth/Trad)

✓ — can you do Simple / Profit sharing

— IRAS and 401K ? (deductability is issue)
count toward
overall limit?
no pt. do safe harbor - cheaper.

✓ math vs. net fee cost, vs. vesting, long term goals + max. limits.
2/3% vs. safe harbor
(ratios ✗)
- safe harbor realistic option (wants to match anyways)
⤷ (if don't want to match + know they'll put in -
may be worth it).